The
French Classical Romances

Complete in Twenty Crown Octavo Volumes

Editor-in-Chief
EDMUND GOSSE, LL.D.

With Critical Introductions and Interpretative Essays by

HENRY JAMES   PROF. RICHARD BURTON   HENRY HARLAND

ANDREW LANG   PROF. F. C. DE SUMICHRAST

THE EARL OF CREWE   HIS EXCELLENCY M. CAMBON

PROF. WM. P. TRENT   ARTHUR SYMONS   MAURICE HEWLETT

DR. JAMES FITZMAURICE-KELLY   RICHARD MANSFIELD

BOOTH TARKINGTON   DR. RICHARD GARNETT

PROF. WILLIAM M. SLOANE   JOHN OLIVER HOBBES

ALEXANDRE DUMAS, PÈRE

1802-1870

The
Black Tulip

TRANSLATED FROM THE FRENCH
BY A. J. O'CONNOR

WITH A CRITICAL INTRODUCTION
BY RICHARD GARNETT, C.B., LL.D.

A FRONTISPIECE AND NUMEROUS
OTHER PORTRAITS WITH
DESCRIPTIVE NOTES BY
OCTAVE UZANNE

P. F. COLLIER & SON
NEW YORK

THE NOVELS OF THE ELDER DUMAS

IF there is any lesson more legibly inscribed than another upon the history of research, it is: beware of generalizations. In matters of mental speculation they are the analogues of " working hypotheses " in material science, most useful for co-ordinating facts and affording platforms, as it were, from which to obtain a general view of the way by which knowledge has travelled and the way that still lies before it, but a positive obstruction in its path if mistaken for ultimate results. M. Renan, for example, seemed to have established a solid principle when he generalized on the monotheistic tendencies of the Semitic race from his observation of the religions of the Jews and the Arabs, but a little consideration would have shown him that any dearth of deities imputable to these nations was more than made up by the singular opulence of the Pantheons of their Phœnician and Assyrian kinsfolk.

By an extraordinary coincidence—for it seems impossible to bring the pair into any relations of cause and effect—two remarkable generalizations founded upon the alleged observation of a triple stage in human development were independently propounded in France in the third decade of the nineteenth century. In 1826, Auguste Comte—whether or no plagiarizing from Schelling, as alleged by the late J. D. Morell—announced the discovery that " each branch of our knowledge passes successively through three different stages: the theological, the metaphysical, and the positive." Whatever Comte's obligations to Schelling may have been, we cannot easily believe that Victor Hugo was under any indebtedness to either for the discovery announced in the preface to his *Cromwell* (1827) that there are three stages in imaginative literature: " The poetry of the world's childhood was lyrical; that of its youth was epic; the poetry of its maturity is dramatic." From this deliverance dates the birth of the Romantic School in France.

Alas for generalizations when the sign-post is mistaken for the road! Comte's had been before the world but twenty-four years, when Martineau, writing amid the British excitement over the " Papal Aggression," was able to point out with an ironic chuckle that " the most practical nation of Europe— the nation in which the high-priest of inductive science was Chancellor nearly two centuries and a half ago— signs requisitions about the grace of baptism, holds county meetings on the doctrine of Apostolicity, demands leading articles on the remission of sins, and listens in crowded town halls to the canon law and the Tridentine decrees. M. Comte's law stands aghast.

The Novels of the Elder Dumas

Since the memorable date of his discovery, the world must have been altered; he found it in its last stage, it is now in its first: it had then for some ages emerged from the last trail of theology; it has now plunged again into the very nucleus of that nebulous light." Victor Hugo's law of three stages did not fare much better. The poet who, having produced but one important work, and that a drama, inferred that all poets must henceforth follow the example he had set, was speedily obliged to recognise a notable exception to his rule in his own person. Within three years he produced a romance which gained fifty times the renown of *Cromwell*, and his chief disciple at that early day, whose *Henri III* (1828) anticipated Hugo himself in making the romantic drama a power on the stage, was to earn contemporary and posthumous fame not as the dramatist, but as the romancer of the time. This disciple was Alexandre Dumas.

If Victor Hugo proposed to confine the definition of poetry to composition in verse, his generalization might not appear entirely unreasonable at the period when it was formulated. Epic poetry in its orthodox form was already regarded as in danger of exhaustion, and the rejuvenescence it had received from Byron, and was to receive from Hugo himself, was not as yet realized or foreseen. Lyric poetry was considered as but a minor department of the art, what then remained but the drama? Hugo's error was the failure to perceive that the drama alone could never fulfil the requisitions which the age was about to make upon poetry; that even poetry could never respond to them except by in some measure disencumbering herself of her singing robes, and consenting to appear as prose. From the moment of the recognition of prose as a medium for the expression of deep sentiment and tragic passion the contest between the drama and the novel becomes unequal. The novelist's opportunities and resources are far greater than the dramatist's. The business of both has been defined for all time by Horace:

> Ille per extentum funem mihi posse videtur
> Ire poeta, meum qui pectus inaniter angit,
> Irritat, mulcet, falsis terroribus implet,
> Ut magus; et modo me Thebis, modo ponit Athenis.

The novelist is evidently in a far more favourable position than the dramatist for accomplishing such a feat. Although the conditions of time and place may be abolished within the action of the drama, the drama itself as a whole is bound by them. The public representation is circumscribed to a particular edifice, and comprised within a definite time. There must be some limit to the number of characters: and in serious drama, the personage can seldom express himself exactly as he would have done in real life. Much of the controversy between the partisans of the romantic and those of the classical drama might have been spared if the romantic drama had been recognised for what, in one point of view, it really was, an effort, conscious or unconscious, on the part of the modern world so to widen the sphere of the ancient drama as to adapt it to modern conditions. To effect this, the consummate artistic standard of Hellas had to be lowered, and its depreciation compensated by an affluence of new life which far transcended the conceptions of a Sophocles. Instead of the narrow field of mythology, the entire domain of human life was to be open to the dramatist. Instead of an inexorable Fate as the universal controller of action, each personage was to determine his own. Instead of two or three types of character, kings, lovers, confidants, parasites made to pattern, there were to be as many types as personages. There was as much difference between the old and the new as between the ancient effigies of the gods which sat with unparted limbs in majestic immobility, and those which Dædalus represented running, walking, and flying.

This emancipation of the drama did not until the nineteenth century extend to France. Before Hugo's time it would have been easy to generalize and prove by specious arguments that it never could, but it is now sufficiently clear that there is no absolute incongruity between the French temperament and the doctrines of the romantic school. That the national genius for the terse, the lucid, and the symmetrical inclines it even more powerfully in the direction of classicism may be readily admitted, but this does not alter the fact that when Hugo wrote *Cromwell* the classical school, deriving its material from an area comparatively limited, was on the verge of exhaustion, and could only be preserved by a temporary retirement from the field of literature. Hugo himself, as we have said, did not then perceive that even the drama in its most emancipated form was unable to represent the agitation and complexity of modern life, and that so surely as the romantic stage had superseded the classical, so surely would it have to give way to romantic fiction. This involved the deduction that Hugo himself was not to be the dominating figure of the new movement: for, though a great poet in prose, he was not a great novelist. The qualities which ennoble his romances are the same as those which constitute his greatness as a poet. As a novelist in the strict sense of the term he is inferior to the three leading representatives of the French prose fiction of his age—Balzac, George Sand, Alexandre Dumas.

Of these great writers the most eminent for purely literary qualities is the least of a force in literature. Great in the lower departments of invention, masterly in devising plot and exhibiting character, George Sand, as respects the originality of her conceptions, affords no answer to the searching inquiry, " When did woman ever yet invent? " She continues the work of Rousseau with equal eloquence and far more fertility: but writes as an idyllist or sentimentalist of the previous century might have written if transported to the more exciting age of Louis Philippe, and contributes little absolutely new to French fiction. Balzac and Dumas, on the other hand, are as novel and original as Hugo himself. Balzac, no doubt, is the greater figure. The spirit in which the *Comédie Humaine* was attempted is that in which religions have been founded. Other writers have done greater things; but, with one exception, they have not achieved them with the like deliberate purpose and clear conception from the first of what they intended to accomplish. Homer, we may be sure, was led through the *Iliad* canto by canto; Milton hesitated among a score of schemes before fixing upon *Paradise Lost*, which even then he postponed for fifteen years; and Shakespeare would probably have dropped dramatic authorship long ere he did, if it had not been daily bread to him. The only parallel to the creator of the Human Comedy is the creator of the Divine. Dante announced his purpose of hymning the apotheosis of Beatrice before a line of the Divine Comedy was written, and pursued it with undeviating constancy amid vicissitudes even more trying than Balzac's privations. But this very loftiness and seriousness of purpose almost disqualifies Balzac for the character of the typical romancer. This part rather belongs to him to whom his vocation is everything, who narrates without *arrière pensée*, who enchains the attention, not by his philosophy or his fidelity to manners, but merely by his story. Hence, while Balzac is a romancer and a great deal more, Dumas is the romancer and nothing more; and if he loses as an author he gains as a novelist. Balzac is deeply significant: Dumas, in the strict etymological meaning of the word, and that only, insignificant; Balzac is a great instructor, Dumas merely amuses. But, on the other hand, Balzac's plan confined him principally to his own country and time, while Dumas is at home in every age and every part of the world. Balzac displays a gallery of pictures, Dumas unrolls a panorama. Balzac is popular nowhere, and Dumas everywhere. Perhaps the nearest affinity to Dumas, in British literature at least, is manifested by Scott. It would be misleading to push the analogy too far; it may, nevertheless, be affirmed that the basis of the genius of each is a genius for story-telling. In everything not strictly definable as narrative power—humour, pathos, all merely intellectual operations—Scott far surpasses Dumas. But in one thing which constitutes the especial excellence of both, Dumas surpasses Scott, surpasses everybody. None can rival the easy grace with which he launches into a story, the affluent invention by which fresh characters and fresh situations arise whenever wanted, the power of compelling assent to whatever the writer pleases, the force with which the reader is riveted from first to last. Nor are these gifts confined to the author in his character as a narrator of fiction. They are fully as conspicuous in his memoirs and in his records of travel. The one thing needful is that he should have a story to tell; whether true or fictitious, or between the two, matters nothing to him.

It is manifest that the stage, where narrative can only be allowed very sparingly, and under severe restrictions, could not be the predilection of an author thus endowed. Dumas' genius for dialogue, nevertheless, was only second to his genius for narrative, and, combined with an inventiveness equally efficient in drama and novel, gained him a fair reputation as a dramatist. He can hardly, however, rank higher than as a very able playwright. To be more than this, the writer of serious drama must be a poet. Poetical feeling is an obvious requisite for tragedies in verse: but it may even be observed that most of the very few tragedies in prose which have gained high literary rank— *Goetz von Berlichingen, The Robbers, The Soul's Tragedy* —have been the work of poets. The same observation will be applicable to Ibsen's later plays, should a place anywhere near *Peer Gynt* be awarded to them by posterity. Dumas, it need not be said, was no poet. Had he worked all his life at the drama, he could have gained no other renown than that of a more rhetorical Scribe. The romance came to his aid, and he entered upon it exactly at the most propitious moment.

It would be an interesting inquiry when France first became firmly impressed with the belief in her supremacy over the rest of the world in arts and letters, no less than in military glory. It is enough for us to carry it back to the age of Louis XIV, when, in the *Combat des Livres*, which gave the model for Swift's *Battle of the Books*, the nations of Europe whose languages are not of Latin origin, including the land of Shakespeare, are excluded from the contest until the said idioms shall be refined to the standard of Gallic politeness. Voltaire's undisputed sovereignty over European literature could but confirm this comfortable conviction; but after him new ideals came in, and the pretension to dominate literature and prescribe a universal standard of taste was temporarily eclipsed by two competing and inconsistent pretensions: first, to bestow universal freedom upon Europe, and afterward, to reduce Europe to universal subjection. The frustration of this latter ideal left the nation with a mass of accumulated and unused energy, which, debarred from its natural vent in conquest and politics, ran impetuously into literature. Alfred de Musset has painted for us the discouragement of the young generation which, born in the latter years of Napoleon's period of glory, found itself as it grew up confronted with national humiliation. But Musset was one of the younger romanticists. The greatest representatives of the movement, born several years earlier, had received their first and keenest impressions under quite different circumstances. Never, perhaps, since the days of Rome had any nation occupied a position of such unquestioned superiority as France held during the first twelve years of the nineteenth century. Not only by her material, but also by her intellectual conquests she saw herself at the head of the world. The pre-eminence of her men of science was as undisputed as that of her soldiers; and the finest works of other nations, in their captivity at the Louvre, made Paris the metropolis of Art. She had enough and more than enough to compensate for the sufferings of the Revolution, which also she counted among her glories. The susceptible youth of that period could not but grow up animated with pride and confidence, fit to conceive and execute vast designs. By the time that disasters came, these feelings had become a part of their being, and the spirit of mastery and aggrandizement, repelled from the spheres of war and conquest, threw itself with all the more vehemence into the fields of the intellect. Napoleon himself, though a patron of science, had been no friend to literature; but for the writings of his adversaries, which he strove to suppress, his own period would have been barren of literary glory; yet his spirit seems to preside over French literature long after the downfall of his power. There is an intensely Napoleonic quality in Victor Hugo, the great Coryphæus of the Romantic movement, who, if he proclaims the new literary principles in the spirit of 1789, enforces them in the fashion of 1796. It was in 1830 that Goethe declared the volcano to be in eruption, not thinking at all of the revocation of the Charter and the consequent overthrow of the legitimate monarchy, but of the memorable discussion on creation and evolution between Cuvier and Geoffroy-Saint-Hilaire. Had Goethe carried his vision a little farther he might have announced an even more volcanic contemporaneous outburst in the realm of literature, more striking to the imagination and destined to produce greater immediate if less permanent effects. The progress of science, if sure, is slow: but the literary conflagration in France blazed forth with a vehemence which devoured everything in its path, and for a time left nothing uncoloured by its light.

The Novels of the Elder Dumas

Europe had seen the counterpart of this in another sphere, when the *furore francese* so hugely dismayed the methodical warriors of Italy. Compared with such an outbreak our literary innovations on the English side of the Channel seem tame affairs, and we must allow that a nation which, judging by particular circumstances in its history and its social arrangements, we are accustomed to regard as conventional and unenterprising in comparison with our own, on occasion displays a genius for the colossal and grandiose to which we can afford no parallel. Nothing is more characteristic of the literary era of the July monarchy than the Titanic proportions of its great men and their ideals, and the extraordinary affluence of their production. This may seem typified in one of its earliest literary performances, the enormous catalogue of objects of beauty or curiosity in the curiosity dealer's stores in Balzac's *Peau de Chagrin*, accumulated until, as in Martin's pictures, the feeling of sublimity is produced by endless space and incessant reiteration. All the great writers we have named work upon the imagination by the magnitude and excessive daring of their conceptions: coming down even as low as Eugène Sue, how vast is the scheme of *The Wandering Jew*! All this, however national, is totally at variance with another quality no less inherent in the race: the feeling for lucidity, measure, propriety, and symmetry, which is after all the dominant note of French manners and French literature. It will perhaps be some day considered that it has been the especial task of the authorship of the latter part of the nineteenth century to reconcile this contradiction as far as possible. The gulf between the conflicting tendencies was never wider than when Hugo and Dumas appeared upon the scene.

We have often speculated whether the overthrow of the classical school by the romantic may not be parabolically set forth in one of the finest poems of the *Légende des Siècles, Pan*. The Olympian divinities sit at their banquet, attired in the most correct mythological costume, partaking of the invariable nectar and the immutable ambrosia, listening to the melodies with which Apollo has regaled them ever since the lyre has been invented, when an uncouth satyr-like creature is brought in by the ear as a contribution to their amusement, who, after having for a space submitted to the refined Olympian raillery, suddenly begins to grow, and reveals himself as no mere Sylvan, but that great Pan of the philosophers of whom visible Nature, including the deities and their palaces, is but the raiment, and by a gesture brings Jupiter to his knees. The conception might serve as the symbol of other than literary revolutions, but is well adapted to set forth the overthrow of a classical school, enfeebled by the constant reproduction of typical excellence, by a return to Nature. If Hugo had any such intention, his vanity was sufficiently colossal to allow him to conceive that in depicting Pan he was embodying himself. No mortal under Shakespeare could really be equal to such a part; but if we were to look merely to external characteristics, and not to the actual performance attributed to the intrusive guest, we should find his counterpart in a writer even more opulent than Hugo, and less prone to the affectation which estranges from Nature, Alexandre Dumas.

Dumas does indeed make such a figure in the bower of the Muses as Pan makes at the table of the Gods. There is perhaps hardly such another instance of a man with so little moral or intellectual claim to rank among the *élite* of men of letters, taking so high a place upon the literary Olympus. Every nation can produce abundant instances of writers, especially of fiction, attaining boundless popularity and realizing vast fortunes, whose works, nevertheless, no person of culture ever dreams of classing as literature. The author himself may be honestly unable to apprehend the reason, the critic may find difficulty in justifying the inexorable exclusion, but, notwithstanding, the trained judgment experiences no more uncertainty in its discrimination than in distinguishing the pure carbon of graphite from the pure carbon of diamond. Dumas exceptionally passed for long as an example of this inferior grade of authorship. At one time it would have been thought absurd to parallel him with deep thinkers like Balzac or exquisite artists like George Sand. *Monte Cristo* and *The Three Musketeers* were ranged along with *The Mysteries of Paris* and *The Wandering Jew*, and the circumstances of their reproduction in England showed that they were expected to appeal to readers of the same class. When

The Novels of the Elder Dumas

Lewes declared that the frequency of translation of French novelists into English was in the inverse ratio of their merit, and adduced Balzac as an example at one end of the scale, he must have visualized Dumas at the other. Yet as time passed, and mere clever melodrama gave place to other clever melodrama, but Dumas retained his power and popularity, it became clear that his work really belonged to the domain of literature.

In adjusting the relations between Dumas and his critics, it must be remembered that he did not, like some of the literary heroes of his age, take the world by storm with his earliest writings. Hugo and George Sand began their career, or nearly so, with productions which could not be overlooked or confounded with the mass. So practically did Balzac, for although, before bursting upon the world with the *Physiology of Marriage* and *La Peau de Chagrin*, he had drudged for ten years at inferior novels, no one had heard of him or them. But Dumas had acquired a good sound reputation as a second-rate romancer before writing *Monte Cristo*, and criticism was naturally slow to accept him as a genius. Born in 1802, he had made his *début* in 1826 with a volume of short stories, one of them, *Blanche de Beaulieu*, " a pearl " in the estimation even of his remorseless antagonist, Quérard. His first efforts, however, were mostly in the dramatic line, and as Hugo's *Cromwell* was incapable of representation, Dumas has the honour of having gained the first dramatic victory for the romantic school by his *Henri III*. *Christine* and *Antony* obtained fair success, notwithstanding the discovery that the first of them was partly stolen from Schiller. According to his own account, his conversion to the romantic drama proceeded from the visit to Paris of a troupe of English performers who acted Shakespeare: if, however, he had not received this impulse from them he certainly would have received it from Hugo.

The early thirties, which brought a brilliant succession of dramatic triumphs to Victor Hugo, were ruinous to his lieutenant in this branch of art. The very names of most of Dumas' numerous pieces are forgotten, though two obtained a place in the repertory of the Comédie Française. About 1835 he convinced himself that his vocation was rather for the novel, and he went on for some years producing very excellent work of a somewhat melodramatic class, until about 1844 he hit upon the further discovery which has made him representative and immortal. It was that melodrama upon a gigantic scale becomes epical, provided that vigour of style, fertility of invention, and ingenuity of construction are on a par with these colossal dimensions. This condition, it may safely be said, was at that time fulfilled by no French author but himself. Victor Hugo may in some measure be deemed an exception, but the period of Dumas' most successful activity was that of Hugo's silence and self-effacement; and there is, moreover, an important distinction to be drawn between the two writers as novelists, entirely to the advantage of Dumas. Hugo is essentially unnatural, few of his personages and incidents are probable, many are not even possible; the poet has continually to be invoked to repair the failures of the romancer. Dumas, on the contrary, granted his premises, is natural and logical in the development of his plot; his characters, if not everyday personages, are yet sufficiently credible; he has no monsters of vice or virtue, but men and women of the world, not less human than the generality for being more picturesque. In a word, the vast scale on which he now wrought did not tempt him to magnify his characters in proportion: the canvas has become colossal, but the figures are at most of heroic size. His great gain in energy and effectiveness is due to his working on a scale more congenial to the fire and vehemence of his temperament: refuting for once a maxim in general most sound, he has become a great painter by painting with a big brush.

The achievement of Dumas' triumph dates from the publication of *Les Trois Mousquetaires*, followed at short intervals by its sequels, *Vingt Ans Après* and *Le Vicomte de Bragelonne*. As historical novels in their own department these have never been surpassed. Their method is not that of *Romola*; they do not carefully and scientifically resuscitate a bygone era for us to examine: they rather grasp the reader himself and throw him into the midst of the action, in which he lives and moves as though he were a contemporary. Dumas' eye for the picturesque is as sure as Napoleon's eye for a battlefield: and could we be certain that the labour of disinterring it from the past was equally his own, we must award him as much credit for diligence as for *coup d'œil*. There can be little doubt, however, that he was largely indebted to collaborators, whose employment raises a grave question. To what extent was he the author of the books that pass under his name? He was for a time at the head of a great literary manufactory, where much work was done, not by himself, but professedly under his direction: a case analogous, he would plead, to that of the great painters who, as regards the subordinate part of their work, have been content with furnishing designs, and have devolved the actual execution on their scholars. But did Dumas always furnish so much as the designs? He was notoriously unscrupulous in such matters: in works even in which he unquestionably had a hand he stands convicted of theft from Schiller, Cooper, and Marryat: and he would attach his name to essays of which he had not written a line on the plea that they had become his property by purchase, as though this mattered anything to the defrauded public. On the issue, however, whether his most famous works were really his own he seems entitled to a verdict from the inability of his chief reputed collaborator, Auguste Maquet, to sustain the test which Bacchus in Aristophanes proposes to apply to Iophon: " Let me shut him up by himself," he says, " and I shall know what to think of him." If Maquet had really written *The Three Mus-*

keteers and *Monte Cristo*, he ought to have produced something remarkable apart from Dumas, but after their breach and separation he wrote nothing worthy of note. By far the most important departments of Dumas' best novels are the plot and the dialogue, and these are precisely the parts which it would give him the least trouble to produce, and which are the most evidently from his hand. That he owed much to Maquet and other assistants may be admitted, but their mutual relations may perhaps be not unfairly compared to those between the great Rothschild and " the army of clerks, money-changers, discounters, and billbrokers," with which, according to Heine, " he conquers the world."

The Three Musketeers was followed by *Monte Cristo* (1846), a romance more popular still, and a proof that Dumas was not bound to history, but that his abounding inspiration was equal to the production of an ideal world. The next eight or ten years were the summit of his activity and his renown. *Les Mémoires d'un Médecin, La Reine Margot, Les Frères Corses, La Tulipe Noire, Isaac Laquedem, Dieu Dispose, Ascanio, Ange Pitou,* and other romances too numerous to mention here, characterized that brilliant epoch. At the same time monitions of the inevitable decay were apparent in the spoiled child of fortune's devouring vanity, growing charlatanism, reckless dissipation, and rapacity after gain; not from covetousness, for no man was more open-handed, but as the necessary consequence of colossal extravagance. It can only be urged in extenuation that every good and bad quality of Dumas was of necessity colossal, and that the man never lived of whom it could be more truly declared that he must needs have the defects of his qualities. In some degree this decadence was profitable to literature, driving Dumas to the production of narratives of travel in which invention had as much scope as observation; and to his wondrous *Memoirs*, which, as it is inconceivable that any one but himself should have written them, alone suffice to establish his genius and his virtual independence of the supports on which he may sometimes have condescended to lean. It was impossible that his brain should perpetually work at such pressure, and as the author declined the charlatan gained ground. Abortive journalistic speculations, farcical adventures in the wake of Garibaldi, schemes even less dignified for attracting public attention, lawsuits, scandals of various kinds, succeeded each other; until at last, all but a wreck, yet not wholly bereaved of prestige and esteem, and affectionately tended by his children, the great Alexandre expired in his country's darkest hour.

The list of Dumas' works in the complete collection published by Michel Lévy comprises three hundred and three volumes. Twenty-five of these are occupied by plays, twenty-nine by travels, ten by memoirs; a few of the remainder are not fiction, or do not properly belong to him, but after every deduction the mass exhibits a fecundity rivalled by very few novelists, and a standard of merit equalled by none who have approached Dumas' productiveness. Lope de Vega is perhaps his nearest literary analogue, but he is a dramatist of a conventional school as regards character, and his inventiveness is chiefly displayed in the variety of his plots.

It cannot be said that Dumas is a Mezzofanti of fiction, transcending by a wide interval the faculties of other men as hitherto ascertained. Balzac might have written as much if he had lived as long; and when Scott's multifarious performances in all kinds of fields literary and non-literary are considered, and it is further remembered that he did not seriously take to novel-writing until he was upwards of forty, it will not appear impossible that his productiveness might, under other conditions, have surpassed that of Dumas. But, taking things as they actually are, Dumas stands out as the first among the truly eminent novelists of the world for exuberance of production. To class him thus is to assign him a high place. Mediocrity may be productive, but cannot be opulent; its work is necessarily formal and mechanical. Exuberance implies a vast fertility of invention; animated, impassioned style; and more particularly great facility in dialogue. All these merits Dumas possesses in the highest degree; and as already remarked, his invention moves within the limits of humanity, his characters are credible personages, neither monsters nor puppets. The nicer shades of psychological analysis are not to be expected from him, nor does he profess to depict the fashion of the times. In intellectual power he is far inferior to his principal contemporaries, but his instinct is often truer than their reason.

Such a writer could not miss popularity with the masses, but the circumstances of his time were long unfavourable to his recognition in higher spheres. It is difficult to be equally attuned to widely differing orders of excellence, and to those who best appreciated the power of the novel in George Eliot's hands as an interpreter of the highest thought, or the psychology of a Hawthorne or a Meredith, the naïve romance of a Dumas might well appear almost childish. A reaction came when men began to weary of introspection, and felt ready to exclaim with Keats, "O for a life of sensations rather than of thoughts!" It seems probable that in the Anglo-Saxon world the rehabilitation of Dumas was due in great measure to Robert Louis Stevenson. Stevenson's restoration of the novel of adventure to the place it had formerly occupied in our literature was greatly aided by his studies of Dumas, and the discovery he made that Dumas was not only a stirring story-teller, but in his own way an artist, contributed much to restore the author of *Monte Cristo* to his place among the masters of fiction. From French criticism of the moment, however, he still endures a neglect which shows no present sign of being removed. It scarcely need be observed that the qualities of the Elder Dumas are rather French than English, and that it is hardly more to be expected that novelists of our ordinary national type should rival his verve and energy than that average

Britons should vie with French vivacity and gesticulation. On this very account, however, he is one of the writers from whom most may be learned. His is not the romance of the future, it is far from indicating the lines along which fiction will progress, but it can teach the writer of more ardent enthusiasm and loftier purpose many a useful lesson in the indispensable requisites of constructive and dramatic art.

The Black Tulip, selected for translation in this series, though not on the extensive scale which in general best suited Dumas, is one of his most delightful and characteristic works, exhibiting within a small compass most of the traits which give him his peculiar place among the masters of fiction. The key to all is the powerful imagination which renders his ideal tulip as interesting to himself as the actual bulb could have been to the personages whose lives and fortunes are represented as depending upon it. With this concur equally exceptional powers of enchaining the attention of the reader, and of throwing his conception into relief by a skilfully devised plot, full of vicissitude and suspense, and by personages entirely sympathetic and in no way overwrought; with the needful contrast of deliberate but not exaggerated villainy, and of disagreeable qualities among subordinate characters so presented as to produce a comic rather than a repulsive impression. Everything is provided for: once started, the story rattles off and chimes through its course like a good air played by a musical box, sure to reach its conclusion without marring a note,

The Novels of the Elder Dumas

and to leave a sense of enjoyment behind it. The only exception to the general artistic finish is occasional repetition, tiresome when the book is read as a whole, but more excusable in its original form as a newspaper *feuilleton*, where the reader, taking his intellectual food in morsels from day to day mixed up with all sorts of other matters, really does need to be reminded of what he has read. A remarkable instance this, how a man's personal defects of character, which seem at first sight to have no relation to his performance as an author, infallibly come home to him. Dumas had great artistic faculty, but little artistic conscience; he was extravagant, and therefore needy; hence he condescended to the *feuilleton* novel as the shortest cut to money-making; and the Muses were offered up by their own priest upon the altar of Plutus.

RICHARD GARNETT.

LIFE OF ALEXANDRE DUMAS
THE ELDER

ALEXANDRE DUMAS *was born at Villers-Cotterets,
in the Aisne, on the 24th of July, 1802. He was the son
of General Alexandre Dumas, who was the illegitimate
son of the Marquis Davy de la Pailleterie by a negress
of St. Domingo; the father died in 1806, leaving the
mother of Dumas poor. The future novelist entered a
lawyer's office in his native town. In 1823, in company
with his mother, he went to Paris, where, through the
help of General Foy, he obtained a clerkship in the offices
of the Duke of Orléans. He had been, up to this time,
ignorant of the elements of literature, but he now began
to study poetry and drama with avidity, and determined
to make literature his profession. In 1825 his first play
was acted at the Ambigu. He became almost immediately
a fertile and a fairly successful playwright; although his
earliest fine play, " Christine," was rejected by the Théâtre
Français. His next tragedy, however, " Henri III.," was
accepted and performed in February, 1829; this was
" more than a success—a frenzy," and brought its author
in a large sum of money. The Duke of Orléans now
appointed Dumas his librarian, and on the strength of*

*his success he plunged into a life of extravagant expend-
itures. "Christine" was acted with great applause, and
Dumas entered into permanent celebrity. He was drawn
into politics by the Revolution, and he has left a thick volume describing his own exploits during the three famous
days of revolution in July, 1830; he left Paris to organ-
ize the National Guard in La Vendée, which he calls " the
heart of the Royalist party." On the accession of Louis
Philippe the joy of Dumas knew no bounds, and he
adopted, in pure absent-mindedness, the title of Marquis
de la Pailleterie, to which he had no sort of claim. He
presently married the actress Ida Ferrier, from whom he
soon obtained a separation. He continued his work for
the stage, and two of his most famous plays, "Antony"
and "Charles VII," belong to 1831. Already the
charge of plagiarism had been brought against him, and
"La Tour de Nesle," which was the great success of
1832, was proved to be only partly his own. The series
of his great plays closes, in 1842, with "Lorenzino"; by
this time Dumas had turned his attention to popular
romance, to be treated with a mixture of historic events
and anecdotic incident. "Monte Cristo" found thou-
sands of readers directly it appeared in 1844, and all Europe began to hang on the lips of Dumas. "The Three
Musketeers" merely added fuel to the fire of his popularity, and from this time forth Dumas poured forth an
immense stream of novels, in which nothing could be too
extravagant, ingenious, or picturesque. He set up a sort
of factory from which he poured forth romances, issu-
ing sometimes as many as forty volumes in a year, in the*

majority of which he had little part beyond directing the plot and generally writing the dialogue. He gained huge sums of money, but squandered them directly in " feasts of Sardanapalus " and other mad forms of extravagance. The last twenty years of his life were spent in alternate splendour and poverty, in violent effort of every kind. At last his health broke down under the intolerable strain, and he was removed, an invalid, to the house of his son, at Puys, near Dieppe. There he died, in the midst of the Franco-German War, on the 5th of December, 1870. In April, 1872, his body was removed to Villers-Cotterets, where a sumptuous monument has been raised above his tomb.

E. G.

CONTENTS

The Black Tulip

THE BLACK TULIP

I

A GRATEFUL PEOPLE

On the 20th of August, 1672, the city of The Hague, so lively, so clean, and so smart that one would have thought every day was a Sunday; the city of The Hague, with its shady park, its tall trees overhanging its Gothic houses, and its broad, mirror-like canals reflecting the almost Oriental cupolas of its bell-towers; the city of The Hague, the capital of the Seven United Provinces, was flooded in all its main thoroughfares by a black and red stream of eager, panting, and excited citizens, who, with knives at their girdles, muskets on their shoulders, or sticks in their hands, were hurrying towards the Buitenhof, a formidable prison, the barred windows of which may still be seen, where, upon a charge of attempted murder brought against him by the surgeon Tychelaer, Cornelius de Witt, brother of the ex-Grand Pensionary of Holland, was lying confined.

If the history of the period, and especially of the year, in which we begin our story were not indissolubly connected with the two names which we have last mentioned, the few explanatory lines which we are about to insert might appear superfluous; but we must explain at the outset to the reader—that old friend whom we always on our first page promise to please, and with whom in the pages that follow we keep our word, more or less—we must explain, we say, to the reader that this introduction is as necessary for the clearness of our story as it is for a proper understanding of the great political events with which the story is interwoven.

Cornelius, or Cornelis, de Witt, Ruart de Pulten, that is to say, Inspector of the Dikes, of his country, ex-burgomaster of his native town of Dort, and deputy in the Assembly of the States of Holland, was forty-nine years of age when the people of Holland, tired of the Republic as it was understood by John de Witt, the Grand Pensionary, were suddenly seized with a violent desire for the Stadtholderate, which the Perpetual Edict, forced by John de Witt on the United Provinces, had abolished utterly and forever in Holland.

Public opinion, in its capricious variations, almost always identifies a principle with a man; and accordingly, behind the Republic the people saw the two stern figures of the brothers De Witt, those Romans of Holland, who would not condescend to flatter the national whims, but acted as inflexible supporters of liberty without license and prosperity without luxury. Similarly, the Stadtholderate was represented in

A Grateful People

their minds by the grave, serious, and thoughtful countenance of the young William of Orange, to whom his contemporaries had given the surname of " the Silent," a name adopted by posterity.

The two De Witts tried to keep on terms with Louis XIV, for they recognised that his moral influence throughout Europe was increasing, and they had recently had experience of his physical superiority in Holland during the marvellous and successful campaign of the Rhine (a campaign sung of by Boileau and made illustrious by the romantic hero known as the Comte de Guiche), which in three months had utterly overthrown the power of the United Provinces.

Louis XIV had long been the enemy of the Dutch, who insulted or ridiculed him to their heart's content, nearly always, it must be admitted, through the instrumentality of French refugees in Holland. The national pride regarded him as the Mithridates of the Republic. Thus the brothers De Witt had to contend with a twofold movement, due partly to the vigorous resistance offered to an authority fighting against the desires of the people, and partly to the weariness which comes naturally to all conquered races when they are hoping that a new leader will be able to save them from ruin and disgrace.

This new leader, quite ready to come forward and measure his strength against that of Louis XIV, gigantic as the power of the latter appeared likely to become in the future, was William, Prince of

The Black Tulip

Orange, son of William II, and grandson, through Henrietta Stuart, of King Charles I of England. In the eyes of the Dutch, this silent youth represented, as we have said, the Stadtholderate. In 1672 William was twenty-two years of age. John de Witt had been his tutor, and had brought him up with a view to making this former prince into a good citizen. His love for his country had prevailed over his love for his pupil, and by the Perpetual Edict he had deprived the young man of all hope of becoming Stadtholder. But God had smiled at the human presumption which thinks to make and unmake earthly potentates without regard to the designs of the King of Heaven; and, by means of the fickleness of the Dutch and the terror inspired by Louis XIV, had overthrown the political schemes of the Grand Pensionary and abolished the Perpetual Edict, re-establishing instead the stadtholdership in the person of William of Orange, with regard to whom He had his own designs, hidden as yet amid the deep mysteries of the future.

The Grand Pensionary bowed to the will of his fellow-citizens; but Cornelius de Witt was less yielding, and in spite of threats of death from the Orangeist mob, which besieged him in his house at Dort, he had refused to sign the act which re-established the Stadtholderate.

The tears of his wife finally induced him to sign, but he added to his name the two letters V. C., *vi coactus*, that is to say, *constrained by force*.

A Grateful People

On that day it was only by a miracle that he escaped from the assaults of his foes.

John de Witt's more rapid and easy submission to the will of his fellow-citizens brought him little or no advantage. A few days later an attempt was made to assassinate him. Stabbed in several places, he barely escaped death.

This was not at all what the Orangeists wanted. The existence of the two brothers was a perpetual obstacle to their projects. They therefore changed their tactics for a moment, and while leaving themselves free to crown at any opportunity the second crime by the first, they attempted to bring about by calumny what they had not been able to achieve by the dagger.

It is but seldom that at a given moment there is found under the hand of God, a great man ready to execute a great action, and that is why, when the providential combination does occur, history both records the name of the chosen hero and, at the same time, holds him up to the admiration of posterity.

But when the devil interferes in human affairs to ruin a life or overthrow a state, it is seldom indeed that he does not find ready to hand some wretched being, into whose ear he has but to whisper a word in order to set him immediately to work as he desires.

The scoundrel who, in the present case, was ready to be the agent of the evil spirit was a surgeon, and his name, as we think we have already mentioned, was Tychelaer.

The Black Tulip

He lodged an information that Cornelius de Witt, furious, as the letters added to his signature proved, at the revocation of the Perpetual Edict, and urged on by hatred of William of Orange, had commissioned an assassin to deliver the Republic from the new stadtholder, and that this assassin was himself, Tychelaer; but that, stung by remorse at the bare idea of the deed which he had been asked to commit, he had preferred to reveal the crime rather than to commit it.

One can easily imagine the outburst which the report of this plot provoked among the Orangeists. The Public Prosecutor, on the 16th of August, 1672, caused Cornelius to be arrested in his own house, and the Ruart de Pulten, the noble brother of John de Witt, underwent in one of the halls of the Buitenhof the preliminary torture designed to drag from him, as from one of the vilest criminals, a confession of his pretended plot against William.

But Cornelius had not only a great mind, but also a great heart. He belonged to that company of martyrs, who, sustained by political, as others have been by religious, faith, laugh at the pains inflicted on them. During the tortures he recited in a firm voice, and scanning the lines according to their metre, the first verse of Horace's *Justum et tenacem*. He confessed nothing, and wore out not merely the physical strength of his executioners, but even their fanaticism.

The judges, nevertheless, dismissed Tychelaer

A Grateful People

without saying anything against him, while they passed sentence on Cornelius, depriving him of all his offices and dignities; and further condemned him to pay the costs of the proceedings, and banished him forever from the territories of the Republic.

To the populace, whose interests Cornelius had always devotedly served, this sentence passed upon one who was not only an innocent man, but also a great patriot, was indeed a certain satisfaction. But, as we shall see, it was not enough.

The Athenians, who have left a bad enough reputation for ingratitude, were surpassed in this quality by the Dutch. They contented themselves with banishing Aristides.

John de Witt, at the first rumour of the charge brought against his brother, had resigned his position of Grand Pensionary. He, also, was fittingly rewarded for his devotion to his country. He carried with him into private life his cares and his wounds, the only return that honest men, as a rule, receive for having laboured for their country without thinking of themselves.

During this time William of Orange, not without using every means in his power to hasten the event which he desired, was waiting until the populace, whose idol he was, should make of the bodies of the two brothers the two steps which he needed to enable him to reach the stadtholdership.

On the 20th of August, then, 1672, the whole town, as we said at the commencement of this chap-

ter, was hastening towards the Buitenhof, to watch
Cornelius de Witt leave his prison on his way into
exile, and to see the traces left by the torture on the
body of this great man, who knew his Horace so
well.

It must not be supposed, however, that all the
multitude which was hastening to the Buitenhof
was doing so merely with the innocent intention of
enjoying a spectacle. Many of the crowd were
anxious to play an active part in it, or rather to do
over again something which they considered had not
been properly carried out—that is to say, the work
of the executioner.

There were others, it is true, who went with less
hostile intentions. All they were concerned about
was a spectacle, always pleasant to the feelings and
flattering to the pride of a mob, that, namely, of the
overthrow of one who has long held a high position.

" Is not this fearless Cornelius de Witt," they
asked, " now under lock and key, and broken down
by torture? Shall we not see him, pale, bleeding,
and disgraced? Was not this a great triumph for the
burghers, whose jealousy was much stronger than
that of the common people, and should not every
good burgher of The Hague take his share in it? "

" And then," said the Orangeist agitators, skilfully mingling with the crowd which they intended
to make use of as an instrument, keen-edged, and at
the same time crushing, " shall we not find between
the Buitenhof and the town-gate some small chance

A Grateful People

of throwing a little mud, or even a few stones, at this inspector of dykes, who not only refused the stadtholdership to the Prince of Orange until *vi coactus,* but also wished to have him assassinated? "

" To say nothing of the fact," added the fanatical enemies of France, " that if things are only well and boldly done at The Hague, Cornelius de Witt will never be allowed to go into exile, where, once free again, he will renew all his intrigues with France and live with his scoundrel of a brother on the gold of the Marquis of Louvois."

Animated by such sentiments, spectators usually run rather than walk, and this is why the inhabitants of The Hague hurried so fast towards the Buitenhof.

In the midst of those who advanced most eagerly, with rage in his heart and no settled plan in his mind, the honest Tychelaer hurried onward, paraded by the Orangeists as a hero of probity, of national honour, and of Christian charity.

This fine scoundrel related, with all the embellishments which his imagination could conjure up, the attempts which Cornelius de Witt had made to corrupt him, the sums which he had promised him, and the infernal machinations by which he had endeavoured to remove beforehand all the difficulties which he, Tychelaer, might meet with in carrying out the assassination.

And each sentence that he uttered, eagerly listened to by the mob, roused enthusiastic shouts in favour of Prince William, and cries of blind rage against the brothers De Witt.

The populace even went so far as to curse the iniquitous judges whose sentence had allowed such an abominable criminal as this Cornelius to escape with life and limb.

Some of the agitators kept muttering:

" He will get away! he will escape from us!"

" A vessel awaits him at Scheveningen, a French vessel. Tychelaer has seen it."

" Brave Tychelaer! Honest Tychelaer!" shouted the mob in chorus. " Don't forget either," added a voice, " that while Cornelius is flying in this way, John, who is just as much a traitor as his brother, will also escape."

" And the two rascals will squander our money in France, money got by selling our ships and arsenals and dockyards to Louis XIV."

" Don't let them go at all!" cried a patriot, more extreme than the rest.

And amid these cries, the burghers, cocking their muskets and brandishing their axes, began, with fury in their eyes, to run still faster towards the Buitenhof.

Still no violence had as yet been done, and the body of horsemen who were guarding the approaches to the Buitenhof remained cool, impassible, silent, more awe-inspiring by their very calmness than the whole crowd of burghers with their shouts, their excitement, and their threats. They sat motionless under the eye of their chief, the captain of the mounted troops of The Hague, who held his sword drawn but lowered, and with its point against the corner of his stirrup.

This troop, the sole defence of the prison, kept in check by its attitude not only the disorderly and shouting masses of the populace, but also the detachment of the town-guard, which, though placed in front of the Buitenhof to share with the horsemen the duty of keeping order, encouraged the seditious rioters by constantly shouting:

" Hurrah for Orange! Down with the traitors! "

The presence of Tilly and his horsemen was, it is true, a salutary check on all these civic soldiers, but in a short time their own shouting excited the town-guard more and more, and as they did not understand that it is possible to be brave without shouting, they attributed the silence of the horsemen to cowardice, and began to move towards the prison, drawing the whole disorderly mob after them.

But at this point the Count de Tilly advanced alone to meet them, and raising his sword, said, with a frown:

" Now, gentlemen of the town-guard, why are you moving, and what do you want? "

The burghers waved their muskets and continued their shouts of " Hurrah for Orange! Death to the traitors! "

" ' Hurrah for Orange! ' certainly," said De Tilly, " although, as a matter of fact, I prefer pleasant faces to gloomy ones. ' Death to the traitors! ' if you like, provided you don't go beyond wishing it in words only. Shout as much as you please ' Death to the traitors! ' but as for actually putting them to death, I am here to prevent that, and I will prevent it." Then, turning towards his men, he cried:

" Soldiers, make ready! "

The soldiers obeyed their commander's order with a precision and calmness which caused an immediate retreat of the burghers and the populace, a retreat accompanied by so much confusion that the officer laughed.

" There! there! " said he in that bantering tone which is peculiar to military men, " don't be alarmed, citizens; my men will not fire a shot, but you on your side will not advance a step towards the prison."

" Let me tell you, sir, that we have muskets," shouted the leader of the burghers, angrily.

" I see well enough that you have muskets," replied Tilly, " you make them flash so under my eyes, but take notice on your side, too, that we have pistols, and pistols carry admirably at fifty yards and you are only twenty-five yards off."

" Death to the traitors! " shouted the furious burghers.

" Bah! you always say the same thing," growled the officer; " it becomes wearisome."

And he resumed his post at the head of the troop, while the tumult continued to rage more and more furiously round the Buitenhof. And yet the enraged

A Grateful People

populace were unaware that, at the very moment
when they were so keenly on the scent of one of their
victims, the other, as though hastening to meet his
fate, was passing at only a hundred yards' distance,
behind the crowd and the horsemen, on his way to
the Buitenhof.

John de Witt had in fact just got down, with one
servant, from his carriage, and was quietly walking
across the fore-court of the prison.

He gave his name to the gatekeeper, who, for the
matter of that, knew him already, and added:

" Good-day, Gryphus. I have come to take away
my brother, Cornelius de Witt, out of the town. He
has been condemned, as you know, to exile."

And the gatekeeper, a kind of bear trained to
open and shut the gate of the prison, bowed and per-
mitted him to enter the building, the doors of which
were shut again behind him.

Ten yards from the door he met a charming
young girl of seventeen or eighteen, dressed in the
Frisian national costume, who made him a graceful
courtesy. Placing his hand lightly under her chin,
he said to her:

" Good-day, my good and fair Rosa; how is my
brother? "

" Oh! Mr. John," replied the young girl, "it is
not the harm which they have already done him that
I fear on his account, for that is past."

" What is it, then, that you are afraid of, my little
friend? "

The Black Tulip

" I am afraid of the harm which they still wish to do him."

" Oh yes," said De Witt, " you refer to the mob outside? "

" You hear them? "

" They are certainly very angry, but when they see us perhaps they will become calmer, as we have never done them anything but good."

" Unfortunately, that is no reason," murmured the girl, as, in obedience to a signal from her father, she retired.

" No! my child, no! you are perfectly right there."

Then, pursuing his way, he said to himself:

" Here is a young girl who probably cannot read, and who consequently has never read anything, yet she has just summed up the history of the world in a single phrase."

And still as calm as when he entered, but more melancholy, the ex-Grand Pensionary continued to walk towards his brother's cell.

II

THE TWO BROTHERS

WHILE John de Witt was ascending the stone
staircase which led to the cell of his brother Cornelius, the presentiment of the fair Rosa was being fulfilled in the action of the burghers, who were doing
their best to get rid of the troop of horsemen which
was in their way.

The populace perceived this, and appreciating the
good intentions of their militia, shouted lustily,
" Hurrah for the burghers!"

M. de Tilly on his side, prudent as well as firm,
was parleying with the burghers, under the protection of the cocked pistols of his squadron, explaining
as clearly as he could that the orders given him by
the States directed him to guard, with three com-
panies, the prison square and its approaches.

" Why this order? Why guard the prison?"
cried the Orangeists.

" Ah!" replied De Tilly, " there you ask more
than I can answer. They gave the order, ' Guard the
prison,' and I guard it. You, gentlemen, being almost soldiers yourselves, will know that an order is
not a matter to be discussed."

"But they have given this order so that the traitors may be able to leave the town."

"That may very well be, since the traitors are condemned to exile," replied Tilly.

"But who gave the order?"

"The States, of course."

"The States are betraying us."

"I know nothing about that."

"And you are a traitor yourself."

"I?"

"Yes, you."

"As to that, let us understand each other, gentlemen. Who am I to betray? The States? I cannot be betraying them, if, being in their pay, I am faithfully carrying out their orders."

Whereupon, as the count was so clearly in the right that it was impossible to discuss his answer, the cries and threats were redoubled; but alarming as they were, the count replied to them with all possible politeness.

"Really, gentlemen, I must ask you to uncock your muskets, if you please. One of them might go off by accident, and if the shot wounded one of my men, we should lay two hundred of you in the dust, a thing we should be truly sorry to do. You would be sorrier still, especially as the event would not be in accordance with the intentions of either party."

"If you were to do that," cried the burghers, "we in our turn should fire upon you."

"Yes, but all the same if you fired on us and

killed us all from the first rank to the last, those of you whom we had killed would not come to life again."

" Give the square up to us then, and you will be acting like a good citizen."

" In the first place," said Tilly, " I am not a citizen, but an officer, which is a very different thing, and next, I am not a Dutchman, but a Frenchman, and in that there is a still greater difference. I look only to the States which pay me. Bring me an order from the States to give up the square and I will march off on the instant, and willingly too, for I am horribly bored here."

" Yes, yes! " cried a hundred voices, instantly re-echoed by five hundred others, " let us go to the Town Hall and find the deputies. Come along! come along! "

" That's right! " muttered Tilly, as he watched the most excited of the throng making off, " go and ask at the Town Hall for your miserable order, and see whether you will get it. Go on, my friends, go on! "

The worthy officer relied upon the honour of the magistrates, as they relied upon his.

" I say, captain," whispered the first lieutenant in Tilly's ear, " it will be a good thing, I fancy, if the deputies refuse these madmen what they ask for, and send us a small re-enforcement instead."

Meanwhile John de Witt, whom we left mounting the stone staircase after his conversation with the jailer Gryphus and his daughter Rosa, had arrived at the door of the cell in which, on a mattress, lay his brother Cornelius, whom the public prosecutor had subjected, as we have said, to the preliminary torture. The decree of banishment having reached the prison, the second stage of the torture was not now necessary.

Cornelius, stretched on his bed, with bruised wrists and crushed fingers, having avowed nothing regarding a crime which he had not committed, was now, after three days of suffering, able to breathe freely once more, for he had been informed that the judges, from whom he had expected a sentence of death, had only condemned him to banishment.

Possessed of a vigorous body and an invincible spirit, he would have grievously disappointed his enemies had they been able, in the deep shadows of that cell in the Buitenhof, to perceive playing over his pale features the smile of the martyr, who, having caught a glimpse of the splendours of heaven, forgets the earth and its miseries.

The Ruart, thanks rather to the power of his will than to any external remedies, had already recovered his strength, and was calculating how much longer the formalities of the law would detain him in prison.

It was just at this moment that the combined clamours of the town militia and the populace were being raised against the two brothers, and were threatening Captain Tilly, who served as a rampart

The Two Brothers

before them. This uproar, which broke against the foot of the prison wall like a rising tide against the rocks, reached the ears of the prisoner.

But threatening as the sound was, Cornelius asked no questions about it; neither did he trouble to raise himself and look out through the iron bars of the narrow window by which light and sound from without penetrated to the cell.

He was so benumbed by his constant pain that he had almost become used to it. With such delight, too, did he feel that his soul and his mind were almost on the point of being released from the clogs of the body, that it seemed to him that this soul and mind of his, already freed from material things, was raised above them like a flame that flickers above an all but extinguished fire, which it is about to quit entirely in order to mount towards the skies.

He was thinking, too, of his brother.

Doubtless the approach of the latter was making itself felt by means of the unknown mysterious force which magnetism has since revealed. At the moment when John was so present to Cornelius that Cornelius was on the point of murmuring his name, John entered, and with hasty step crossed the cell to the bed of the prisoner, who extended his injured arms and his hands, still wrapped in linen, towards his great brother, whom he had succeeded in surpassing, not indeed in services to his country, but in the hatred which the Dutch felt towards him.

John tenderly kissed his brother on the forehead,

and replaced the injured hands gently on the mattress.

" My poor Cornelius," said he, " you are in great pain, are you not? "

" I suffer no longer, brother, now that I see you."

" Oh, my poor dear Cornelius, then I can only say that I suffer in your stead when I see you like this."

" I, too, have thought more of you than of myself, and while they were torturing me I did not think of complaining, except once, and then I said, ' My poor brother! ' But now you are here, let us forget all that. You have come to fetch me, have you not? "

" Yes."

" I am cured already. Help me up, brother, and you will see how well I can walk."

" You will not have to walk very far, my friend, for I have my carriage here, by the fish-pond, behind Tilly's dragoons."

" Tilly's dragoons? Why are they at the fish-pond? "

" Oh," said the Grand Pensionary, with his usual melancholy smile, " it is because it is thought that the people of The Hague will wish to see you set out, and they fear some slight disturbance."

" Disturbance? "

" Yes, Cornelius."

" So that is what I heard just now," said the prisoner, as though speaking to himself. Then, again addressing his brother, he said:

The Two Brothers

"There is a crowd on the Buitenhof, is there not?"

"Yes, brother."

"But then, to come here . . ."

"Well?"

"How was it they let you pass?"

"You know we are scarcely favourites, Cornelius," said the Grand Pensionary, in a tone both melancholy and bitter. "I came by the back streets."

"You hid yourself, John?"

"I wanted to reach you without loss of time, and I did what one does in politics and at sea, when the wind is against one—I tacked."

At this moment the shouts rose more furious than ever from the square to the prison. Tilly was arguing with the burgher-guard.

"Oh," said Cornelius, "you are a very good pilot, John, but I doubt whether you will take off your brother in this storm and through these breakers, as successfully as you conducted the fleet of Van Tromp to Antwerp, through the shallows of the Scheldt."

"With the help of God, Cornelius, we will try, nevertheless," replied John. "But one word first of all."

"Say on."

The shouts rose again.

"Ho! ho!" continued Cornelius, "how angry those fellows are! Is it with you? or is it with me?"

"I think it is with both of us, Cornelius. I was going to say just now that what these Orangeists chiefly reproach us with is that we opened up negotiations with France."

"The idiots!"

"Yes, but still they bring it against us."

"But if these negotiations had succeeded they would have been spared the defeats of Rees, Orsay, Vesel and Rheinberg; they would have escaped the crossing of the Rhine, and Holland would still have been able to believe herself invincible in the midst of her marshes and canals."

"All that is true, brother, but what is still truer is, that if at this moment they were to discover our correspondence with M. de Louvois, I should not be able, good pilot though I may be, to save the frail skiff which is to carry the De Witts and their fortunes out of Holland. That correspondence, which would prove to honest men how much I love my country and what sacrifices I offered to make personally for her liberty, that correspondence, I say, would destroy us with the Orangeists, who have got the better of us. Therefore, my dear Cornelius, I hope you burnt it before quitting Dort to come and join me at The Hague."

"Brother," replied Cornelius, "your correspondence with M. de Louvois proves that you are the greatest, the most generous, and the most enlightened citizen that the Seven Provinces have had in recent times. I love the glory of my country, and I love your good name, more than anything else, and I took good care not to burn the correspondence."

"Then we are lost, as far as this world goes," said the Grand Pensionary quietly; and he went towards the window.

"No; on the contrary, John, we shall save our lives and also recover our popularity."

"What have you done with the letters, then?"

"I have intrusted them to my godson Cornelius van Baerle, whom you know. He is living at Dort."

"Unfortunate young man! You have delivered to this dear honest soul, this scholar who, though he knows so much, thinks, strangely enough, of nothing but the flowers which bow their heads to God and of God who makes the flowers grow, you have delivered this fatal packet to him! Then our poor dear Cornelius is ruined, brother!"

"Ruined?"

"Yes, for either he will be strong or he will be weak. If he is strong—and however unaware he may now be of what is happening to us, buried as he is at Dort, and however absent-minded, it will be a miracle but he will know sooner or later what is happening to us—if he is strong, he will boast of our friendship for him, if he is weak, he will be afraid to acknowledge it; if he is strong, he will publish the secret, if he is weak, he will let it be discovered. In either case he is ruined, and so are we. So let us fly at once, brother, if there is yet time."

Cornelius raised himself on the bed, and taking

the hand of his brother, who shuddered at the touch of the bandages, he said:

"Do I not know my godson? Have I not learnt to read every thought in Van Baerle's mind, every feeling of his heart? You ask me whether he is weak, whether he is strong? He is neither the one nor the other. But what does it matter what he is? The point is that he will keep the secret for the simple reason that he does not know it."

John turned round in surprise.

"Oh," said Cornelius, with his sweet smile, "the Inspector of the Dikes is a politician, trained in the school of John de Witt. I repeat, brother, that Van Baerle is quite ignorant of the nature and the importance of the packet which I intrusted to him."

"Quick! then," cried John, "since there is yet time, send him an order to burn the bundle of papers."

"By whom can I send the order?"

"By my servant, Craeke. He was to have accompanied us on horseback, and came with me into the prison to help you down the stairs."

"Think well, John, before you burn these title-deeds of your fame."

"I think first of all, my dear Cornelius, that the brothers De Witt must save their lives if they wish to save their reputations. When we are dead, who will defend us, Cornelius? Who are they who alone have understood us?"

"You believe, then, that they would kill us if they found those papers?"

The Two Brothers

John, without answering his brother, extended his hand towards the Buitenhof from which at that moment bursts of ferocious yells were rising towards the prison.

" Yes, yes," said Cornelius, " I hear the shouting well enough, but what do they say? "

John opened the window.

" Death to the traitors! " yelled the mob.

" Do you understand now, Cornelius? "

" And we are the traitors! " said the prisoner, looking upwards and shrugging his shoulders.

" We are," replied John de Witt.

" Where is Craeke? "

" At the door of your cell, I believe."

" Bring him in then."

John opened the door; the faithful servant was waiting on the threshold.

" Come in, Craeke, and remember well what my brother is going to say to you."

" No, no! it will not be enough to say it, John. I must write it, unfortunately."

" Why so? "

" Because Van Baerle will not give up the deposit, or burn it, without a definite order."

" But can you write, my dear friend? " asked John, looking at the burnt and maimed hands of the prisoner.

" Oh, if I had pen and ink, you would see," said Cornelius.

" Here is a pencil, at any rate."

The Black Tulip

"Have you any paper? they have left me none here."

"This Bible—tear out the first leaf of it."

"Very well."

"But your writing will be illegible."

"Come now," said Cornelius, looking at his brother, "the fingers which have withstood the executioner's fire, and the will which has conquered agony, will unite in a common effort, and trust me, brother, the lines will be traced without a tremor."

Cornelius took up the pencil and began to write.

The pressure of the fingers on the pen forced out from the still unhealed wounds drops of blood which became visible under the white linen bandages.

A cold sweat broke out on the forehead of the Grand Pensionary.

Cornelius wrote:

"DEAR GODSON—Burn the packet which I intrusted to you. Burn it without looking into it, without opening it, so that you remain quite ignorant of its contents. Secrets of the kind which it contains are fatal to those with whom they are deposited. Burn it, and you will have saved John and Cornelius. Farewell, and love me.

"CORNELIUS DE WITT.

"August 20th, 1672."

John, with tears in his eyes, wiped away a drop of blood which had fallen on the leaf. Then giving the paper and some final directions to Craeke, he turned again to Cornelius, who had grown very pale and was almost fainting from the pain which the act of writing had caused.

"Now," said John, "when our worthy Craeke lets us hear his old boatswain's whistle, we shall know that he has got through the crowd and is on the other side of the fish-pond. Then we will start in our turn."

Five minutes had not elapsed when a long, steady, and rippling whistle pierced the dark dome-like tops of the elms and was heard above the clamour of the Buitenhof.

John lifted his arms to heaven in thanksgiving.

"And now, Cornelius," said he, "let us set off."

III

THE PUPIL OF JOHN DE WITT

WHILE John de Witt, in consequence of the increasing fury of the crowd on the Buitenhof, was hastening the departure of his brother Cornelius, a deputation of burghers had gone, as we have seen, to the Town Hall to demand the removal of Tilly's dragoons.

It is not very far from the Buitenhof to the Hoog Straat, and a stranger, who from the commencement of the scene had followed all its details with the greatest interest, now made his way with the others, or rather in the wake of the others, towards the Town Hall, in order to learn more quickly what was going to take place there.

This stranger was a very young man, barely twenty-two or twenty-three years of age, and he seemed deficient in vigour. Doubtless he did not wish to be recognised, for he hid his long pale face under a handkerchief of fine Frisian linen, with which he incessantly wiped his damp forehead or his burning lips.

With his fixed and steady eye, which was like that

The Pupil of John de Witt

of a bird of prey, his long aquiline nose, and his thin straight mouth, which was open, or rather split, like the lips of a wound, this man would have provided Lavater, if Lavater had been living at the time, with a subject for physiognomical study, the results of which would not at first sight have been very favourable to the possessor of the features.

Between the face of a conqueror and that of a pirate, asked the ancients, what difference is to be found? The same as will be found between an eagle and a vulture, between calmness and restlessness.

The sallow face, the thin and sickly body, and the uneasy walk of the stranger, who followed the shouting mob from the Buitenhof to the Hoog Straat, were the very type and image of a suspicious master or an uneasy thief; and a police officer would certainly have inclined towards the latter supposition, by reason of the care which the subject of our remarks took to escape notice.

For the rest, he was simply dressed and apparently carried no weapon. His arm, thin but sinewy, and his hand, dry, but white, elegant and aristocratic, rested, not on the arm but on the shoulder of an officer, who, with hand on sword, had watched, with an interest that will be readily understood, the whole scene on the Buitenhof. When the young man moved towards the Hoog Straat, he drew his companion with him.

Arrived on the square of the Hoog Straat, the pale-faced man pushed the other under the shelter of

31

an open window shutter, and fixed his eyes on the balcony of the Town Hall.

At the furious cries of the populace, a window in the Hoog Straat was opened, and a man came out to speak to the crowd.

"Who is that coming onto the balcony?" asked the young man of the officer, indicating by a glance the speaker, who seemed to be greatly agitated and rather held himself up by the balustrade than leant upon it.

"That is the Deputy Bowelt," replied the officer.

"What sort of a man is this Deputy Bowelt? Do you know anything of him?"

"A very worthy man, as far as I know, my Lord."

The young man, hearing this description of Bowelt's character from the officer, made so strange a gesture of disappointment and showed such evident dissatisfaction that his companion noticed it, and hastened to add:

"That is what is commonly said, at least, my Lord. I cannot myself state anything positively about him, as I know nothing personally of M. Bowelt."

"A worthy man!" repeated he who had been addressed as "my Lord." "An honest man, do you mean, or a brave man?"

"Ah! you will excuse me, my Lord, I cannot venture to settle that question regarding a man whom, I repeat, I know only by sight."

"Well," murmured the young man, "wait, and we shall soon see."

The Pupil of John de Witt

The officer bowed his head in token of assent, and remained silent.

" If this Bowelt is an honest man," continued his Highness, " he will give the request of these madmen a very queer reception."

And, in spite of his efforts to control it, the nervous twitching of his hand on the shoulder of his companion, like the fingers of a player on the keys of an instrument, betrayed the burning impatience which at times, and especially at this moment, was so ill-concealed under the icy and sombre expression of his face.

One could hear the head of the deputation of burghers questioning the deputy as to where the other deputies, his colleagues, were to be found.

" Gentlemen," repeated M. Bowelt for the second time, " gentlemen, I tell you that at this moment I am alone with M. d'Asperen, and I cannot decide anything by myself."

" The order! the order! " cried a thousand voices.

M. Bowelt tried to make a speech, but one could not hear a word he said, though one could tell from his gesticulations that he did not know what to do.

Seeing that he could not make himself heard, he turned again towards the window and called M. d'Asperen.

M. d'Asperen appeared in his turn on the balcony and was received with shouts still more vociferous than those which had welcomed M. Bowelt ten minutes earlier. Nevertheless, he attempted the difficult task of addressing the multitude, but the mob, rather than listen to M. d'Asperen's harangue, preferred to overpower the State guard, which, as a matter of fact, offered no resistance to the Sovereign People.

" Come," said the young man coldly, while the people poured into the principal door of the building, " come, colonel, the discussion is apparently going to take place inside. Let us go and listen to it."

" Ah! my Lord, my Lord, be careful."

" What of? "

" Among the deputies there are many who have had to do with you, and it would be enough if a single one recognised your Highness."

" Yes, to accuse me of being the instigator of all this! You are right," said the young man, whose cheeks reddened for an instant with shame at having shown his wishes so eagerly. " You are right, let us stay here. From here we shall see them come out again, with or without the order, and we shall be able to tell from the result whether M. Bowelt is an honest man or a brave man, a thing I am very anxious to discover."

" But," said the officer, looking with astonishment at him whom he had addressed as " my Lord," " your Highness does not suppose for a moment, I presume, that the deputies will order Tilly's cavalry to leave? "

" Why not? " asked the young man, coldly.

" Because to order that would be simply to sign the death-warrants of John and Cornelius de Witt."

The Pupil of John de Witt

"We shall see," replied the prince coldly. "God alone knows what passes in the hearts of men."

The officer, who was both a brave and an honest man, glanced stealthily at the impassible face of his companion and turned pale.

From the spot where they were standing they could hear the noise and the trampling of the people on the staircases of the Town Hall. Then, through the open windows of the room on the balcony of which M. Bowelt and M. d'Asperen had appeared, the noise issued and spread all over the square. The two deputies had gone in again, fearing no doubt that the rush of people would push them right over the balustrade.

Almost immediately afterward the figures of the mob appeared, like whirling shadows, behind the windows of the Town Hall.

The council chamber was filling.

Suddenly the noise ceased; then, as suddenly, it began again louder than ever, and increased to such a degree that the old building shook with it to the roof.

Then, finally, the torrent rolled back again through the galleries and down the staircase to the door, under the arch of which it poured forth like water out of a spout.

At the head of the first group there flew, rather than ran, a man whose face was hideously disfigured by ferocious joy. It was the surgeon Tychelaer.

The Black Tulip

"We have it! we have it!" he cried, waving a paper in the air.

"They have the order!" muttered the officer in amazement.

"Well, now I am answered," said the prince, quietly. "You did not know, my dear colonel, whether M. Bowelt was an honest man or a brave man. He is neither the one nor the other."

Then, still keeping his eye steadily on the multitude which surged past him, he said:

"Now come to the Buitenhof, colonel. I think we shall see a strange sight there."

The officer bowed, and followed his master without replying.

On the square and about the approaches of the prison, the crowd was enormous. But the horsemen of Tilly still kept it in check with the same good humour and the same firmness as before.

Very soon the count heard the increasing uproar caused by the approaching torrent of humanity; and immediately afterward he saw the foremost waves of it, rolling onward with the rapidity of a cataract. At the same moment he perceived the paper waving in the air above the moving arms and the glittering weapons.

"Eh!" said he, rising in his stirrups and touching the lieutenant with the pommel of his sword, "I believe the wretches have got the order."

"Cowardly scoundrels!" cried the lieutenant.

It was indeed the order; the burgher-guard re-

The Pupil of John de Witt

ceived it with shouts of joy. They immediately began to march forward, with lowered arms and loud shouts, to meet Tilly's horsemen.

But the count was not the man to allow them to approach too near. "Halt!" he cried, "halt! and stand away from the heads of the horses, or I will give the word ' Forward! ' "

"Here is the order!" replied a hundred insolent voices.

He took it with amazement, cast a rapid glance over it, and said in a loud voice:

"Those who have signed this order are the real executioners of M. Cornelius de Witt. As for me, I would not have written a single letter of this infamous order, to save my two hands."

And repulsing with the pommel of his sword a man who wanted to take back the order from him, he said:

"One moment! a document like this is important and must be preserved."

He folded the paper and put it away carefully in the pocket of his doublet.

Then, turning towards his men:

"Tilly's horse!" he said, "right wheel!"

And in a lower tone, yet so that his words were not entirely lost to the bystanders, he added:

"And now, murderers, do your work!"

A furious yell, inspired by all the fierce hatred and ferocious delight which inspired those on the Buitenhof, greeted the departure of the troops.

As the horsemen slowly filed off, the count remained behind facing till the last moment the maddened populace, who advanced step by step as the captain's horse backed.

As one sees, John de Witt had not exaggerated the danger when he helped his brother to rise and pressed him to set out at once.

Cornelius, leaning on the arm of the ex-Grand Pensionary, descended the stairs leading to the courtyard.

At the foot of the staircase he found the fair Rosa, trembling.

" Oh, Mr. John," said she, " what a misfortune! "

" What is the matter, my child? "

" They say that some of them have gone to the Hoog Straat to get an order for the removal of Count Tilly's horsemen."

" Oh! oh! " said John. " Indeed, my child, if the horsemen go we shall be in a bad way."

" I have, therefore, some advice to give you," said the young girl, still trembling.

" Give it, my child. There is no reason why I should be surprised at God's speaking to me through you."

" Well, Mr. John, I would not go out by the main street."

"And why do you say that, since Tilly's horsemen are still at their post? "

" Yes, but the order, even if it is not revoked, is to remain in front of the prison."

" Quite so."

The Pupil of John de Witt

" Have you got an order that they should accompany you out of the town? "

" No."

" Well, then, as soon as you have passed the first horsemen, you will fall into the hands of the people."

" But the burgher-guard? "

" Oh, the burgher-guard is more furious than all the others."

" What is to be done, then? "

" In your place, Mr. John," continued the young girl timidly, " I would go out of the prison by the postern gate. The door opens onto a street which is quite deserted, for every one is in the main street, waiting at the chief gate of the prison. Then I would go to that gate of the city by which you wish to leave."

" But my brother will not be able to walk," said John.

" But you have your carriage, have you not? " asked the girl.

" The carriage is waiting at the chief gate of the prison."

" No," replied the girl. " I thought your coachman could be trusted, so I told him to wait for you at the postern."

The two brothers looked at her tenderly and the eyes of both, resting together on the young girl, expressed their thanks.

"Now," said the Grand Pensionary, "it remains to be seen whether Gryphus will open this door for us."

The Black Tulip

" Oh, no, he will not," said Rosa.

" Well, what are we to do, then? "

" Ah, I foresaw his refusal and just now, while he was talking at the prison window with one of the troopers, I took the key from his bunch."

" And you have it—this key? "

" Here it is, Mr. John."

" My child," said Cornelius, " I have nothing to give you in exchange for this service which you are doing me, except the Bible which you will find in my room; it is the last present of an honest man; may it bring you good fortune! "

" Thank you, Mr. Cornelius, I will never part with it," replied the girl. Then to herself she added with a sigh:

" What a pity it is I do not know how to read! "

" The shouting grows louder, my child," said John. " I think we have not a moment to lose."

" Come, then," said the fair Frisian, and she led the brothers by an inner passage to the other side of the prison.

Still guided by Rosa, they descended a staircase of about a dozen steps, crossed a small court with castellated ramparts, and the arched gate being opened for them, they found themselves outside the prison in a deserted street, opposite a carriage which was waiting for them, with the step already lowered.

" Oh, quick! quick! my masters, do you hear them? " cried the terrified coachman.

The Pupil of John de Witt

But the Grand Pensionary, having made Cornelius get into the carriage first, turned towards the young girl.

"Good-bye, my child," said he; "all that we could say would be but a feeble expression of our gratitude. We commend you to God. He will remember, I trust, that you have this day saved the lives of two men."

Rosa took, and respectfully kissed, the hand extended to her by the Grand Pensionary.

"Go! go!" she said, "it sounds as if they were breaking in the door."

John de Witt mounted in haste, took his seat beside Cornelius, and fastened the apron of the carriage, calling out:

"To the Tol-Hek!"

The Tol-Hek was the iron gate which closed the road leading to the little port of Scheveningen, where a small boat was awaiting the two brothers.

The carriage, drawn by two strong Flemish horses, set off with the fugitives at a gallop.

Rosa followed it with her eyes till it turned the corner of the street. Then she went in, shut the door behind her, and threw the key into a well.

The noise which had made Rosa think that the populace were breaking in the door of the prison was, indeed, caused by the mob, which, after clearing the prison square, had precipitated itself against the door of the prison.

In spite of its thickness, and of the fact that the

The Black Tulip

jailer Gryphus, to do him justice, obstinately refused to open it, it was easy to see that the door could not long withstand the attack made upon it, and Gryphus, growing paler and paler, was asking himself whether it would not be better to open the gate than to have it broken in, when he felt himself gently pulled by the coat.

He turned and saw Rosa.

"You hear these madmen?" said he.

"I hear them so well, father, that in your place . . ."

"You would open, would you not?"

"No, I would let them break the door in."

"But they will kill me."

"Yes, if they see you."

"How can they miss seeing me?"

"Hide yourself."

"Where?"

"In the secret cell."

"But you, my child?"

"I will go down into it with you, father. We will shut the door on ourselves, and when they have left the prison we will come out of our hiding-place again."

"Blest if you aren't right!" cried Gryphus; then he added, "it is amazing what a lot of sense there is in that little head."

Then, as the door, to the great delight of the mob, began to give way,

"Come, father, come," said Rosa, opening a small trap-door.

The Pupil of John de Witt

" But still, our prisoners? " said Gryphus.

" God will take care of them, father," said the girl. " Let me take care of you."

Gryphus followed his daughter, and the trap-door shut down over their heads, just at the moment when, through the broken door, the mob gained entrance to the prison.

This cell, the secret cell as it was called, into which Rosa had induced her father to descend, afforded the two persons we have just mentioned a safe refuge, in which we must now leave them for a little while. The secret cell was known only to the authorities, who sometimes used it for the safe-keeping of important prisoners when a rising or a rescue was to be feared.

The mob rushed into the prison, crying:

" Death to the traitors! To the gallows with Cornelius de Witt! Death! Death!"

IV

THE MURDERERS

THE young man, still wearing his large hat, still leaning on the officer's arm, still wiping his forehead and lips with his handkerchief, remained motionless in a corner of the Buitenhof, hidden in the shadow of an awning which overhung a closed shop. He kept his eyes fixed on the spectacle afforded by the infuriated crowd, whose proceedings seemed to be rapidly coming to a crisis.

"Ah," said he to the officer, "I think that you are right, Van Deken, and that the order signed by the deputies is really the death-warrant of Cornelius. Do you hear the crowd? They are decidedly angry with the De Witts."

"Truly," said the officer, "I never heard such yells in my life."

"They must have found the cell, I think. Look! is not that the window of the room in which Cornelius was detained?"

One of the mob had seized with both hands, and was violently shaking, the iron bars of the window of the cell which Cornelius had left barely ten minutes earlier.

The Murderers

"Halloa! halloa!" cried the man, "he is not here!"

"What! not there!" cried those who were still in the street and who, having arrived last, could not get into the prison, which was already over-crowded.

"No! no!" repeated the man in a fury, "he is not here. He must have escaped."

"What does he say?" asked the prince, growing pale.

"Oh, my Lord, he gives them a piece of news which would be very good, if it were true."

"Yes, no doubt, it would be good news if it were true," said the young man; "only, unfortunately, it cannot be true."

"But look . . ." said the officer.

And, in fact, other furious faces, distorted with rage, showed themselves at the windows, crying:

"Escaped! Rescued! They have got him out!"

And the crowd in the street repeated, with frightful imprecations:

"Gone! escaped! After them! follow them!"

"My Lord," said the officer, "it seems that M. Cornelius de Witt has really escaped."

"Yes, from the prison, perhaps, but not from the town. You will see, Van Deken, that the poor man will find the gate of the town locked, which he thought to find open."

"Has the order been given to shut the gates, then, my Lord?"

" No, I think not. Who would have given such
an order? "

" What makes you suppose it, then? "

" There are fatalities," replied the prince carelessly, " and the greatest men sometimes fall victims
to them."

The officer, at these words, felt a shudder pass
through his veins, for he understood that, in one way
or another, the prisoner was doomed.

At this moment the roar of the mob broke out
like a thunder-clap, for they saw that Cornelius de
Witt was really no longer in the prison. Cornelius
and John, in fact, after having skirted the fish-pond,
had taken the main road leading to the Tol-Hek,
directing the coachman to moderate the speed of his
horses so that the passing of the carriage might not
arouse any suspicion.

But when he had gone half-way down the road
and saw the iron gate in the distance, the driver, feeling that he was leaving behind him prison and death,
and had before him life and liberty, disregarded all
precautions and urged his horses to a gallop.

Suddenly he stopped.

" What is it? " asked John, putting his head out
of the window.

" Oh! my masters," cried the coachman,
" the . . ."

Terror choked the worthy man's voice.

" Come, say on! " said the Grand Pensionary.

" The gate is shut."

The Murderers

" What? the gate shut! It is not usual to shut the gate in the daytime."

" Look at it yourself."

John de Witt leaned out of the carriage and saw that the gate was really closed.

" Go on, all the same," said he. " I have the order of commutation here; the gatekeeper will open for us."

The carriage resumed its course, but it was evident that the driver had lost confidence.

Moreover, when John de Witt put his head out of the window, he had been seen and recognised by an innkeeper, who, left behind by his comrades, was hastily shutting his door in order to go and join them on the Buitenhof.

He uttered a cry of astonishment and ran after two other men who were running on ahead of him.

At the end of a hundred yards he caught them up, and spoke to them; then all three stopped and looked after the receding carriage, still uncertain as to who were in it.

The carriage meanwhile reached the Tol-Hek.

" Open! " cried the driver.

" Open? " said the gatekeeper, appearing at the door of his lodge, " open? and what with, pray? "

" With the key, of course," said the coachman.

" With the key, yes; but for that one must have the key."

47

"What!" said the coachman, "you have not the key of the gate?"

"No."

"What have you done with it, then?"

"Why, it has been taken away from me."

"By whom?"

"By some one who probably did not want anybody to leave the town."

"My friend," said the Grand Pensionary, putting his head out of the window, and risking everything to gain everything, "it is for me, John de Witt, and for my brother Cornelius, whom I am taking away into exile."

"Oh! Mr. de Witt, I am indeed sorry," said the gatekeeper, running to the carriage, "but on my honour, the key has been taken from me."

"When was that?"

"This morning."

"By whom?"

"By a pale, thin young man of about twenty-two."

"And why did you give it up to him?"

"Because he had an order, signed and sealed."

"From whom?"

"From the gentlemen at the Town Hall."

"Well, then," said Cornelius quietly, "it appears that we are undoubtedly doomed."

"Do you know if the same precaution has been taken at the other gates?"

"I do not."

The Murderers

"Come," said John to the coachman, "God commands man to do everything he can to preserve his life. Try another gate."

Then, while the driver was turning the carriage round, John said to the gatekeeper:

"Thank you for your goodwill, my friend; the will is as good as the deed. You wished to save us, and in the eyes of God it is the same as if you had succeeded."

"Ah, look!" said the gatekeeper, "do you see? Down there!"

"Gallop through this group of men," cried John to the driver.

The nucleus of the group which John referred to was composed of the three men, whom we saw looking after the carriage. They had since been joined, while John was talking to the gatekeeper, by seven or eight newcomers.

The latter evidently had hostile intentions with regard to the carriage. Seeing the horses coming upon them at a gallop, they spread themselves out across the road, waving their arms and sticks, and shouting, "Stop! stop!" The coachman, however, leaned over his horses and lashed them violently with his whip.

Carriage and men came together with a crash.

The brothers De Witt, shut in as they were, could see nothing. But they felt the horses rear, and then experienced a violent jolt. For a moment vehicle and horses hesitated and rocked, and then, passing over something round and yielding, which seemed like the body of a prostrate man, started off afresh, followed by oaths and curses.

" Oh," said Cornelius, " I greatly fear we have injured some one."

" Gallop! gallop! " cried John.

But, in spite of the order, suddenly the driver pulled up.

" Well, what now? " asked John.

" Do you see them? " asked the coachman.

John looked out.

The whole crowd from the Buitenhof appeared at the end of the road which the carriage had to pass through, and advanced like a howling storm.

" Stop, and save yourself," said John; " it is useless to proceed; we are lost."

" There they are! there they are! " cried five hundred voices together. " Yes, there they are, the traitors, the murderers, the assassins! " shouted those who were running after the carriage to those who were advancing to meet it. The former carried in their arms the mangled body of one of their comrades, who had been knocked down by the horses as he tried to clutch at the reins. It was over his body that the carriage had passed.

The coachman stopped, but in spite of the entreaties of his master made no effort to escape.

In a moment the carriage was caught between those who were following and those who came to meet it.

The Murderers

For an instant it overtopped the whole agitated crowd, like some floating island.

Suddenly the floating island became stationary. A blacksmith with a blow of his hammer had killed one of the horses, which fell in the traces.

At this moment the shutter of a window opened and one could see the ghastly face of the young man, and his gloomy eyes fixed on the scene which was being enacted. Behind him appeared the face of the officer, almost as pale as his own.

" My God! your Highness, what is going to happen? " murmured the officer.

" Something very terrible, you may be sure," replied his companion.

" Ah! do you see, my Lord, they are dragging the Grand Pensionary from the carriage, and beating and tearing him."

" Indeed, those people must be urged on by violent indignation," said the young man, in the same impassive tone which he had hitherto preserved.

" Now they are dragging Cornelius from the carriage, injured as he is already, and mutilated by the torture. Oh, look! look! "

" Yes, that is Cornelius, beyond a doubt."

The officer uttered a low cry and turned away his head.

For, while still on the last step of the carriage and even before he had set foot on the ground, the Ruart had received a blow from an iron bar, which fractured his skull.

The Black Tulip

Yet he rose again, but only to fall immediately.

Then some of the mob took him by the feet and dragged him along through the crowd, in the midst of which one could follow the bloody track left by the body. The mob closed up behind him with howls and yells of triumph.

The young man became still paler, though one would not have thought it possible, and for an instant closed his eyes.

The officer noticed this sign of pity, the first which his stern companion had allowed to escape him, and wishing to take advantage of this softening of the heart, said:

"Come, my Lord, come, they are going to assassinate the Grand Pensionary also."

But the young man had already opened his eyes.

"Indeed," said he, "the people are implacable. It is fatal to betray them."

"My Lord," said the officer, "could we not save this poor man, who taught your Highness? If there is any way tell me what it is, and though I should lose my life . . ."

William of Orange, for it was he, frowned in a sinister fashion, and suppressing the angry glitter which showed itself in his eyes, replied:

"Colonel van Deken, go, if you please, and find my troops, so that they may be ready to meet any emergency."

"But shall I leave your Lordship alone here, close to these murderers?"

The Murderers

"Do not trouble yourself about me more than I trouble myself," said the prince sharply. "Go!"

The officer set out with a rapidity which was less a sign of his obedience than of his pleasure at not being a witness of the abominable murder of the second of the two brothers.

He had not shut the door of the room before John, who by a supreme effort had reached the steps of a house situated almost opposite to that in which his pupil was hidden, began to stagger under the blows which rained upon him from all sides, and called out:

"My brother! where is my brother?"

One of the ruffians struck off his hat with a blow of his fist. Another held up before his eyes a hand covered with blood; this man had been tearing the body of Cornelius, and while the others were dragging the dead body of the latter to the gibbet, he had run as fast as he could so as not to lose the chance of doing the same to the Grand Pensionary, as he had done to his brother.

John uttered a pitiable groan and put his hand before his eyes.

"Ah, you shut your eyes, do you?" said one of the soldiers of the burgher-guard. "Well, I am going to put them out for you."

And with a pike he struck him a blow in the face so that the blood spurted out.

"Brother!" cried De Witt, trying, through the blood which blinded him, to see what had become of Cornelius.

The Black Tulip

"Go and join him," yelled another assassin, holding a musket to his temple and pulling the trigger.

But the gun did not go off.

Then the murderer reversed his weapon, and taking it with both hands by the barrel, struck down the Grand Pensionary with a blow from the butt-end.

John de Witt staggered and fell at his feet.

But immediately, raising himself by a supreme effort, he cried out " Brother! " in so pitiable a manner that the young man drew the shutter in front of him.

Little, however, remained to be seen, for a third assassin fired a shot at the Grand Pensionary at close quarters, and blew out his brains.

John de Witt fell, to rise no more.

Encouraged by his fall the wretches all became eager to strike at the body. Each wished to give a blow with a hammer, with a sword, or with a knife; each wished to draw his drop of blood, to tear off his shred of clothing.

Then, when both were quite dead, and torn, and stripped, the populace dragged the naked and bleeding bodies to an improvised gibbet from which some amateur executioners suspended them by the feet.

Then came the turn of the greatest cowards and scoundrels of all. They had not dared to strike the living flesh, but they now hacked at the dead, and went about the town selling small pieces of the bodies of John and Cornelius at ten sous apiece.

We cannot say whether, through the almost imperceptible chink in the shutter, the young man saw the end of this terrible scene, but at the moment when they were hanging the two martyrs on the gibbet, he passed through the crowd, which was too much engaged on the joyous task it was accomplishing to trouble itself about him.

He soon reached the Tol-Hek.

"Ah, sir," cried the gatekeeper, "have you brought me back the key?"

"Yes, my friend, here it is," replied the young man.

"It is a great pity you did not bring it back just half an hour sooner," said the gatekeeper, with a sigh.

"And why so?" asked the young man.

"Because I could then have opened for M. de Witt and his brother. As it was they were obliged to retrace their steps. They fell into the hands of those who were pursuing them."

"Gate! gate!" cried a voice which seemed to be that of a man in a great hurry.

The prince turned and recognised Colonel van Deken.

"Is that you, colonel?" said he. "Not yet set out from The Hague! This is taking a very long time to carry out my orders!"

"My Lord," replied the colonel, "this is the third gate I have been to. I found the other two closed."

"Well, this good man will open this one for us. Open it, my friend," said the prince to the gatekeeper, who was quite amazed at the title of "my Lord," given by Colonel van Deken to this pale young man, to whom he himself had been speaking so familiarly.

Accordingly, to make up for his presumption, he made as great haste as he could to open the Tol-Hek, which rolled back, creaking on its hinges.

"Will you take this horse, my Lord?" asked the colonel, of William.

"No, thank you, colonel, I should have one waiting for me a short distance from here."

And taking from his pocket a golden whistle such as was used for calling servants at that time, he blew a long and shrill call upon it. At the sound a mounted equerry came riding up, leading a second horse.

William vaulted to the saddle without touching the stirrup, and using both spurs soon reached the road to Leyden.

When he had gained it, he turned round.

The colonel was following at a horse's length behind.

The prince made him a sign to ride alongside.

"Do you know," said he, without drawing rein, "that those scoundrels killed John de Witt as well as Cornelius?"

"Ah, my Lord," said the colonel sadly, "I should have been better pleased, even on your account, if those two difficulties in the way of your becoming stadtholder had still remained."

"Certainly, it would have been better," said the

The Murderers

young man, "if what has happened had not happened. But anyhow what is done is done, and we were not the cause of it. Let us spur on quickly, colonel, so as to arrive at Alphen before the message which the States will certainly send me at the camp there."

The colonel bowed and let the prince ride ahead, himself resuming the place behind him which he had occupied before William addressed him.

"Ah! I should like," muttered William of Orange spitefully, compressing his lips and driving his spurs into his horse, "I should like very much to see the face of 'Louis the Sun King' when he learns how his good friends, the De Witts, have been served. Ah! Sun, Sun, well am I named William the Silent; Sun, look to your beams!"

And so saying he rode quickly onward, this young prince, the bitter rival of the great king; this stadt-holder, who had been so insecure the evening before in his new position, but for whom the burghers of The Hague had now made two stepping-stones with the corpses of the two noble princes, the brothers De Witt.

V

THE AMATEUR TULIP-GROWER AND HIS NEIGHBOUR

Meantime, while the citizens of The Hague were tearing in pieces the corpses of John and Cornelius, and while William of Orange, having assured himself that his antagonists were really dead, was galloping along the road to Leyden followed by Colonel van Deken, whom he found a little too compassionate to deserve a continuance of the confidence with which he had hitherto honoured him, Craeke, the faithful servant, also mounted on a good horse, had been riding along the tree-shaded roads which led out of the town and past the neighbouring villages.

Once out of danger, he determined, in order to avoid suspicion, to leave his horse at a livery-stable; having done this he continued his journey quietly by water. Boats carried him by stages to Dort, skilfully taking advantage of the shortest cuts through the sinuous arms of the river which bathed with limpid caresses the charming islands, bordered with willows, rushes and flowering grasses, and covered with herds of fat cattle, that browsed peacefully in the sunshine.

From afar Craeke recognised the fair city of Dort,

The Tulip-Grower and his Neighbour

situated at the foot of a low hill dotted with wind-mills. He saw the handsome red houses, ornamented with white lines, bathing their bricky feet in the water. He saw the silk tapestries, embellished with golden flowers, marvels of Indian and Chinese art, hung out over the open balconies above the river; and near these tapestries, the long fishing-lines set to catch the voracious eels that were attracted round the houses by the fragments thrown every day from the kitchen windows into the water.

From the deck of the boat Craeke saw, across the turning sails of the windmills, on the slope of the hill, the red and white house which marked his journey's end. The ridges of its roof were lost amid the yel-lowish foliage of a curtain of poplar trees, and the whole house stood out against a dark background of gigantic elms. It was so placed that the sun falling upon it, as though into a funnel, warmed, dried, and even made fruitful, the slight fogs which, in spite of the barrier of verdure, the breeze from the river car-ried there every morning and evening.

Landed in the midst of the ordinary bustle of the town, Craeke immediately directed his steps towards the house which we shall later describe to the reader. Bright, trim, and elegant, more scrupulously clean and more carefully waxed in the hidden corners than in those parts which were easily seen, this house was occupied by a happy mortal.

The happy mortal—a *rara avis*, as Juvenal says—was Dr. van Baerle, the godson of Cornelius de

The Black Tulip

Witt. From his childhood he had lived in the house which we have referred to, for in it had been born both his father and his grandfather, former merchant princes of the famous town of Dort.

M. van Baerle, the father, had amassed in the India trade three or four hundred thousand florins, and M. van Baerle, the son, on the death of his good and dear parents, in 1668, had found these florins quite unworn, although, as the dates showed, some of them had been struck in 1610 and the rest in 1640— which proved that some of them were the florins of M. van Baerle the father and the others the florins of M. van Baerle the grandfather. These four hundred thousand florins, we must add, were merely the purse or pocket-money of Cornelius van Baerle, the hero of our story, for his landed property in the province brought him in an annual sum of about ten thousand florins.

When the worthy man who was the father of Cornelius was on the point of death, three months after the funeral of his wife, who seemed to have gone before to make the way of death easy for him, as she had made the way of life, he said to his son, embracing him for the last time:

" Eat, drink, and spend your money, if you wish to live a real life; for to labour all day on a wooden stool or a leather chair, in a laboratory or a shop, is not living. You will die in your turn, and if you are not fortunate enough to have a son our name will become extinct, and my florins will be amazed to find

The Tulip-Grower and his Neighbour

themselves owned by a strange master, my new florins which have never been handled except by my father, myself, and the man who struck them. Above all things, do not follow the example of your godfather, Cornelius de Witt, who has thrown himself into politics, the most thankless of all careers, and who will undoubtedly come to a bad end."

And then the worthy M. van Baerle died, leaving his son Cornelius overwhelmed with grief, for he had little love for the florins, but a great love for his father.

Cornelius, then, remained alone in the big house. It was in vain that his godfather Cornelius offered him employment in the public service; it was in vain that he tried to give him a taste for glory. Cornelius, out of obedience to his godfather, embarked with De Ruyter on the ship The Seven Provinces, which was at the head of the hundred and thirty-nine vessels with which the illustrious admiral set out to measure his strength against that of France and England combined. When, conducted by the pilot Leger, he had been within a musket-shot of the ship Prince, on which was the Duke of York, brother of the King of England, at the moment when the attack of De Ruyter, his patron, was so rapid and skilful that, seeing his ship on the point of being taken, the Duke of York had only just time to withdraw onto the St. Michael; when he had seen the St. Michael so battered and crushed under the cannon-balls of the Dutch that it had to leave the line; when he had seen a ship, the Earl of Sandwich, blow up, and four hundred sailors perish in the waves or in the fire; when he had seen, at the end of all this, after twenty ships had been battered to pieces, after three thousand men had been killed and five thousand wounded, that nothing was decided on one side or the other; that each claimed the victory; that everything had to be begun again, and that the only result was that another sea-fight, that of Southwold Bay, had been added to the list of battles; when he had calculated what a loss of time it is to have to stop one's eyes and ears if one wishes to think, while one's fellows desire to cannonade each other, Cornelius bade adieu to De Ruyter, to the Ruart de Pulten, and to glory, took leave of the Grand Pensionary, for whom he had a profound admiration, and retired to his home at Dort, rich in the repose which he had regained, in his twenty-eight years, his excellent constitution, his perfect eyesight, his four hundred thousand florins of capital and his ten thousand of income, and, moreover, with this conviction, that a man has always received from Heaven more than enough to make him happy, and enough to prevent him from being so.

Consequently, in order to have some pleasure of his own choosing, Cornelius began to study plants and insects. He collected and classified all the flora of the Dutch islands; got together specimens of all the insects of the province, on which he wrote a manuscript treatise with plates drawn by himself; and, finally, not knowing what further to do with his time,

The Tulip-Grower and his Neighbour

and, above all, with his money, which was increasing at an alarming rate, he ended by selecting from among all the follies of his country and his age, one of the most delightful and the most costly—he fell in love with tulips.

This, as is well known, was the period when the Dutch and the Portuguese, emulating one another in this kind of horticulture, had become almost to worship the tulip and to regard this Oriental flower as no naturalist had ever dared to regard the human race, for fear of encroaching on the rights of God.

Soon from Dort to Mons, the tulips of M. van Baerle were the general topic of conversation; and his flower-beds, his pits, his drying-rooms, and his catalogues of offset bulbs were inspected by visitors, as in former times the galleries and libraries of Alexandria had been visited by distinguished Roman travellers.

Van Baerle began by spending his yearly revenue in setting up his collection; then he dipped into his store of new florins in order to perfect it. His labours were rewarded by magnificent results: he produced five new species of tulips, which he named the Jane, after his mother; the Baerle, after his father; the Cornelius, after his godfather—the other names we have forgotten, but experts will certainly be able to find them in contemporary catalogues.

In 1672, at the beginning of the year, Cornelius de Witt went to Dort to stay three months in the old mansion of his family, for not only was Cornelius born, as we know, at Dort, but the family of the De Witts came originally from that city.

Cornelius, at that time, as William of Orange observed, was beginning to enjoy the completest unpopularity. Nevertheless, in the eyes of his fellow-citizens, he had not yet become a scoundrel fit to be hanged, and although they were not very well satisfied with his republicanism, which was a little too pure for them, they were proud of his important position in the state, and were willing enough to offer him the loving-cup when he entered their town.

Having returned thanks to his fellow-citizens, Cornelius went to see the family residence, and gave orders that certain repairs should be done before his wife, Mme. de Witt, came to stay there with her children.

Then the Ruart made his way to the house of his godson, the only person, perhaps, in Dort who was still unaware of the presence of his godfather in the town.

Van Baerle had gained as much sympathy by completely neglecting the cultivation of politics in favour of the cultivation of tulips, as Cornelius de Witt had gained hatred by dealing with the maleficent seeds which are called political passions.

Hence Van Baerle was beloved by his servants and his workmen; hence, too, he was unable to imagine that there was in the world any man who wished to injure another.

And yet, to the shame of humanity be it said,

The Tulip-Grower and his Neighbour

Cornelius van Baerle, without knowing it, had an enemy more bitter, more irreconcilable, more ferocious, than any of those Orangeists whom the Ruart and his brother had hitherto met with, even including those who were most hostile to the two great brothers, whose devotion to each other, unclouded during life, was to remain famous even after their death.

When Cornelius began to devote himself to tulips, he did not spare in the enterprise his yearly income or the florins of his father.

There was at that time living at Dort, next door to Cornelius, a burgher named Isaac Boxtel, who, from the day when he had attained the use of reason, had devoted himself to the same hobby, and was ready to go into ecstasies at the mere mention of the word *tulban*, which the Floriste Français, that is to say, the most learned treatise on the flower, assured him was the first word used in the Cingalese language to signify that masterpiece of the creation which we call the tulip.

Boxtel had not the good fortune to be as rich as Van Baerle. It was therefore only with great trouble and by the exercise of much patience and care that he had succeeded in making at his house in Dort a garden suited to the cultivation of the tulip; he had parcelled out the ground according to the recognised principles, and given to his beds exactly that amount of heat and of cool fresh air which the code of gardeners laid down as correct.

The Black Tulip

To the twentieth part of a degree almost, Isaac knew the temperature of his glass-frames. He knew the force of the wind and tempered it so as to accommodate it to the waving of the stems of his flowers. And, consequently, his productions began to please the public. They were good, nay, choice. Several connoisseurs had been to see Boxtel's tulips. Finally, Boxtel had launched into the world of Linnæus and the Tourneforts a tulip bearing his own name. This tulip had made its way across France, had entered Spain and had penetrated even to Portugal, and the King, Alphonso VI, who, after being chased from Lisbon, had retired to the island of Terceira and there amused himself, not, like the great Condé, by watering carnations, but by cultivating tulips, had exclaimed, on seeing the Boxtel tulip, " Not at all bad! "

Suddenly, after all the studies to which he had given himself up in succession, Cornelius van Baerle was seized with a passion for tulips. Thereupon he altered his house at Dort, which, as we have seen, was next door to that of Boxtel, and caused one of the buildings in his court-yard to be raised one story. This cut off about half a degree of heat from Boxtel's garden and added, instead, half a degree of cold, to say nothing of the fact that it cut off the wind and upset all the calculations and horticultural arrangements of his neighbour.

After all, in the eyes of Boxtel, this was the whole extent of his misfortune. Van Baerle was merely a painter, that is to say, a kind of lunatic, who disfigures the marvels of Nature in trying to reproduce them on canvas. The painter had raised his studio one story in order to have a better light; he certainly had a right to do so. M. van Baerle was a painter, just as M. Boxtel was an artist in tulips; he wanted more sun for his pictures, and so he took half a degree of it from the tulips of M. Boxtel. The law was on the side of M. van Baerle. *Bene sit.*

Besides, Boxtel had discovered that too much sun injures the tulip, and that the flower grew better and had more colour if exposed to the temperate heat of the morning and evening sun than if exposed to the burning sun of midday. He was almost grateful, therefore, to Cornelius van Baerle for having built him a screen for nothing.

Perhaps this was not altogether the truth, and what Boxtel said with regard to his neighbour Van Baerle was not the complete expression of his thoughts. But great minds in the midst of catastrophes find surprising consolations in philosophy.

But alas! what a state of mind the unfortunate Boxtel was in, when he saw the windows of the newly built story ornamented with bulbs, suckers, tulips in open mould, tulips in pots, in fact with everything connected with the business of a tulipomaniac.

There were packets of labels, pigeon-holes, boxes divided into compartments, wire-gratings to close the pigeon-holes, so as to allow the air to enter while excluding mice, dormice, field-mice, weevils and rats, anin.als strangely fond of tulips that were worth a thousand florins a bulb.

Boxtel was much amazed at the sight of all these stores, but he did not yet understand the full extent of his misfortune. It was well known that Van Baerle loved everything that was pleasing to the eye. He studied Nature deeply for his pictures, which were as finished as those of his master, Gerard Dow, and his friend, Miéris. Possibly he had to paint a scene in the interior of a tulip-fancier's house and had therefore got together in his new studio all the accessories necessary for the scene. However, though buoyed up by this illusion, Boxtel could not overcome the burning curiosity which was devouring him. When evening came he placed a ladder against the party wall, and looking into his neighbour's garden, convinced himself that a large square flower-bed, lately filled with plants of different kinds, had been dug up, arranged in beds of leaf mould mixed with river mud, a compound particularly suitable to tulips, the whole being surrounded by a border of grass to keep the mould to a proper level. Moreover, the beds were so placed as to receive the warmth of the rising and the setting sun; the shade was so arranged as to temper the sun at midday; there was water in abundance close at hand, exposure to the south-southwest, in fact every condition requisite not only for success but for progress. There could no longer be any doubt about it—Van Baerle had become a tulip-grower.

The Tulip-Grower and his Neighbour

Boxtel immediately pictured to himself this learned man, with his capital of four hundred thousand florins and his income of ten thousand, using all his mental and material resources in cultivating tulips on a grand scale. He foresaw his success in a future, which was near, though vague; and he felt beforehand such anguish at this success that, his hands giving way and his knees failing, he rolled in despair to the bottom of his ladder.

So then, it was not for the sake of painted tulips, but for real ones that Van Baerle had deprived him of half a degree of heat. So then, Van Baerle was going to have the most admirable exposure to the sun, in addition to a vast room in which to keep his bulbs and his suckers, a room airy, well lighted, and well ventilated—a luxury beyond the reach of Boxtel, who had been obliged to devote his bed-room to this purpose, and, in order not to injure his suckers and bulbs by sleeping in the same room with them, had resigned himself to sleeping in the loft.

Thus, immediately next to him, on the other side of the wall, Boxtel was to have a rival, a competitor, a conqueror perhaps; and this rival, instead of being some obscure unknown gardener, was the godson of Master Cornelius de Witt, that is to say, one who was already a celebrity.

Boxtel, one sees, had a soul inferior to that of Porus, who consoled himself for his defeat at the hands of Alexander by the thought of his conqueror's fame.

The Black Tulip

What would happen if Van Baerle produced a new kind of tulip and named it the John de Witt, after having named one the Cornelius! It was enough to make one choke with rage.

Thus did Boxtel, a prophet of evil to himself, guess with jealous foresight what was to happen in the future.

And having made this discovery, he passed the most execrable night one can possibly imagine.

VI

A TULIP-FANCIER'S HATRED

FROM this time onward Boxtel was no longer interested merely; he was afraid. Thinking of all the injury which his neighbour's new idea was to do him, he abandoned that which gives vigour and nobility to bodily and mental efforts, the pursuit of an ideal.

Van Baerle, as one would expect, from the moment when he applied to this new design the perfect intellect with which Nature had endowed him, was successful in raising most admirable tulips.

He succeeded in varying the tints, in modifying the forms, in multiplying the varieties, better than any one at Haarlem or at Leyden, although those towns afforded the best soil and the most suitable climates.

He belonged to that ingenious yet simple school which, from the seventh century, adopted the following aphorism, developed in 1653 by one of its members:

" To despise flowers is to offend God."

On this foundation the school of tulip-growers—

The Black Tulip

the most exclusive of all schools—built up in 1653 the following syllogism:

" To despise flowers is to offend God;

" The more beautiful the flower is, the more is God offended by contempt of it;

" Now, the tulip is the most beautiful of all flowers;

" Therefore he who despises the tulip, offends God exceedingly."

By means of this piece of reasoning the three or four thousand tulip-fanciers of Holland, France, and Portugal, not to speak of those of Ceylon, India, and China, had maliciously outlawed the universe, and had declared schismatics, heretics, and worthy of death several hundreds of millions of men who were not interested in tulips.

In this cause Boxtel, although the mortal enemy of Van Baerle, would undoubtedly have marched under the same flag as the latter.

Van Baerle, then, had many successes, and obtained so great a reputation that Boxtel disappeared forever from the list of notable Dutch tulip-fanciers, and the tulip-growers of Dort were represented by the modest, inoffensive, and learned Cornelius van Baerle.

Thus on the humblest stock the proudest shoots are grafted, and the sweetbrier with its four colourless petals originates the large perfumed rose. Thus royal houses have sometimes taken their rise in a woodman's cottage or a fisherman's hut.

A Tulip-Fancier's Hatred

Van Baerle, entirely given up to his work of sow-ing, planting, and culling, flattered by all the tulip-world of Europe, did not even suspect that he had next door to him an unfortunate man whose throne he had usurped. He continued his experiments and consequently his victories, and in two years covered his flower-beds with such marvellous productions that, after God, no one, excepting perhaps Shake-speare and Rubens, had ever before created so much.

To have an idea of a damned soul, overlooked by Dante, it was only necessary to observe Boxtel dur-ing this period. While Van Baerle was weeding, ma-nuring, and watering his flower-beds, while he knelt on his grassy slopes and analyzed each vein of the flowering tulip, considering the modifications he might make and the colours he might try to unite, Boxtel, hidden behind a small sycamore which he had planted beside the wall and which he used as a screen, followed, with blazing eye and with foaming mouth, each step and each gesture of his neighbour; and when he thought he perceived signs of joy in his looks, when he surprised a smile on his lips or a gleam of satisfaction in his eyes, then he sent forth so many curses, so many furious threats that it is difficult to imagine how these infected blasts of rage and jealousy failed to penetrate the stems of the flowers, and to carry into them the principles of decay and the germs of death.

Soon, so rapidly does evil when once master of a human soul make progress in it, soon Boxtel was

The Black Tulip

not content to see Van Baerle only, he wished to see his flowers also—for he was an artist at heart and the masterpiece, even of a rival, appealed to him.

He bought a telescope, by the aid of which he could follow as easily as the owner himself, every change in the flower from the moment when, during the first year it thrust its pale shoot above the surface, till that in which, after completing its period of five years, it spread out its splendid and graceful volute, on which appeared the uncertain shading of its colour, and there were developed the petals of the flower, which then only revealed the hidden treasures of its calyx.

How often did the miserable and envious man, perched on his ladder, perceive in the flower-beds in Van Baerle's garden, tulips which blinded him by their beauty and suffocated him by their perfection.

Then, after a short period of uncontrollable admiration, he felt the fever of jealousy, a passion which gnaws at the breast and changes the heart into a myriad of serpents, which devour each other and become the abominable source of horrible anguish.

How often, in the midst of his torments, of which no description can give any idea, was Boxtel tempted to leap during the night into the garden, to ravage the plants, to tear the bulbs with his teeth, and to sacrifice to his rage even the proprietor himself, should he venture to defend his tulips.

A Tulip-Fancier's Hatred

But then, to destroy a tulip was, in the eyes of a tulip-fancier, a horrible crime.

To destroy a man, that was nothing much.

However, thanks to the continuous progress which Van Baerle made in the science which he seemed to understand by instinct, Boxtel at last worked himself up to such a state of fury that he thought of flinging sticks and stones into the tulip-beds of his neighbour.

But when he reflected that on the following day, at the sight of the devastation, Van Baerle would give information; that it would then be pointed out that the road was a long way off, and that sticks and stones no longer fell from heaven as in the days of the Amalekites; that the author of the outrage, although he had committed it in the night-time, would be discovered and would not only be punished but would also be disgraced forever in the eyes of tulip-loving Europe, Boxtel brought cunning to the aid of malice, and sought to devise another plan which would not compromise him.

He sought long, it is true, to discover such a plan, but at last he found one.

One evening he fastened two cats together, attaching by a cord, ten feet long, the hind leg of one to the hind leg of the other, and threw them from the top of the wall into the middle of the chief, the princely, the royal flower-bed, which contained not only the *Cornelius de Witt*, but also the *Lady of Brabant*, milk-white, purple and red; the marble-coloured tulip of Rotre, gridelin, red and brilliant carnation-coloured; and the *Marvel* of Haarlem, a tulip of dark and light dove-colours.

The terrified animals, falling from the top of the wall to the bottom, first rushed across the flower-bed, each trying to escape on its own side, until the cord which joined them was stretched to its full extent; then, finding it impossible to go any farther, they ran hither and thither with frightful mewlings, and mowed down with the cord the flowers in the midst of which they were struggling. At last, after a quarter of an hour of desperate efforts, they succeeded in breaking the cord which entangled them, and disappeared.

Boxtel, hidden behind his sycamore, saw nothing, owing to the darkness of the night, but at the enraged howls of the cats, he imagined everything, and his heart, eased of its gall, was filled with joy.

Boxtel's desire to assure himself of the ravage committed was so great that he stayed till daybreak to enjoy the sight of the devastation caused by the two cats in the flower-beds of his neighbour.

He was half frozen by the morning fog, but he did not feel the cold; the hope of vengeance kept him warm.

The anguish of his rival would repay him for all his sufferings. At the first rays of the sun, the door of the elegant house opened; Van Baerle appeared and approached his tulips, smiling like a man who has passed the night in his bed in the midst of pleasant dreams.

A Tulip-Fancier's Hatred

Suddenly he perceived furrows and hillocks in the mould which on the evening before had been smoother than a mirror; suddenly he saw that the symmetrical ranks of his tulips were all disordered, like the spears of a battalion in the midst of which a bomb has fallen. He ran forward, pale with excitement.

Boxtel trembled with joy. Fifteen or twenty tulips, torn and lacerated, were lying about, some bent over, others quite broken off and already faded; from their wounds flowed the sap, the blood of the tulip, which Van Baerle would willingly have restored at the price of his own.

But, to the surprise and joy of Van Baerle, and the inexpressible grief of Boxtel, not one of the four tulips specially threatened by the attack of the latter was even touched. They still raised their proud heads above the corpses of their companions. It was enough to console Van Baerle, enough to infuriate the assassin, who tore his hair at the sight of the crime which he had uselessly committed.

Van Baerle, while deploring the misfortune which had befallen him, a misfortune which at any rate was, through the mercy of God, less great than it might have been, could not guess what was the cause of it. He made inquiries, and learnt that the whole night had been disturbed by hideous mewlings. He discovered, moreover, traces of the cats in the marks left by their paws, and in the fur which remained on the scene of battle, and on which the

77

drops of impartial dew still trembled as they did on the leaves of the broken flowers. To prevent a repetition of such a misfortune, he ordered a boy gardener to sleep every night in the garden, in a kind of sentry-box near the flower-beds.

Boxtel heard the order given. He saw the sentry-box put up the same day, and, delighted at having escaped suspicion, though more enraged than ever against the fortunate grower, he awaited a better opportunity.

It was about this time that the Society of Tulip-growers of Haarlem offered a prize for the discovery, we dare not say the fabrication, of a black tulip, free from spots, a discovery which had not then been made and which was regarded as an impossibility, considering that at the time no species existed in Nature even of a dark tan colour.

This last fact made every one say that the founders of the prize might just as well have offered two million florins as a hundred thousand, success being quite impossible.

None the less the whole tulip-growing world was profoundly moved. Some amateurs took up the idea though they did not believe it feasible; but such is the power of imagination in horticulturists that, although they regarded the enterprise as foredoomed to failure, they no longer thought of anything but the great black tulip, which was considered as chimerical as the black swan of Horace or the white blackbird of French tradition.

A Tulip-Fancier's Hatred

Van Baerle was one of those tulip-fanciers who were taken with the idea of a black tulip. Boxtel was one of those who thought of it as a speculation. From the moment when Van Baerle set his clear and ingenious mind to work on this task, he began slowly and carefully the sowings and other operations which were necessary to reduce from red to brown, and from brown to dark-brown, those tulips which he had hitherto cultivated.

In the following year he succeeded in producing flowers of a very dark tan colour, and Boxtel saw them in the flower-bed, at a time when he himself had found only the light-brown.

Perhaps it would be desirable to explain to our readers the beautiful theories which tend to prove that the tulip derives its colours from the elements; perhaps they would be obliged to us if we showed that nothing is impossible to the grower who, by patience and genius, lays under contribution the heat of the sun, the clearness of water, the juices of the earth and the breath of the wind. But it is not a treatise on tulips in general; it is a history of one particular tulip, that we have determined to write. We will therefore confine ourselves to the latter, however attractive the charms of the subject connected with it may be.

Boxtel, once again surpassed by his enemy, was disgusted with tulip-growing; and, almost out of his mind with vexation, devoted himself entirely to spying.

The Black Tulip

The house of his rival was quite open to view; the garden was exposed to the sun; the rooms had glass sides easily seen through; the pigeon-holes, the cupboards, the boxes and the packets of labels, could be minutely inspected with the aid of the telescope. Boxtel allowed his bulbs to rot in their beds, his seeds to dry up in their cases, his tulips to die in the garden, and from that time onward, wearing out his sight and his life, he occupied himself solely with what took place at Van Baerle's. He breathed by the stems of the latter's tulips, quenched his thirst with the water thrown upon them, and satisfied his hunger with the soft fine earth which his neighbour sprinkled on his cherished bulbs.

But the most interesting part of the work was not carried on in the garden.

As soon as one o'clock in the morning arrived, Van Baerle went up to his laboratory, the glazed cabinet so easily penetrated by Boxtel's telescope, and there, as soon as the light of the scholar had taken the place of daylight, Boxtel saw the inventive genius of his rival at work.

He watched him sorting his seeds and watering them with substances destined to modify or to colour them. He tried to follow Cornelius's thoughts as he observed him heating certain seeds, then moistening them, then combining them with others by a kind of grafting, an operation marvellously delicate and adroit, then shutting up in darkness those which were to give tulips of a black colour, exposing to the

A Tulip-Fancier's Hatred

sun, or to the lamp, those which were to be red, and submitting to the uninterrupted action of light reflected from a surface of water, those which were to give white tulips, representative of the watery element.

This innocent magic, the fruit of childlike dreams and of manly genius combined, this patient and never-ceasing labour, of which Boxtel knew that he himself was incapable, made the jealous man concentrate his whole life and all his thoughts and hopes on his telescope.

Strange to say, his interest in the art and his great love for it did not extinguish in Isaac's heart his fierce jealousy and thirst for vengeance. Sometimes, when he had his telescope directed straight at Van Baerle, he fancied to himself that he was levelling at him an unerring musket, and felt with his finger for the trigger in order to give the fatal shot. But it is time that we connected with this period, of labour on the one side and of spying on the other, the visit which Cornelius de Witt, the Ruart de Pulten, made to his native town.

VII

THE HAPPY MAN BECOMES ACQUAINTED WITH MISFORTUNE

AFTER attending to his family affairs, Cornelius de Witt made his own way to the house of his godson, Cornelius van Baerle. It was the month of January and the day was closing in.

De Witt, though not much of a horticulturist or an artist, went over every part of the house, from the studio to the greenhouses, and examined everything, from the pictures to the tulips. He thanked his godson for having found him a place on the deck of the flagship The Seven Provinces during the battle of Southwold Bay, and for having given his name to a magnificent tulip; and all this with the kindness and affability of a father for a son; and while he was inspecting Van Baerle's treasures, the crowd, curious and yet respectful, remained standing before the door of the happy man's house.

All this disturbance arrested the attention of Boxtel, who at the time was taking a meal by his fireside.

He inquired what was going on, and having

found out, he climbed up to the usual scene of his labours. There, despite the cold, he installed himself, with his telescope to his eye.

The telescope had not been of much use to him since the autumn of 1671. Tulips, true daughters of the East, dislike the cold and cannot be grown in the open ground in winter time. They need the interior of the house, the downy bed in the drawer, and the soft caresses of the stove. Cornelius therefore spent the whole of the winter in his laboratory, amid his books and his pictures. Seldom did he go to the room where the bulbs were stored, except to give entrance to a few rays of the sun which he had surprised in the heavens, and which, by opening a glass trap-door, he compelled to fall, whether they wished it or not, into his house.

On the evening of which we speak, after the two Corneliuses had together visited the various rooms, followed by some of the domestics, De Witt said to Van Baerle, in a low voice:

" My son, send your servants away, so that we may be alone for a few minutes."

Cornelius bowed his head in sign of assent, and then said, in a loud voice:

" Sir, would you now like to go and see my drying-room? "

The drying-room was the tabernacle and *sanctum sanctorum* of tulip-worship and, like Delphi of old, was forbidden ground to the uninitiated.

As the great Racine, who flourished at this

period, would have said, no servant had ever placed an audacious foot within it. Cornelius admitted there only the harmless broom of an old Frisian servant, his nurse, who, since Cornelius had devoted himself to the cultivation of tulips, no longer dared to put onions in the stews for fear of picking to pieces and serving up some of the treasures of her nurse-child. Accordingly, at the mere mention of the word *drying-room*, the servants who were carrying the lights stood aside respectfully. Cornelius took the candles from the hand of the first of them and went into the room, followed by his godfather.

We must add that the drying-room was the glass-fronted room towards which Boxtel was continually directing his telescope.

The jealous man was watching more closely than ever.

First he saw the walls and panes of glass lighted up.

Then two shadows appeared.

One of them, tall, stern, and majestic, seated itself near the table on which Cornelius van Baerle had deposited the light.

Boxtel recognised the pale face of Cornelius de Witt, whose long black hair, divided in front, fell on to his shoulders.

After having said to Van Baerle something which the jealous spy tried in vain to understand from the movement of the lips, the Ruart de Pulten drew from his breast, and handed to his godson, a white packet carefully sealed. From the manner in which Cornelius took this packet and put it away in a drawer, Boxtel concluded that it contained papers of the greatest importance.

At first he thought that the precious parcel contained bulbs newly arrived from Bengal or Ceylon; but he soon remembered that Cornelius de Witt did not cultivate tulips and that he occupied himself solely with man, an evil plant much less agreeable to see and much more difficult to bring to a satisfactory condition. He therefore came to the conclusion that the packet contained papers, pure and simple, and that these papers were political.

But why should papers connected with politics be given to Van Baerle, who not only was, but even boasted of being, an utter stranger to this science, which, in his opinion, was more obscure than chemistry or even than alchemy?

Evidently Cornelius de Witt, already menaced by the unpopularity with which his compatriots were beginning to honour him, had intrusted this packet to his godson to keep for him; and the expedient was the more artful on the part of the Ruart from the fact that no one would look for such a deposit in the house of Van Baerle, who was an utter stranger to political intrigues.

Besides, if the packet had contained bulbs, Boxtel knew his neighbour well enough to be quite sure that he would not have delayed for a moment before inspecting them and examining, as an expert, the present which he had received.

But Van Baerle, on the contrary, had taken the packet from the hands of his godfather with every sign of respect, and had in the same manner placed it in a drawer, pushing it right to the back, firstly, no doubt, that it might not be seen, and secondly, that it might not take up too much of the space reserved for his bulbs.

As soon as the packet had been put away in the drawer, Cornelius de Witt rose, shook hands with his godson, and moved towards the door.

Van Baerle hastened to pass first with the lamp, showing his godfather the way.

Then the light gradually disappeared from the glass-fronted room, to reappear on the staircase, then in the hall, and finally in the road, where the crowd was still waiting to see the Ruart re-enter his carriage.

The jealous Boxtel was not wrong in his conclusions. The packet intrusted by the Ruart to his godson, and carefully put away by the latter, contained the correspondence of John de Witt with M. de Louvois.

But Cornelius de Witt, it must be added, had intrusted this correspondence to his godson without giving the latter the least idea of its political importance. The only direction that he gave with regard to it was, that no matter who asked for it, it should not be given up, except to himself or to some one authorized by him to receive it. And Van Baerle, as we have seen, had thereupon put away the packet in the cabinet in which he kept his rare bulbs.

Then, when the Ruart had departed, and the lights had been put out, our hero thought no more about the packet. Boxtel, on the other hand, thought a great deal about it, and like a skilful pilot saw in it the distant and almost imperceptible cloud which would grow as it moved onward, and which contained within it the germs of a storm.

And now we have marked out in the rich fertile land that stretches from Dort to The Hague the whole ground-plan of our story. Let those who wish follow it up in the succeeding chapters. As for us, we have kept our word, and proved that neither John nor Cornelius de Witt ever had such ferocious enemies in the whole of Holland, as Van Baerle had in his neighbour, Mynheer Isaac Boxtel.

Nevertheless, the happy tulip-grower, ignorant of this enmity, continued to make great progress towards the end proposed by the Haarlem Society. He had advanced from the dark tan-coloured or bistre tulip to a tulip of the colour of roasted coffee; and coming back to him again, on the very day on which the great political event that we have described took place at The Hague, we shall find him, towards one o'clock in the afternoon, removing from a flower-bed the as yet unproductive bulbs derived from a sowing of tulips of the colour of roasted coffee, tulips the flowering of which, hitherto prevented, would take place in the spring of the year 1673, and would undoubtedly give to the world the wonderful black tulip desired by the Haarlem Society.

On the 20th of August, then, 1672, at half past one in the afternoon, Cornelius van Baerle was in his drying-room, with his feet on the cross-bar of the table and his elbows on the table-cloth, gazing with delight at three suckers or offset bulbs, which he had just detached from the parent bulb. These suckers, unspotted, perfect and intact, contained hidden within them the principles of one of the most marvellous productions of Science and Nature combined, the success of which was to render illustrious for all time the name of Cornelius van Baerle.

"I shall find the great black tulip," said Cornelius to himself, as he detached his young bulbs. "I shall receive the hundred thousand florins offered as a prize. I will distribute them among the poor of Dort; in this way I shall appease the hatred which riches always inspire during times of civil dissension, and I shall be able, without fearing anything from the Republicans or the Orangeists, to continue to keep up my flower-beds in perfect style. I shall no longer be afraid lest on some day of riot, the shopkeepers and the sailors of Dort should carry out the muttered threats which they have sometimes made, on hearing that I had bought a bulb for two or three hundred florins, and should come and seize on my bulbs to feed their families. It is settled, then, that

The Happy Man Meets Misfortune

I am to give the Haarlem prize of a hundred thousand florins to the poor of Dort.

" Although . . ."

And at this *although* Cornelius stopped and sighed.

" Although," continued he, " it would have been delightful to spend these hundred thousand florins in raising my parterre, or even in going a journey to the East, the native land of beautiful flowers. But alas! I must not think of such things as these: muskets, flags, drums, and proclamations, are everything at the present time."

Van Baerle looked up to heaven and sighed.

Then, looking again at his bulbs, which in his opinion were far more important than muskets, drums, flags, and proclamations, things good for nothing except disturbing honest men's minds, he said:

" These are very fine bulbs, at any rate; how smooth they are and how beautifully formed! they have about them an air of melancholy that promises an ebony-black to my tulip; on their skin the veins of circulation are not even visible to the naked eye. It is certain that not a single spot will spoil the mourning robe of the flower which I shall produce.

" How shall this child of my vigils, my labours, and my thoughts be named? *Tulipa nigra Baerlensis.* Yes, Baerlensis, a good name. All tulip-loving Europe, that is to say, all intellectual Europe, will thrill when the report is carried upon the winds to the four

The Black Tulip

quarters of the globe that ' THE GREAT BLACK TULIP IS FOUND!' 'It's name?' the connoisseurs will ask. '*Tulipa nigra Baerlensis*,' will be the answer. 'Why *Baerlensis?*' 'Because of its discoverer, Van Baerle.' 'And this Van Baerle, who is he?' 'He is the man who has already discovered five new species—the Jane, the John de Witt, the Cornelius, etc.' Well, that is my ambition. It will not cost any one a tear. And the *Tulipa nigra Baerlensis* will still be spoken of when that wonderful politician, my godfather, will very likely be known only from the tulip to which I have given his name.

"What beautiful bulbs! . . .

"When my tulip has flowered," continued Cornelius, "if things are quiet again in Holland, I will give only fifty thousand florins to the poor: that, after all, is a good deal for a man who is not really bound to give anything. Then, with the remaining fifty thousand florins I will make experiments. With these fifty thousand florins I shall try to give an odour to the tulip. Oh! if I could only give it the scent of the rose or of the carnation! or even a completely new scent, that would be better still. If I restored to this queen of flowers that natural generic fragrance, which it has lost in exchanging its Eastern throne for a European one, that fragrance which it must have in the Indian peninsula, at Goa, at Bombay, at Madras, and, above all, in that island which, as we are assured, was formerly the terrestrial paradise and which is now called Ceylon, what glory I should attain! I would rather, yes, I would rather then be Cornelius van Baerle than Alexander, Cæsar, or Maximilian.

"What admirable bulbs! . . ."

And Cornelius became absorbed in his contemplation of the bulbs, and in delightful dreams.

Suddenly the bell in his room was rung much more loudly than usual.

Cornelius started, stretched out his hand over his bulbs, and turned round.

"Who is there?" he asked.

"Sir," replied the servant, "it is a messenger from The Hague."

"A messenger from The Hague? What does he want?"

"It is Craeke, sir."

"Craeke, the confidential servant of M. John de Witt? Very good, tell him to wait."

"I cannot wait," said a voice in the passage, and at the same time, disregarding the order, Craeke burst into the drying-room.

This violent incursion was such an infraction of the rules established in Van Baerle's house, that Cornelius, perceiving Craeke as he rushed into the room, made an almost convulsive movement of his hand and sent two of the precious bulbs rolling, one under a small table, the other into the fire-place.

"The devil take you, Craeke!" said Van Baerle, diving after his bulbs, "what is the matter?"

"It is, sir," said Craeke, laying the paper on the large table on which the third bulb was still lying,

" it is that you are asked to read this paper without a moment's delay."

And Craeke, who thought he had noticed in the streets of Dort signs of a tumult like that which he had just left at The Hague, made off again without looking back.

" Very good, very good, my dear Craeke," said Cornelius, stretching his arm under the table to feel for the precious bulb, " your paper shall be read."

Then picking up one of the bulbs and holding it in the hollow of his hand to examine it, he added:

" Good, here is one of them still intact. What a ruffian that Craeke is, to come into my drying-room in that fashion! . . . Now let us look for the other one."

And without putting down the bulb which he had just recovered, Van Baerle went to the fire-place, and going down on his knees, began to feel with the tips of his fingers in the ashes, which fortunately were quite cold.

In a moment or two he felt the second small bulb.

" Good!" said he, " here it is."

And looking at it with an almost paternal affection, he added:

" Intact, like the first."

At the same instant, as Cornelius, still on his knees, was examining the second bulb, the door of the drying-room was again so violently pushed, and flew open so quickly in consequence, that Cornelius

The Happy Man Meets Misfortune

felt rising to his cheeks and his ears the flame of that evil counsellor called Anger.

"What is it now?" he asked. "Heavens! are they all gone mad in this house?"

"Sir! sir!" cried a servant rushing into the drying-room, with a face paler and more alarmed than Craeke's had been.

"What is it?" asked Cornelius, fearing, at this double breach of all rules, that some disaster had occurred.

"Oh, sir! fly, fly quickly!" cried the servant.

"Fly? what for?"

"Sir, the house is full of State guards."

"What do they want?"

"They are looking for you."

"What for?"

"To arrest you."

"Me? To arrest me?"

"Yes, sir, and they have a magistrate with them."

"What can this mean?" asked Van Baerle, covering up the two bulbs in his hand, and looking with alarm towards the staircase.

"They are coming up, they are coming up!" cried the servant.

"Oh, my dear child, my worthy master," cried the nurse, running into the drying-room, "take your gold and your jewels and fly! fly!"

"But which way can I fly, nurse?" asked Van Baerle.

The Black Tulip

" Jump out of the window! "

" Twenty-five feet down! "

" You will fall on six feet of soft mould."

" Yes, but I shall fall on my tulips."

" No matter, jump! "

Cornelius picked up the third bulb, approached the window and opened it; but at the sight of the havoc which he would work in his flower-beds, rather than at the sight of the distance which he would have to descend, he took a step backward, saying, " Never! "

At this moment the halberds of the soldiers began to be seen through the banisters of the staircase.

The nurse raised her hands to heaven.

As for Cornelius van Baerle, to the honour, it must be admitted, not of the man but of the tulip-fancier, his sole anxiety was for his precious bulbs. He looked round for a paper to wrap them in, perceived the leaf of the Bible which Craeke had placed upon the table, took it up, without remembering, so great was his agitation, whence it had come, wrapped the three bulbs in it, hid them in his bosom, and waited. Almost at the same moment the soldiers entered, with the magistrate at their head.

" Are you Dr. Cornelius van Baerle? " asked the magistrate, although he knew the young man perfectly well. But in this he only observed the rules laid down by the law, and in so doing added to the solemnity of the proceedings.

The Happy Man Meets Misfortune

" I am," replied Cornelius, bowing politely to the magistrate, " and you are well aware of it, Master van Spennen."

" Then deliver up to us the seditious papers which you have in your house."

" Seditious papers? " replied Cornelius, quite bewildered by the words addressed to him.

" Oh, do not pretend to be astonished."

" I swear to you, Master van Spennen," replied Cornelius, " that I entirely fail to comprehend your meaning."

" Then I will put you in the way of understanding it," said the magistrate; " deliver up to us the papers which the traitor Cornelius de Witt deposited with you in the month of January last."

A light broke on the mind of Cornelius.

" Ho! ho! " said Van Spennen, " you begin to remember, don't you? "

" Certainly, but you spoke of seditious papers, and I have no paper of that sort."

" Ah, you deny it? "

" Certainly."

The magistrate turned about, and looked all round the room.

" Which room in your house is called the drying-room? "

" This very room in which we now are, Master van Spennen."

The magistrate glanced at a short note written at the top of his papers.

The Black Tulip

"Very well," said he, like a man who is satisfied. "Will you give up these papers to me?"

"But I cannot, Master van Spennen. The papers are not mine. They have been intrusted to me to take care of, and a deposit of that kind is sacred."

"Dr. Cornelius," said the magistrate, "in the name of the States I order you to open this drawer, and to hand over to me the papers contained in it."

And with his finger the magistrate indicated precisely the third drawer in a cabinet near the fireplace.

"Ah, you will not?" said Van Spennen, seeing that Cornelius remained motionless with surprise. "I shall open it myself, then."

And opening the drawer to its fullest extent, the magistrate disclosed, first, about a score of bulbs, carefully arranged and ticketed; and next, the packet of papers which remained in precisely the same state as it had been in when delivered by the unfortunate Cornelius de Witt to his godson.

The magistrate broke the seals, tore open the envelope, cast an eager eye over the first sheets that he came to, and exclaimed in a portentous voice:

"Ah! justice has not been deceived, then."

"Why," said Cornelius, "what is this?"

"Ah, don't go on pretending ignorance, M. van Baerle," replied the magistrate; "you must come with us."

"What! come with you?" cried the doctor.

The Happy Man Meets Misfortune

"Yes, for in the name of the States, I arrest you."

They had not yet begun to arrest in the name of William of Orange; he had not been stadtholder long enough.

"Arrest me!" cried Van Baerle; "but what have I done?"

"That has nothing to do with me, doctor; you must discuss that with your judges."

"Where?"

"At The Hague."

Cornelius, quite bewildered, embraced his nurse, who fainted away, gave his hand to his servants, who were all in tears, and followed the magistrate. The latter put him into a closed carriage and ordered him to be taken, as a prisoner of state, with all possible speed to The Hague.

VIII

AN INCURSION

WHAT had happened was due, as will be guessed, to the machinations of Mynheer Isaac Boxtel.

It will be remembered that, aided by his telescope, he had followed every detail of the interview between Cornelius de Witt and his godson, and that, though he had heard nothing, he had seen everything.

It will be remembered also that he had guessed the importance of the papers confided by the Ruart to his godson, when he saw the latter put them away so carefully in the drawer in which he kept his most valuable bulbs.

The result was that when Boxtel, who followed the course of political affairs much more attentively than his neighbour Cornelius did, learnt that Cornelius de Witt had been arrested on a charge of high treason against the States, he thought to himself that it only needed a word to bring about the arrest of the godson at the same time as that of the godfather.

But, elated as Boxtel was at this idea, he shuddered at first at the thought of denouncing a man, when the denunciation might lead to the scaffold.

But the worst of evil thoughts is, that bad hearts soon become quite habituated to them.

Moreover, Mynheer Isaac Boxtel encouraged himself with this sophism:

Cornelius de Witt is a bad citizen, since he is accused of high treason and arrested;

Now I am a good citizen, since I am not accused of anything at all, and am as free as the air;

But if Cornelius de Witt is a bad citizen, as he certainly must be, since he is accused of high treason and arrested, his accomplice, Cornelius van Baerle, is equally a bad citizen;

Therefore, as I am a good citizen and it is a part of the duty of good citizens to denounce bad ones, it is clearly a duty incumbent on me, Isaac Boxtel, to denounce Cornelius van Baerle.

Perhaps this reasoning, specious as it was, would not have entirely prevailed with Boxtel, and perhaps that envious man would not have yielded merely to the desire for vengeance which was eating into his heart, if the demon of greed had not joined forces with the demon of envy.

Boxtel was aware how far Van Baerle had advanced in his search after the great black tulip.

Modest as Dr. Cornelius was, he had not been able to conceal from his more intimate friends that he was practically certain to gain, in the year 1673, the prize of a hundred thousand florins offered by the Horticultural Society of Haarlem.

Now this practical certainty of Cornelius van Baerle was the fever which was devouring Isaac Boxtel.

If Cornelius were arrested the event would be certain to cause a great commotion in his house. On the night which followed the arrest no one would think of watching over the tulips in the garden.

And on this night Boxtel would climb over the wall, and as he knew whereabouts in the garden the bulb which would produce the black tulip was to be found, he would carry it off. Instead of flowering in Cornelius's house, it would flower in his; and he and not Cornelius would have the hundred thousand florins, to say nothing of the supreme honour of calling the new flower *Tulipa nigra Boxtellensis*.

This was a result which would satisfy not only his vengeance, but also his greed.

When awake, he thought only of the great black tulip; when asleep, he dreamt of it.

Finally, on the 19th of August, the temptation grew so strong that Mynheer Isaac could no longer resist it. Consequently he drew up an anonymous denunciation, which made up for its want of authentication by its preciseness of detail, and threw the denunciation into the post-box.

Never did a venomous paper slipped into the bronze jaws at Venice produce a more speedy, or a more deadly result.

An Incursion

The chief magistrate received the communication on the same evening, and at once summoned a meeting of his colleagues for the following morning. The next day they met, decided on the arrest, and intrusted the execution of their orders to Master van Spennen, who performed the duty as a true Hollander should and arrested Cornelius van Baerle just at the moment when the Orangeists of The Hague were roasting pieces of the dead bodies of Cornelius and John de Witt.

But, either through shame or through faint-heartedness, Isaac Boxtel had not the courage that day to direct his telescope towards the garden or towards the studio or towards the drying-room. He knew too well what was about to happen in the house of poor Dr. Cornelius to have any need of looking. He did not even rise when his only servant, who envied the lot of Van Baerle's servants as much as Boxtel envied that of their master, came into his bedroom. Boxtel said to him:

"I shall not get up to-day; I am ill."

About nine o'clock he heard a great noise in the street and shuddered on hearing it; at that moment he was paler than a person who was really ill, and trembled more than any fever-patient.

His servant came in. Boxtel hid himself under the bed-clothes.

"Ah, sir!" cried the servant, not without suspecting that while deploring the misfortune that had happened to Van Baerle, he was bringing good news to his master, "ah, sir! you do not know, then, what is going on at this moment?"

"How do you suppose I can know?" replied Boxtel in a voice that was scarcely intelligible.

"Well, then, at this very moment, Mynheer Boxtel, your neighbour, Cornelius van Baerle, is being arrested on a charge of high treason."

"Bah!" muttered Boxtel in a faint voice, "impossible!"

"Indeed, then, that is what people are saying, at any rate; besides, I have just seen Judge van Spennen and the police officers go into his house."

"Ah! if you have seen it yourself," said Boxtel, "that is different."

"In any case, I am going out to get some more news," said the servant. "Do you remain quietly here. I will keep you informed of what happens."

Boxtel contented himself with encouraging by a gesture of assent the zeal of his servant.

The latter went out and returned in about a quarter of an hour.

"Oh, sir! all that I told you is quite true."

"How do you mean?"

"M. van Baerle is arrested and has been sent off in a carriage to The Hague."

"To The Hague?"

"Yes, and there it will go badly with him, if what they say is true."

"And what do they say?" asked Boxtel.

"Why, sir, they say, but it is not quite certain,

An Incursion

that the burghers of The Hague are at this moment on the point of assassinating M. Cornelius and M. John de Witt."

"Oh!" muttered Boxtel in a choking voice, at the same time shutting his eyes to keep away the terrible picture which without doubt presented itself to his mind.

"The devil!" said the servant, as he went out, "Mynheer Isaac Boxtel must be very ill indeed not to have jumped out of his bed at such a piece of news."

Isaac Boxtel was in fact very ill, as ill as a man who has just assassinated another.

But he had assassinated this man with two objects: the first was accomplished; it remained to accomplish the second.

The night came. It was night that Boxtel was waiting for. When it arrived, he got up.

Then he climbed into his sycamore.

He had been quite right in his calculations: no one thought of keeping watch in the garden: house and servants were all in confusion.

He heard ten o'clock strike; then, eleven; then, midnight. At midnight, with beating heart, trembling hands and face deadly pale, he came down from his tree, took a ladder, raised it against the wall, mounted to the top step but one, and listened.

All was still: not a sound disturbed the silence of the night. A single light only remained in the whole house. It was that of the old nurse.

The Black Tulip

The silence and the darkness emboldened Boxtel.

He got astride of the wall, stopped for a moment on the top, then, quite sure that he had nothing to fear, he transferred the ladder from his own garden into that of Cornelius and went down.

Next, as he knew, to an inch almost, the place where the bulbs of the future black tulip were to be found, he ran towards it, following, nevertheless, the gravelled pathways, so as not to be betrayed by his footprints. Arrived at the exact spot, he plunged his hands, with the eagerness of a tiger, into the soft mould.

He found nothing, and thought he must have made some mistake.

Nevertheless, a cold sweat stood out in beads on his forehead.

He felt at one side—nothing!

He felt on the right, on the left—nothing!

He felt in front and behind—nothing!

He became almost mad on perceiving at last that on that very day the ground had been dug up.

In fact, while Boxtel was still in bed Cornelius had gone down into the garden, had dug up the parent bulb, and, as we have already seen, had divided it into three suckers, or young bulbs. Boxtel could not make up his mind to leave the spot. He had turned up with his hands more than ten square feet of mould.

At last he no longer felt any doubt about his misfortune.

Mad with rage, he went back to his ladder, got

An Incursion

on to the wall, dragged up the ladder from Cornelius's garden, threw it into his own, and jumped after it.

All at once a last gleam of hope broke on his mind.

Perhaps the new bulbs were in the drying-room!

If so, it was only a matter of getting into the drying-room, as he had got into the garden. There he would find them.

Besides, it was almost as easy as the other. The windows of the drying-room opened like those of a greenhouse. Cornelius had opened them in the morning and no one had thought of shutting them again. All that was necessary was to procure a ladder long enough—one twenty feet long instead of twelve.

Boxtel had noticed in the street in which he lived a house under repair; by the side of this house a very long ladder was lying.

This ladder would just serve Boxtel's purpose, provided the workmen had not taken it away.

He ran to the house; the ladder was still there.

Boxtel seized the ladder and, with great difficulty, succeeded in carrying it into his garden; with still greater difficulty he raised it against the wall of Cornelius's house.

The ladder just reached the casement.

Boxtel put a dark lantern, already lighted, into his pocket, mounted the ladder, and got into the drying-room.

The Black Tulip

When he found himself in this sanctuary, he stopped and leant against the table; his legs were giving way and his heart beat as though it would suffocate him.

Here it was much worse than in the garden; one would say that the open air makes property less entitled to respect; he who jumps over a hedge, or climbs over a wall, stops at a door or at the window of a room.

In the garden Boxtel was only a trespasser; in the room Boxtel was a thief.

However, he regained his courage; he had not come that far only to go home again with empty hands.

But it was in vain that he searched high and low, and opened and shut all the drawers, even the particular one in which had been put away the packet that had just proved so fatal to Cornelius; he found, duly ticketed, as though in a botanical garden, the Jane, the De Witt, the bistre tulip, and the tulip of the colour of roasted coffee, but of the black tulip, or rather of the bulbs in which it was still sleeping, hidden and as yet undeveloped, there was not a trace.

And yet in the register of seeds and of young bulbs, kept in double columns by Van Baerle with more methodic accuracy than the ledgers of the chief commercial houses of Amsterdam could show, Boxtel read these lines:

"To-day, August 20th, 1672, I dug up the bulb

of the great black tulip and divided it into three perfect young bulbs."

"Those bulbs! those bulbs!" shouted Boxtel, tossing about everything in the drying-room, "where can he have hidden them?"

Then suddenly striking himself violently on the forehead, he cried out:

"Oh, wretched man that I am! Oh, thrice-accursed Boxtel! would any one separate himself from his bulbs? would any one leave them at Dort when he set out for The Hague? Can a man live without his bulbs, when they are those of the great black tulip? He would have had time to take them, the scoundrel! He has them on him, he has taken them to The Hague!"

This was a flash of lightning which revealed to Boxtel the abyss of useless crime into which he had sunk.

He fell forward on the table on the very spot where, a few hours earlier, the unfortunate Van Baerle had admired so long and with such delight the bulbs of the black tulip.

"Well, after all," said the jealous Boxtel, raising his ghastly face, "if he has them he can only keep them while he is alive, and . . ."

The rest of this horrible thought was lost in a frightful smile.

"The bulbs are at The Hague," said he; "then I can no longer live at Dort. To The Hague for the bulbs! to The Hague!"

The Black Tulip

And, paying no attention to the immense riches he was leaving behind him, so much was he taken up with another inestimable treasure, Boxtel got out through the window, let himself slide down the ladder, took back the instrument of his crime to the place from which he had brought it, and, like a beast of prey, returned growling to his own house.

The Family Cell

IX

THE FAMILY CELL

It was about midnight when poor Van Baerle was entered in the register of prisoners at the Buitenhof.

Rosa's anticipations had been fulfilled. The rage of the populace, when they found Cornelius's cell empty, knew no bounds; and if Gryphus had then fallen into the hands of these madmen, he would certainly have paid dearly for the escape of his prisoner.

But the fury of the people expended itself on the two brothers, whom the assassins had overtaken in their flight, thanks to the precaution which William, a man of precautions, had taken in closing the gates of the town.

A time soon came, therefore, when the prison was empty, and silence succeeded to the thunder of terrifying shouts that had rolled along the staircases.

Rosa took advantage of this moment and came out of her hiding-place, bringing her father with her.

The prison was quite deserted. What was the use of remaining in the prison when throats were being cut at the Tol-Hek?

Gryphus came out trembling behind the coura-

The Family Cell

geous Rosa. They went and shut the great door as well as they could—we say as well as they could, for it was half-destroyed. It was evident that a furious torrent of anger had poured through the doorway. Towards four o'clock they heard the noise coming nearer again, but it had no terrors now for Gryphus and his daughter. It was caused by the mob which was coming back, dragging along the dead bodies to hang them up at the ordinary place of execution.

Rosa hid herself again, but this time it was in order not to see the horrible spectacle.

At midnight there was a knock at the door of the Buitenhof, or rather on the barricade which had taken its place.

It was Cornelius van Baerle, who was being brought to the prison.

When the jailer Gryphus received his new guest and read on the order of committal the description of the prisoner, "Godson of Cornelius de Witt," he muttered with his jailer's smile, "Ah! young man, we have the family cell here; we will give it you."

And, delighted with the joke he had made, the savage Orangeist took up his lantern and keys, to conduct Cornelius to the cell which, on the same day, Cornelius de Witt had left to go into what is termed exile by those great philosophers who, in times of revolution, repeat as a high political maxim:

"It is only the dead who do not return."

Gryphus, then, prepared to conduct the godson to the cell of the godfather.

The Black Tulip

As he went along the passages which led to the cell, the unfortunate tulip-grower heard nothing but the barking of a dog, saw nothing but the face of a young girl.

The dog came out of a niche hollowed in the wall, shaking a heavy chain, and sniffed at Cornelius so as to be able to recognise him at once if ordered to attack him.

The young girl, hearing the rail of the staircase creak under the heavy hand of the prisoner, opened the upper part of the door of a room which she occupied in the thick wall of the stairway. In her right hand she held a lamp, which lit up her rosy features framed in thick coils of beautiful fair hair, while with her left hand she held close to her breast her white night-dress, for she had been wakened out of her first sleep by the unexpected arrival of Cornelius.

It would have made an excellent picture, worthy of being painted by Rembrandt, this dark spiral staircase lighted up by the reddish lantern of Gryphus, with the sombre figure of the jailer at the top, next the melancholy face of Cornelius, who was leaning over the rail to look round, and then below him, framed in the luminous half-open doorway, the sweet face of Rosa, rather troubled apparently at being thus seen by Cornelius, whose wandering and melancholy glance fell on her from above.

Then lower still, quite in the shadow, at a part of the staircase where details were indistinguishable in the darkness, there gleamed the fierce eyes of the watch-dog shaking his chain, the links of which sparkled here and there under the double light of Rosa's lamp and Gryphus's lantern.

But what even the great master himself could not have shown in his picture was the sorrowful look which appeared on the face of Rosa when she saw this pale handsome young man slowly mounting the stairs, and applied to him the sinister words of her father, " You shall have the family cell."

This vision lasted but a moment, a much less time than we have taken to describe it. Then Gryphus proceeded on his way, Cornelius perforce followed him, and five minutes later entered the cell, which we need not describe, as the reader knows it already.

Gryphus, after pointing out to the prisoner with his finger the bed on which the martyr, who had that day surrendered his soul to God, had suffered so much, took up his lantern and went out.

As for Cornelius, left alone, he threw himself on the bed; but he did not sleep. He kept his eyes fixed on the narrow iron-barred window which looked out upon the Buitenhof until he saw appearing beyond the trees those first beams of light which the heavens let fall like a white mantle upon the earth.

From time to time during the night horses had passed at a gallop across the Buitenhof, the tramp of the patrols had re-echoed from the cobblestones of the square, and the matches of the arquebusiers, flaring up at the southwest wind, had thrown intermittent gleams of light on the window-panes of the prison.

But when the growing day had lit up the coping stones of the roofs of the houses, Cornelius, impatient to find out whether there was any sign of life around him, approached the window and looked sorrowfully about.

At the extremity of the square a dark mass, to which the morning mist lent a bluish tint, showed its irregular outlines against the pale houses beyond.

Cornelius recognised the gibbet.

On this gibbet there hung two shapeless figures, which were now little more than bleeding skeletons.

The good people of The Hague had hacked off the flesh of their victims, but had taken care to bring back what remained, in order to have an excuse for setting up a large placard bearing a twofold inscription.

On this placard Cornelius, with his young eyes, succeeded in making out the following lines, traced by the thick brush of some sign-dauber:

" Here hang the great scoundrel, John de Witt, and the little rascal, Cornelius de Witt, his brother, both enemies of the Prince of Orange, but very good friends of the King of France."

Cornelius uttered a cry of horror, and in the height of his terror and agitation beat so wildly and vehemently on the door with hands and feet that Gryphus came running up in a fury, his immense bunch of keys in his hand. He opened the door uttering hid-

The Family Cell

eous imprecations against the prisoner for disturbing him at an hour when he was not used to being disturbed.

"Ah! but he must be mad, this new De Witt," he cried; "but, then, all the De Witts are possessed by the devil."

"Sir, sir," cried Cornelius, seizing the jailer by the arm and dragging him towards the window, "what is that which I have just read down there?"

"Down there? where?"

"On that placard."

And breathless, pale, and trembling, he showed him at the end of the square the gibbet with its cynical inscription.

Gryphus began to laugh.

"Ha, ha!" replied he. "So you've read it! Well, my dear sir, that is what happens to people who have dealings with the enemies of the Prince of Orange."

"The De Witts assassinated!" murmured Cornelius. The sweat stood out on his forehead and he let himself fall on his bed, with his arms hanging down and his eyes closed.

"The De Witts have fallen before the justice of the people," said Gryphus. "You say they were assassinated; I say, executed."

And seeing that the prisoner had become not merely calm, but almost unconscious, he went out of the room, slamming the door and noisily pushing the bolts.

Cornelius on coming to himself found that he

was alone, and recognised that the cell in which he had been placed, the family cell, as Gryphus called it, was, as it were, a fatal passage destined to lead him to a miserable death.

And as he was a philosopher, and above all a Christian, he first prayed for the soul of his godfather, then for that of the Grand Pensionary, and lastly resigned himself to all the ills which it might please God to send upon him.

Then, having descended from heaven to earth, and having returned from the outer world to his cell, in which he assured himself that he was quite alone, he took from his breast the three bulbs of the black tulip, and hid them at the back of a stone shelf, on which was placed the traditional pitcher, in the darkest corner of the cell.

" Useless labour of so many years! destruction of such sweet hopes! His discovery, then, was to come to nothing, just as he himself was to come to a miserable end. Here in this prison there was not a blade of vegetation, not an atom of mould, not a ray of sunshine! "

At this thought Cornelius fell into deep despair, from which he was only aroused by an extraordinary circumstance.

What was the circumstance?

That we will reserve for the next chapter.

X

THE JAILER'S DAUGHTER

THE same evening, when bringing the prisoner his daily allowance, Gryphus, as he opened the cell door, slipped on the damp flagstones, and fell. As he did so, he tried to save himself, but failing to get his hand exactly beneath him, he broke his arm above the wrist.

Cornelius made a step towards the jailer; but Gryphus, not suspecting the gravity of the accident, said to him:

" It is nothing; do not stir."

And he tried to raise himself, leaning on his arm; but the bone yielded, and Gryphus, feeling the pain for the first time, cried out.

He perceived that his arm was broken, and fell back fainting on the door-step, where he remained cold and inert, like a dead man.

During this time the door of the cell remained open, and Cornelius found himself almost at liberty.

But it never occurred to him to take advantage of the accident; he recognised, from the way in which the arm had bent, and from the sound which accompanied the bending, that this was a case of fracture and of pain; he thought only of assisting the injured man, in spite of the ill-will towards himself which the latter had shown in the only interview he had yet had with him.

At the noise made by Gryphus in falling, and the cry which he had uttered, a hurried step was heard on the staircase, followed immediately by the appearance of a young girl, at the sight of whom Cornelius uttered an exclamation.

She who had thus appeared was the fair Frisian. Seeing her father stretched on the ground and the prisoner bending over him, she at first thought that Gryphus, whose brutality she knew well, had fallen in an encounter with the prisoner.

Cornelius saw what was passing in the young woman's mind at the very moment when the suspicion occurred to her.

But the first glance showed her the truth, and, ashamed of what she had thought, she raised her beautiful eyes, filled with tears, and said to the young man:

" Forgive me, sir, and thank you. Forgive me for thinking as I did, and thank you for what you are doing."

" In assisting a fellow-creature," said Cornelius, with a blush, " I am only doing what, as a Christian, I am bound to do."

" Yes, but in helping him this evening, you are forgetting the insults which he offered you this

The Black Tulip

morning. That, sir, is more than humanity and than Christianity."

Cornelius looked up at the handsome young woman, quite astonished to hear from the lips of a girl in her position words at once so dignified and so full of feeling.

But he had not time to express his surprise. Gryphus, having recovered consciousness, opened his eyes, and his usual brutality returning with his senses, he said:

"Ah! that's how it is. I hasten to bring the prisoner's supper, I fall down in my hurry, in falling I break my arm, and you leave me here on the floor."

"Be quiet, father," said Rosa. "You are unjust to this gentleman. I found him engaged in assisting you."

"He?" said Gryphus, doubtingly.

"It is quite true, sir, and I am ready to help you still further."

"You?" said Gryphus; "are you a doctor, then?"

"That was my original profession," said the prisoner.

"So that you can set my arm?"

"Certainly."

"And what will you need for that, eh?"

"Two wooden splints, and some linen bandages."

"You hear, Rosa," said Gryphus; "the prisoner is going to set my arm. That will be a saving, at any rate. Come, help me up, I feel like lead."

The Jailer's Daughter

Rosa leant down towards the injured man; he put his uninjured arm round the girl's neck, and with an effort got on to his feet, while Cornelius, to save him the trouble of walking, pushed an arm-chair towards him. Gryphus sat down in the chair; then turning towards the girl,

"Well," said he, "don't you hear? Go and get what you are asked for."

Rosa went downstairs, and in a minute or two came back with two staves of a cask and a large linen bandage.

Cornelius, in the meantime, had removed the jailer's coat and rolled up his own sleeves.

"Is this what you want, sir?" asked Rosa.

"Yes, miss," said Cornelius, looking at the things she had brought, "yes, that's just it. Now push the table here, while I lift up your father's arm."

Rosa pushed forward the table. Cornelius laid the broken arm flat upon it, and with great skill re-adjusted the fracture, applied the splints, and fastened the bandage.

As he was inserting the last pin, the jailer fainted a second time.

"Go and get some vinegar," said Cornelius; "we will rub his temples with it and he will come round."

But instead of doing as she was directed, Rosa, having assured herself that her father was quite unconscious, approached Cornelius, and said:

"Service for service, sir."

"What do you mean, my good girl?" asked Cornelius.

"I mean, sir, that the judge who will interrogate you to-morrow, came here to-day, to ask what room you were in; he was told that you had M. Cornelius de Witt's room, and on hearing the answer he gave a sinister smile, which makes me think that nothing good awaits you."

"But," asked Cornelius, "what can they do to me?"

"You can see the gibbet from here."

"But I am not guilty," said Cornelius.

"Were they guilty who are hanging there, mutilated and torn?"

"That is true," said Cornelius, gloomily.

"Besides," continued Rosa, "the public wants you to be guilty. Anyhow, guilty or not guilty, your trial will begin to-morrow; the day after you will be condemned—things are done very quickly, nowadays."

"Well, and what do you conclude from all this?"

"I conclude that I am alone, that I am weak, that my father has fainted, that the dog is muzzled, so that nothing prevents your getting away. Escape, then, that's my conclusion."

"What do you say?"

"I say that, unfortunately, I could not save M. Cornelius or M. John de Witt, and that I want to save you. Only, be quick, my father is coming to: in another moment, perhaps, he will open his eyes, and it will be too late. Do you hesitate?"

Cornelius indeed remained motionless, looking at Rosa, as though he saw her but did not hear anything she said.

"Don't you understand?" asked the girl impatiently.

"Oh yes, indeed, I understand," said Cornelius, "but . . ."

"But what?"

"I refuse; they would accuse you of it."

"What does that matter?" said Rosa, blushing.

"Thank you, my child," replied Cornelius, "but I will stay here."

"Stay here! My goodness! don't you understand then that you will be condemned . . . condemned to death, executed on a scaffold, perhaps assassinated and torn to pieces, as M. John and M. Cornelius were. In Heaven's name, do not trouble about me, but fly from this cell. Beware of it, it is fatal to the De Witts."

"Eh?" cried the jailer, coming to, "who is speaking of those wretches, those scoundrels, the De Witts?"

"Don't excite yourself, my good man," said Cornelius, with his sweet smile; "the worst thing for a fracture is to heat the blood."

Then, in a low voice, he said to Rosa, "My child, I am innocent. I will await my judges with the tranquility and calmness of an innocent man."

The Black Tulip

"Hush!" said Rosa.

"Hush? Why?"

"My father must not suspect that we have been talking."

"What would it matter if he did?"

"What would it matter? Why, he would prevent me from ever coming here again."

Cornelius received this artless confidence with a smile; it seemed to him that he was, after all, to have some slight consolation in the midst of his misfortunes.

"Well, what are you two mumbling about?" said Gryphus, rising, and holding up his right arm with his left.

"Nothing," said Rosa; "this gentleman is telling me what regimen you must follow."

"What regimen I must follow, indeed! And you, too, young woman, you have one to follow also."

"What is that, father?"

"It is not to come into the prisoners' rooms, or if you do come, then to go out again as soon as possible; so be off with you, in front of me, and be quick about it."

Rosa and Cornelius exchanged a look.

That of Rosa meant: "You see how it is."

That of Cornelius signified: "God's will be done."

XI

THE WILL OF CORNELIUS VAN BAERLE

ROSA was not mistaken. The judges came the next day to the Buitenhof and interrogated Cornelius van Baerle. As a matter of fact, the examination did not last long. It was proved that Cornelius had kept at his house the fatal correspondence of the De Witts with France.

He did not deny it.

The only doubt in the minds of the judges was whether this correspondence had been delivered to him by his godfather, Cornelius de Witt.

But as, since the death of the two martyrs, Cornelius van Baerle no longer feared to compromise them, he not only admitted that the letters had been given into his charge by Cornelius de Witt in person, but he further related exactly how, when, and where the packet had been intrusted to him.

This trust implicated the godson in the crime of the godfather; the guilt of both was clear.

Van Baerle did not confine himself to this avowal; he told the whole truth with regard to his sympathies, his habits, and his ways of life. He spoke of his indifference to politics, his love of study, of art, of science, and of flowers. He stated that, since the day when Cornelius de Witt came to Dort and gave him the packet, he had never looked at it or touched it.

It was objected that in saying this he could not be speaking the truth, inasmuch as the papers had been kept in the very drawer into which he looked, and in which he placed his hand, every day.

Cornelius replied that this was true, but that he had only put his hand into the drawer to assure himself that his bulbs were keeping dry, and had only looked into it to see whether they were beginning to sprout.

It was objected that this pretended indifference with regard to the packet intrusted to him could not reasonably be credited, because it was impossible that he could have received such a charge from his god-father without being aware of its importance.

To this he replied that his godfather Cornelius loved him too well and, moreover, was too wise a man, to have said anything to him with regard to the nature of these papers, since a knowledge of their character would only have worried him.

It was objected that if M. de Witt had taken this course he would have placed with the papers, in case of accidents, a certificate of the fact that his godson was quite ignorant of the character of the correspond-ence; or, at any rate, would, during his trial, have written him a letter by means of which he would be able to exculpate himself.

The Will of Cornelius van Baerle

Cornelius replied that doubtless his godfather had not imagined that his packet would be in any danger, hidden away as it was in a cabinet which was held as inviolable as the ark by every one in the Van Baerle household; that with regard to a letter, he had some idea that, a few moments before his arrest, while he was absorbed in the contemplation of a very rare bulb, a servant of M. John de Witt had come into his drying-room and had given him a paper; but that his recollection of the incident was very vague and uncertain, that the servant had disappeared, and that, as for the paper, it might perhaps be found if a careful search were made for it.

As for Craeke, it was impossible to find him again, seeing that he had left the country.

As for the paper, its recovery was considered so improbable that no one took the trouble to look for it.

Cornelius himself did not insist much on this point, since, even supposing the paper were found, it might have nothing at all to do with the correspondence which was the foundation of the charge.

The judges wished to appear as though urging Cornelius to make a better defence than he was doing; they showed with regard to him that kindly patience which is a sign either that a magistrate is interested in a prisoner, or that he regards himself as a conqueror who has so completely overthrown and mastered his adversary that he has no need to adopt harsh measures in order to destroy him.

The Black Tulip

Cornelius would not accept this hypocritical assistance, and in a last reply, made with all the dignity
of a martyr and the calmness of an innocent man, he
said:

"You ask me, gentlemen, questions to which I
have no answer except the plain truth. Now the
plain truth is this. The packet came into my hands
in the way I have described. I protest before God
that I did not know, and do not know now, what it
contains. It was only on the day of my arrest that I
was told this packet consisted of the correspondence
of the Grand Pensionary with the Marquis de Louvois. Finally, I protest that I cannot conceive how
it became known that the packet was in my house,
and especially, how I can be held guilty of a crime in
having received that which my illustrious and unfortunate godfather brought to me."

That was the whole of Cornelius's defence. The
judges then began to discuss their decision.

They laid stress on the fact that every offshoot of
civil dissension is most injurious, in that it revives
hostilities which in the public interest should be put
an end to.

One of them—and he was a man who passed for
being a great observer—gave it as his opinion that
this young man, so phlegmatic in appearance, must
be very dangerous in reality, inasmuch as under an
icy exterior he must be concealing an ardent desire to
avenge his relatives, the De Witts.

Another observed that the love of tulips agrees

The Will of Cornelius van Baerle

very well with politics, and that it is shown by history that many men very dangerous to the State have engaged in gardening neither more nor less than if it had been the business of their lives, while in reality they were occupied with very different matters. Examples of this were Tarquinius Priscus, who cultivated poppies at Gabii, and the great Condé, who watered his carnations in the keep at Vincennes, and this at the very time when the former was planning his re-entry into Rome, and the latter his escape from custody.

The judge concluded with this dilemma:

" Either M. Cornelius van Baerle is very fond of politics, or he is very fond of tulips. In either case he has lied to us; first, because it has been proved that he was engaged in politics, and that by the letters which have been found at his house; and second, because it has been proved that he occupied himself with tulips. The bulbs are there to show it. Finally—and this is the worst part of his offence—since Cornelius van Baerle occupied himself at one and the same time with tulips and with politics, the accused must be of a hybrid nature, of an. amphibious organization, working with equal ardour in regard to tulips and in regard to politics, and therefore must have all the characteristics of a class of men particularly dangerous to the public tranquility, affording a certain, or rather a complete, analogy with the famous characters of whom Tarquinius Priscus and M. de Condé have just been cited as examples."

The Black Tulip

The result of all these reasonings was that the Prince-Stadtholder would undoubtedly be very much obliged to the magistrates of The Hague if they simplified the administration of the Seven Provinces for him, by destroying to the last germ all conspiracies against his authority.

This argument capped all the others, and in order effectually to destroy the germs of conspiracy, the penalty of death was unanimously decreed against M. Cornelius van Baerle, accused and convicted of having, under the pretence of being an innocent fancier of tulips, participated in the detestable intrigues and abominable plots of the two De Witts against the Dutch national life, and in their secret relations with the French enemy.

As a corollary to the sentence, it was ordered that the said Cornelius van Baerle be removed from the prison of the Buitenhof, and conducted to the scaffold erected on the square of the same name, and that there the public executioner should sever his head from his body.

As the deliberation had been a serious matter, it had lasted half an hour, and during this half hour the prisoner had been taken back to his cell.

There the Recorder of the States came to read the sentence to him.

Master Gryphus was confined to his bed with a fever brought on by the breaking of his arm. His keys had, therefore, been handed over to one of the assistant jailers; and behind this assistant, who had

The Will of Cornelius van Baerle

ushered in the Recorder, Rosa, the beautiful Frisian, had placed herself in the angle of the doorway, with a handkerchief to her lips to stifle her sighs and sobs.

Cornelius heard the sentence with a look rather of amazement than of sadness.

After the sentence had been read, the Recorder asked him if he had anything to say.

" No, indeed," replied he, " except that among all the causes of death which a cautious man might foresee and guard against, that is one which I never should have thought of."

At this answer the Recorder bowed to Cornelius van Baerle with all the ceremony which functionaries of his class accord to great criminals of any kind.

As he was about to retire, Cornelius said:

" By the way, Mr. Recorder, what day is fixed for this, please? "

" Why, to-day," replied the Recorder, a little taken aback by the calm indifference of the condemned man.

A sudden sob was heard from behind the door.

Cornelius leant forward to see who had given utterance to it, but Rosa, foreseeing that he would do so, had flung herself back.

" And," added Cornelius, " at what hour is the execution to take place? "

" At midday, sir."

" The devil! " said Cornelius; " I think I heard it strike ten at least twenty minutes ago. I have no time to lose."

The Black Tulip

" Not if you wish to reconcile yourself with God, sir," said the Recorder, bowing to the ground; " and you may ask for any minister you choose."

Saying this he went out backwards, and the assistant-jailer was about to follow him and to shut the door on Cornelius, when a white and trembling hand was placed between him and the heavy door.

Cornelius saw only the head-dress of cloth of gold with white lace hanging from it over the ears—the cap usually worn by Frisian maidens—and heard only a whisper in the turnkey's ear; but the jailer immediately gave up his heavy keys into the white hand stretched out to him, and descending a few steps, sat down in the middle of the staircase, which was thus doubly guarded, by him above and by the dog below.

The golden cap turned round and Cornelius recognised Rosa; her face was distorted with grief and her large blue eyes were filled with tears.

The young girl approached Cornelius, holding her hands to her broken heart.

" Oh, sir! sir! " she said; and she stopped short.

" My dear child," replied Cornelius, much moved, " what do you desire from me? I am not able to do much for any one now."

" Sir, I come to ask a favour from you," said Rosa, holding her hands stretched out, partly towards Cornelius, partly towards heaven.

" Do not weep thus, Rosa," said the prisoner,

The Will of Cornelius van Baerle

" for your tears affect me far more than does my approaching death. And, you know, the more innocent a prisoner is, the more calmly and joyfully ought he to meet death, since he dies a martyr. Come, do not cry any more, my dear Rosa, but tell me what it is you wish."

The young girl fell on her knees.

" Forgive my father," she said.

" Your father? " said Cornelius, astonished.

" Yes, he has been so hard on you, but it is his nature to be so, and you are not the only one to whom he has been brutal."

" He is punished, my dear Rosa, more than punished, by the accident which has happened to him, and I forgive him."

" Oh, thank you," said Rosa. " And now, tell me, can I do anything for you? "

" You can dry your beautiful eyes, my dear child," said Cornelius with a sweet smile.

" But for you, for you? "

" He who has only an hour to live is a great sybarite, dear Rosa, if he needs anything."

" The minister whom they have offered you? "

" I have adored God all my life, Rosa, and been blessed by his goodness. I have adored him in all his works. God has nothing against me. Therefore I shall not ask for any minister. The last thought which occupies my mind, Rosa, is connected with the glory of God. Help me, my dear, I beg of you, to carry out this last thought."

The Black Tulip

"Ah! M. Cornelius, speak, speak!" cried the young girl, bathed in tears.

"Give me your hand, child, and promise not to laugh at me."

"Laugh!" cried Rosa, despairingly, "laugh! at such a time! Why, you cannot have looked at me, M. Cornelius."

"I have, indeed, looked at you, Rosa, both with the eyes of the body and with those of the soul. Never have I met with a more beautiful woman, or a purer heart. And if from this moment I no longer look at you, it is because, being on the point of leaving this world, I wish to have nothing to regret here."

Rosa began to tremble, for, as the prisoner said these words, the clock in the belfry of the Buitenhof struck eleven.

Cornelius understood her agitation.

"Yes, yes, you are right, Rosa," he said. "Let us be quick."

Then taking from his breast (where he had again hidden it, now that he no longer feared being searched) the paper containing the three bulbs, he said:

"My dear little friend, I have loved flowers very much. That was at a time when I did not know that one could love something else. Oh! do not blush, do not turn away, Rosa. Even were I to make you a declaration of love, poor child, it would lead to nothing; there is, down there on the Buitenhof, a sword which, in sixty minutes from now, will put an end to my boldness. I loved flowers, then, Rosa, and I had found, at least I believe I had, the secret of the wonderful black tulip which it was thought impossible to produce, and for which, as you may or may not know, a prize of a hundred thousand florins has been offered by the Horticultural Society of Haarlem. These hundred thousand florins—and God knows it is not the money that I regret—these hundred thousand florins I have in this paper; they are won by the three bulbs which it contains, and which you may take, Rosa, for I make you a present of them."

" M. Cornelius! "

" Oh! you may take them, Rosa; you are not robbing any one. I am alone in the world; my father and mother are dead; I never had a brother or sister. I have never been in love with any one, and if any one has thought of being in love with me, I have not been aware of it. You see clearly, then, Rosa, that I am abandoned by all, since you alone are in my cell at this hour, consoling and helping me."

" But, sir, a hundred thousand florins! "

" Now, let us be serious, my dear child," said Cornelius. " A hundred thousand florins will be a good dowry, such as your beauty deserves; you shall have them, these hundred thousand florins, for I am sure of my bulbs. You shall have them, Rosa. I only ask of you in exchange a promise that you will marry a good young man, whom you will love and who will love you, as much as I have loved my flowers. Do not interrupt me, Rosa, I have only a few minutes more."

The sobs of the poor girl almost choked her.

Cornelius took her hand.

"Listen to me," he continued; "this is how you must proceed. Take some mould from my garden at Dort. Ask Butruysheim, my gardener, for some of the earth in bed number six; then plant in it, in a deep box, these three bulbs; they will flower next May, that is to say, in seven months, and when you see the flower appearing on the stem, shield it during the night from the wind, and during the day from the sun. It will flower black, I am certain. Then you must give notice to the President of the Haarlem Society. He will have the colour of the flower certified by the committee, and they will then pay you the hundred thousand florins."

Rosa sighed heavily.

"Now," continued Cornelius, wiping away a tear which trembled on the edge of his eye-lid, and which was a tribute rather to the beautiful black tulip which he was never to see than to the life he was about to lose, "I desire nothing more, except that the tulip be called the *Rosa Baerlensis*, that is to say, that it may bear your name and mine together; and as you do not, of course, know Latin, and may therefore forget this name, try to get me a pencil and paper that I may write it down for you."

Rosa began to sob anew, and handed to Cornelius

The Will of Cornelius van Baerle

a book bound in shagreen and bearing the initials
C. W.

"What is this?" asked the prisoner.

"Alas!" replied Rosa, "it is the Bible which
belonged to your godfather, Cornelius de Witt.
From it he obtained strength to undergo the torture, and to hear his sentence without turning
pale. I found it in this room after the martyr's
death, and kept it as a relic. To-day I brought it to
you, for it seems to me that this book has in it a
power quite divine. You were not in need of
strength from this source, for God himself had already given it to you. God be praised for it! Write
in this that which you have to write, M. Cornelius,
and though, unfortunately, I cannot read, what you
write shall nevertheless be done."

Cornelius took the Bible and kissed it reverently.

"What shall I write with?" he asked.

"There is a pencil in the Bible," said Rosa. "It
was there and I did not remove it."

It was the pencil which John de Witt had lent to
his brother, and which he had forgotten to take back
again.

Cornelius took it, and on the second page—for
the first, it will be remembered, had been torn out—
in a hand not less firm than his godfather's, though,
like him, he was about to die, he wrote:

"On this 23d day of August, 1672, being on the
point, though innocent, of surrendering my soul to

God on the scaffold, I bequeath to Rosa Gryphus the only piece of property remaining to me in this world, all the rest having been confiscated. I bequeath, I say, to Rosa Gryphus three bulbs, which I am absolutely convinced will produce, in the month of May next, the great black tulip for which the Haarlem Society has offered a prize of one hundred thousand florins, desiring that she may receive these hundred thousand florins in my place and stead and as my sole heiress, on the single condition that she shall marry a young man of about my age, whom she will love and who will love her, and that she shall give to the great black tulip, which will originate a new species, the name of *Rosa Baerlensis*, that is to say, her name and mine united.

"May God grant me grace, and her, health.

"CORNELIUS VAN BAERLE."

Then, giving the Bible to Rosa, he said, "Read it."

"Alas!" replied the young girl, "I have already told you I cannot read."

Then Cornelius read to Rosa the will which he had just made.

The sobs of the poor girl redoubled.

"Do you accept the conditions?" asked the prisoner, with a sad smile, kissing the tips of the trembling fingers of the beautiful Frisian.

"Oh! I do not know, sir," she murmured.

"You do not know, my child? and why not?"

The Will of Cornelius van Baerle

" Because there is one of the conditions which I cannot fulfil."

" Which one? I thought we had arranged it all by our treaty of alliance."

" You give me a hundred thousand florins as a dowry? "

" Yes."

" So that I may marry a young man whom I love? "

" Precisely."

" Well, then, sir, I cannot have the money; I shall never love any one, and I shall never marry."

And after uttering these words in a pitiable tone, Rosa sank to her knees and almost fainted away with grief.

Cornelius, alarmed at seeing her so pale and deathlike, was about to take her in his arms when a heavy step, followed by other ominous sounds, re-echoed on the stone staircase, accompanied by the barking of the dog.

" They are coming to fetch you! " cried Rosa, wringing her hands. " My God! my God! have you nothing more to say to me? "

And she fell on her knees, with her head buried in her arms, quite choked with sobs and tears.

" I have to tell you to hide your three bulbs most carefully, and to treat them according to the directions I have given you, and this, for love of me— farewell, Rosa."

" Oh! yes," she replied, without raising her head,

"yes, everything you have told me I will do. Except marry," she added, in a low voice, "for that, oh! that I can never do now."

And she hid away in her throbbing bosom the precious treasure of Cornelius.

The noise which Cornelius and Rosa had heard was made by the Recorder, who was coming to fetch the prisoner. He was followed by the executioner, by the soldiers who were to form the guard round the scaffold, and by the officials of the prison, curious to see the condemned man. Cornelius, without weakness and without ostentation, received them rather as friends than as persecutors, and allowed them to make such preparations as they thought necessary in the execution of their duties.

Casting a glance through the small barred window, he saw the scaffold, and twenty yards from the scaffold the gibbet, from which, by order of the Stadtholder, the outraged remains of the two brothers had been removed.

When he had to descend in order to follow the guards, Cornelius tried to exchange a look with Rosa, but he only saw, behind the swords and pikes, a form stretched out near a wooden bench and a pale face half hidden by long hair.

But Rosa, as she fell senseless, was still obedient to her friend; she placed her hand on her velvet corset and, although quite unconscious of everything around her, continued to clasp instinctively the precious charge intrusted to her by Cornelius.

The Will of Cornelius van Baerle

And as he quitted the cell, the young man could see, between the tightly clinched fingers of the girl, the yellowish leaf of the Bible, on which Cornelius de Witt had written with such pain and distress the few lines which, had Cornelius van Baerle read them, would undoubtedly have saved both a man and a tulip.

XII

THE EXECUTION

To reach the foot of the scaffold from the prison Cornelius had not to take three hundred steps.

At the bottom of the staircase the dog looked quietly at him. Cornelius even thought that he noticed in the animal's eyes a sort of kindly expression, which was almost one of pity. Perhaps the dog could recognise a condemned man, and bit those only who went forth free.

It will be readily understood that the shorter the road to be traversed between the prison door and the scaffold, the more closely was it packed with inquisitive spectators.

Their thirst for blood had not been quenched by that which they had shed three days before. They were now eager for a new victim. Scarcely had Cornelius appeared when a torrent of yells arose in the street and covered the whole surface of the square, spreading thence in different directions along the crowded roads which converged on the scaffold.

Thus the scaffold seemed like an island at the meeting point of four or five turbulent rivers.

The Execution

In the midst of these threats, howls, and vociferations, in order no doubt to avoid hearing them, Cornelius buried himself in his own thoughts.

What was this innocent man thinking of on his way to death?

It was not of his enemies, or his judges, or his executioners.

It was of the beautiful tulips which, from the heights of heaven, he would see in Ceylon, and Bengal, and elsewhere, when, seated with the just at God's right hand, he would be able to look down with pity on this earth, on which M. John and M. Cornelius de Witt had been murdered for having thought too much of politics, and on which M. Cornelius van Baerle was about to be murdered for thinking too much of tulips.

" One stroke of the sword," said the philosopher, " and my beautiful dream will commence."

It only remained to be seen whether, as in the cases of M. de Chalais, and of M. de Thou, and of other clumsily executed persons, the executioner was reserving more than one stroke, that is to say, more than one martyrdom, for the poor tulip-grower.

But Van Baerle mounted the steps of the scaffold none the less resolutely for that.

He mounted them proud of having been the friend of the illustrious John, and the godson of the noble Cornelius, de Witt, whom the ruffians now thronging to witness his own execution had hacked to pieces and burnt three days before.

The Black Tulip

He knelt down and prayed, and when he had done so, observed not without joy that, when he placed his head on the block, he would be able, by keeping his eyes open, to see till the end the barred window of the Buitenhof.

At last the moment arrived for the fatal stroke. Cornelius placed his chin on the cold damp block. But at this instant he closed his eyes in spite of himself, so as to withstand more resolutely the horrible avalanche which was about to fall upon his head and sweep away his life.

A gleam of light flashed on the floor of the scaffold; the executioner was raising his sword.

Van Baerle said farewell to the black tulip, convinced that he would awake to greet God in another world very different in light and in colour from this.

Three times he felt the cold wind of the sword pass over his shrinking neck.

But, to his amazement, he felt neither pain nor concussion. Neither did he perceive any change in his surroundings.

Then, suddenly, he felt himself raised by gentle hands, he knew not whose, and found himself again on his feet, still staggering a little.

He reopened his eyes.

Some one near him was reading aloud from a large parchment, sealed with a huge seal of red wax.

And the same sun, yellow and pale as a Dutch sun usually is, shone in the sky, and the same barred window faced him at the end of the Buitenhof, and

The Execution

the same ruffians, no longer howling but struck dumb
with amazement, were watching from the square
below.

By dint of reopening his eyes, looking round, and
listening, Van Baerle began to understand what had
happened.

The Prince of Orange, fearing no doubt that the
seventeen pounds (more or less) of blood which were
in Van Baerle's body might more than fill up the cup
of divine justice, had taken pity on the prisoner,
because of his good character, and of the fact that
appearances were in his favour.

Consequently, his Highness had granted him his
life. This was the reason why the sword which had
been raised with sinister gleam had whirled thrice
round his head, as the bird of ill-omen had done
round the head of Turnus, and had hung suspended,
but had not fallen, and had left his vertebræ intact.

This was the reason why he had felt neither pain
nor concussion, and why the sun continued to smile
in the sky—a sky the colour of which was but an
indifferent one, though Cornelius found it agreeable
enough.

The prisoner, who had hoped that he would
shortly see God and be able to admire all the tulips of
the universe spread out in a panorama before him,
was really a little disappointed; but he felt somewhat
consoled as, with a certain feeling of satisfaction, he
moved the muscles of that part of the body which the
Greeks call *trachelos*, and we, more simply, the neck.

The Black Tulip

And then, too, Cornelius hoped that the pardon would be complete, and that he would be restored to liberty and to his flower-beds at Dort.

But Cornelius was mistaken, for, as Mme. de Sévigné expressed it at about the same time, there was a postscript to the letter, and the most important part of the letter was contained in the postscript.

By this postscript, William, Stadholder of Holland, condemned Cornelius van Baerle to perpetual imprisonment.

He was not guilty enough to be put to death, but he was too guilty to be set free.

Cornelius listened to the reading of this postscript, and then, after the first feeling of disappointment which it caused had passed away, he said to himself:

" Bah! all is not lost; there is some good even in perpetual imprisonment. There is still Rosa, and there are still my three bulbs of the black tulip."

But Cornelius forgot that the Seven Provinces might perhaps have seven prisons, one for each province; he also forgot that food for prisoners would be cheaper at other places than at a capital like The Hague.

His Highness could not, it seemed, afford to feed Van Baerle at The Hague, and so sent him to undergo his perpetual imprisonment in the fortress of Loevestein, very close to Dort, but also, alas! very far from it. For Loevestein, geographers tell us, is situated at the point of the island which lies at the

The Execution

junction of the Waal and the Maas, opposite Gorcum.

Van Baerle knew the history of his country well enough to be aware that the famous Grotius had been shut up in this castle, after the death of Barneveldt, and that the States, in their generosity to the celebrated publicist, jurist, historian, poet, and theologian, had allowed him for maintenance a sum of twenty-four Dutch halfpence a day.

" I am far from being as important a person as Grotius," said Van Baerle to himself; " they will hardly give me more than twelve halfpence, and I shall fare badly—still, I shall be alive."

Then suddenly a terrible thought occurred to Cornelius: " Ah!" he cried out, " what a damp and cloudy district! and the ground there, how bad it will be for tulips!

" And Rosa, too! Rosa will not be at Loevestein," he murmured, letting his head fall on his breast —that head which he had very nearly let fall still lower.

XIII

THE THOUGHTS OF ONE OF THE SPECTATORS DURING THE LAST SCENE

WHILE Cornelius was thus reflecting on his future lot, a carriage approached the scaffold. This carriage was for the prisoner. He was directed to get into it; he obeyed.

His last look was towards the Buitenhof. He hoped to see at the window the face of Rosa, and to perceive in it the relief which she would feel at his reprieve; but the horses in the carriage were swift, and speedily carried Van Baerle out of reach of the vociferous shouts with which the multitude either honoured the magnanimity of the Stadtholder, or railed against the De Witts and their godson, who had just narrowly escaped death.

This escape led the spectators to say:

" It is very lucky that we lost no time in doing justice on that great scoundrel John, and that little rascal Cornelius; otherwise the clemency of his Highness would most certainly have snatched them from us just as it has this one."

Among the spectators whom the execution of Van

One Spectator's Thoughts

Baerle had drawn to the Buitenhof, and whom the upshot of the affair had somewhat disappointed, the most disappointed of all was certainly a soberly dressed burgher, who during the morning had made such good use of his hands and feet that by midday he found himself separated from the scaffold only by the file of soldiers which surrounded that structure.

Many had shown themselves eager to witness the shedding of the traitorous blood of the guilty Cornelius, but none had expressed this desire with such vehemence as the burgher we have referred to.

The most furious of the mob had come to the Buitenhof at break of day to secure good places, but he, outstripping even the most eager of them, had passed the night on the steps of the prison and, as we have said, had reached the first row, *unguibus et rostro*, cajoling some and striking others.

And when the executioner brought the condemned man on to the scaffold, the burgher, mounted on the stone basin of a fountain so as to see and be seen better, made a sign to the executioner which seemed to mean:

" It is agreed, is it not? "

To this gesture the executioner replied by another, which signified:

" Yes, don't be uneasy about it."

Who was this burgher who seemed so much at home with the executioner? and what was the meaning of the signs exchanged between them?

Nothing more natural: the burgher was Mynheer

147

The Black Tulip

Isaac Boxtel, who, after the arrest of Cornelius, had, as we have seen, come to The Hague to try and get hold of the three bulbs of the black tulip.

Boxtel had at first tried to get Gryphus on his side, but the latter was equal to a bulldog in fidelity, suspiciousness, and biting power. He had consequently refused to believe in Boxtel's hatred of the prisoner, and had set Boxtel down as an earnest friend of Van Baerle's, who was merely asking questions about things which were of no consequence in order to arrive at some means of facilitating the prisoner's escape.

Accordingly, to the first propositions which Boxtel made to Gryphus with a view to the abstraction of the bulbs which Cornelius van Baerle must be hiding, if not in his breast, at any rate in some corner of his cell, Gryphus made no reply except by a forcible eviction, which was assisted by the caresses of the dog.

Boxtel was not discouraged by the fact that the end of one leg of his trousers remained within the teeth of the watch-dog. He returned to the charge; but this time Gryphus was in bed with the fever brought on by the breaking of his arm, and did not even see Boxtel. The latter therefore applied to Rosa, offering the young girl in exchange for the three bulbs, a head-dress of pure gold. But the young girl, though as yet ignorant of the value of the property which she was asked to purloin, and for which she was offered so great a reward, advised the tempter to go to the executioner, who was not only

148

One Spectator's Thoughts

the final judge, but also the last heir, of condemned prisoners.

This advice started an idea in Boxtel's mind.

Things had just arrived at this stage when the sentence was pronounced, a prompt sentence, as we have already observed. Isaac therefore had no time to bribe anybody. He adopted the idea which Rosa had suggested to him, and went to interview the executioner.

He did not doubt for a moment that Cornelius would die with the tulips next to his heart.

In fact, Boxtel left two things out of account: Rosa, that is to say, love; and William, that is to say, clemency.

Leaving Rosa and William out of account, the calculations of the envious Boxtel were quite correct.

Leaving out William, Cornelius would die; leaving out Rosa, Cornelius would die with the bulbs next his heart.

Mynheer Boxtel, therefore, went to see the executioner, gave himself out to the latter as a great friend of the condemned man, and, for the rather exorbitant sum of one hundred florins, bought everything that might be found on the body of his friend after the execution, gold and silver ornaments excepted; these last he allowed the executioner to retain.

The sum seemed a large one, but what was a hundred florins to a man who, by expending it, was almost certain to obtain the prize offered by the Haarlem Society?

It was money lent at one hundred thousand per cent, which, it must be admitted, was a good enough investment.

The executioner, on his side, had nothing, or next to nothing, to do to gain his hundred florins. He had merely, when the execution was over, to allow Mynheer Boxtel to ascend the scaffold with his servants, and to remove the dead body of his friend. This, as a matter of fact, was commonly done by faithful servants, when a master died publicly on the Buitenhof.

A fanatic like Cornelius might very well have for a friend another fanatic who would give a hundred florins for his remains.

The executioner accordingly agreed to the proposal. He only imposed one condition, and that was that he should be paid in advance.

Boxtel might be like some people who go into side-shows at fairs; he might be dissatisfied and decline to pay afterwards. Boxtel paid in advance, and waited.

After this one can guess whether Boxtel was excited; whether he kept his eyes on the guards, the Recorder, the executioner; whether the movements of Van Baerle interested him. How would he place his head on the block? how would he fall? would he not, in falling, crush under him the inestimable bulbs? had he at least taken care to inclose them in a box—a gold box, for instance, as gold is the hardest of metals?

We will not attempt to describe the effect produced on this worthy man by the delay in the execution.

What was the use of the executioner losing his time in making his sword flash above Cornelius's head, instead of cutting the head off at once? But when he saw the Recorder take the hand of the condemned man and raise him up, at the same time taking the parchment from his own pocket; when he heard the public reading of the pardon granted by the Stadtholder, Boxtel was no longer human. The rage of the tiger, the hyena, and the serpent, burst forth in his eyes, his voice, and his features. If Van Baerle had been within reach he would have flung himself on him, and murdered him.

So then, Cornelius would live, Cornelius would go to Loevestein; there, in his prison, he would still have his bulbs, and there, perhaps, he would find a garden in which he would succeed in making the black tulip flower!

There are some catastrophes which the pen of the unfortunate writer cannot describe. He is obliged to leave them, after stating the simple facts, to the imagination of his readers.

Boxtel, growing faint, fell from the edge of the stone basin on to some Orangeists, who, like himself, were disgusted with the turn which the affair had taken. Thinking that the cries of Mynheer Boxtel

The Black Tulip

were cries of joy, they overwhelmed him with blows and thumps, which certainly would not have been given with more vigour even on the other side of the Channel.

But what were a few thumps to the pain already felt by Boxtel?

He wanted to run after the coach which was carrying off Cornelius and his bulbs. But in his haste he overlooked a paving-stone, stumbled, lost his balance, rolled ten yards, and did not succeed in getting up again till he had been bruised and trampled upon by the feet of the whole filthy populace of The Hague.

Boxtel was thus experiencing a run of ill-luck; his clothes were torn, his back was bruised, his hands were scratched.

One would have thought that this was enough for Boxtel.

But in this one would have been mistaken.

Once more on his feet, Boxtel tore out as much of his hair as he could lay hold of, and flung it from him as a holocaust to that savage and heartless deity who is called Jealousy.

It was no doubt an offering very acceptable to that goddess, whose hair, according to mythology, takes the form of serpents.

XIV

THE PIGEONS OF DORT

It was certainly a great honour for Cornelius van Baerle to be shut up in the very prison in which the learned Grotius had been confined.

But when he arrived at the prison he found that a still greater honour awaited him. The cell once occupied by the illustrious friend of Barneveldt was empty, as it happened, when the clemency of the Prince of Orange sent the tulip-fancier Van Baerle to Loevestein.

This cell had had a very bad reputation in the fortress since the day when Grotius, thanks to his wife's ingenious idea, had escaped in the famous box of books which was allowed to pass without examination.

Van Baerle, for his part, however, regarded it as a good omen that he should have been placed in this room, for to his mind, a jailer should never have placed a second pigeon in a cage from which a first had so easily escaped.

The cell is historic. We will therefore not waste time in giving a detailed account of it here. Except for an alcove, which had been fitted up for Mme. Grotius, it was like the other cells in the prison, though perhaps farther from the ground. It had, too, a very pleasant view from the barred windows. The interest of our story, moreover, does not consist in descriptions of a number of interiors. To Van Baerle life was something far different from a mere exercise in respiration. There were two things which the poor prisoner loved far more than he did his own personal comfort, things which henceforth he could possess only in imagination, by the aid of thought which no prison can restrain.

These two things were a flower and a woman, both lost to him forever.

Happily he was mistaken in this idea, our good Van Baerle. God, who had looked down on him with fatherly pity when he was walking towards the scaffold, was reserving for him in the very heart of the prison, in the cell of Grotius, the most adventurous existence which ever fell to the lot of a tulip-fancier.

One morning, while he was enjoying at his window the fresh breeze which rose from the Waal, and while he was admiring in the distance, behind a forest of chimneys, the wind-mills of his native Dort, he perceived some pigeons flying towards him in a body, from that point of the horizon. They perched, fluttering in the sunshine, on the pointed gables of Loevestein.

"These pigeons," said Van Baerle, "come from Dort, and consequently they can go back there. Now,

The Pigeons of Dort

a person who fastened a message to the wing of one of these pigeons would have a very fair chance of conveying news of himself to Dort, and to his friends there who might be grieving for him."

Then, after a moment's thought, he added:

"That person shall be myself."

One is not in a hurry at twenty-eight, if condemned to perpetual confinement, that is to say, to twenty-two or twenty-three thousand days of imprisonment.

Van Baerle, still thinking of his three bulbs, for this thought was always stirring in the recesses of his mind, as the heart is ever beating in the recesses of the breast—Van Baerle, we say, still thinking of his three bulbs, made a snare for the pigeons. He tempted these airy beings with all the resources of his larder—which cost eighteen Dutch, that is twelve French, halfpence a day—and after a month of fruitless efforts, he succeeded in capturing a female bird.

He took two months more to catch a male: then he placed them together, and towards the beginning of the year 1673, having obtained some eggs, he let the female bird go. Trusting to the male bird which was sitting on the eggs in her place, the female went off joyfully to Dort, with the note under her wing.

She returned in the evening: the note was still in its place. This continued to happen for fifteen days, at first to the great disappointment, and later to the utter despair, of Van Baerle.

155

The Black Tulip

On the sixteenth day she returned without the note.

Now Van Baerle had addressed the note to his nurse, the old Frisian woman, begging any charitable soul who might find it to send it on to her as safely and as quickly as possible.

In this letter addressed to his nurse he had placed a little note addressed to Rosa.

God, who causes the wind to carry the seeds of wall-flowers to the walls of old castles, and makes them flower there by the aid of a little rain, allowed this letter to reach the nurse. And in this way:

On quitting Dort for The Hague and The Hague for Gorcum, Mynheer Isaac Boxtel had abandoned not only his house and his servant, his observatory and his telescopes, but also his pigeons.

The servant, whom he had left without wages, at first lived on his own scanty savings; then he went on to eat the pigeons.

And the pigeons, perceiving this, emigrated from Isaac Boxtel's roof to Cornelius van Baerle's. The nurse was a kindly soul, who found it absolutely necessary to love something. She became very friendly with the pigeons that had come to beg her hospitality; and when Isaac's servant demanded the twelve or fifteen remaining pigeons in order to eat them, as he had eaten the others, she offered to buy them from him at the rate of six Dutch halfpence apiece.

This was double the value of the birds, and accordingly the servant accepted her offer with great alacrity.

Thus the nurse found herself the legitimate owner of the jealous Boxtel's pigeons.

These pigeons, with others, visited in their wanderings The Hague, and Loevestein, and Rotterdam, seeking no doubt for wheat of a fresh kind, and hempseed of a different flavour.

Chance, or rather God, God whom we, for our part, see at the bottom of everything, brought it about that Cornelius van Baerle captured just one of these particular pigeons. The result was that had the envious man not left Dort to follow his rival, first to The Hague and then to Gorcum—or Loevestein, which you will, for the two places are only separated by the junction of the Waal and the Maas—it would have been into his hands, and not into those of the nurse, that the note written by Van Baerle would have fallen, and consequently the poor prisoner, like the raven of the Roman cobbler, would have lost both his time and his labour, and instead of having to relate the various events which, under our pen, will be unrolled like a many-coloured tapestry, we should have had nothing to describe but a long series of days, lifeless, sad, and gloomy as the mantle of night.

The note fell, then, into the hands of Van Baerle's nurse.

And, accordingly, towards the end of February, as the first hours of the evening were coming on, and the new-born stars were appearing in the sky, Cor-

The Black Tulip

nelius heard on the staircase of the tower a voice which made him tremble.

He held his hand to his heart, and listened.

It was the soft and musical voice of Rosa.

We must admit that Cornelius was not so amazed or so wild with joy as he would have been but for the story of the pigeon. In exchange for his letter the pigeon had brought him hope under its empty wing, and knowing Rosa, he had been expecting every day, provided the letter had reached her, to hear news of his love and of his tulips.

He rose, listening eagerly and leaning towards the door.

Yes, those were indeed the accents which had so moved him at The Hague.

And now Rosa, who had journeyed from The Hague to Loevestein and had succeeded, Cornelius knew not how, in getting into the prison, might happily succeed also in reaching the prisoner himself.

While Cornelius, at this idea, was building up thought upon thought and hopes upon misgivings, the shutter of the opening in the door of his cell was withdrawn, and Rosa, radiant with joy and still beautiful, in spite of the grief which during the last five months had paled her cheeks, Rosa pressed her face against the iron bars of the opening and said:

" Sir! sir! here I am! "

Cornelius stretched out his arms, looked up to heaven and uttered a cry of joy.

" Oh! Rosa, Rosa! " he cried.

The Pigeons of Dort

"Hush! speak low, my father is following me," said the young girl.

"Your father?"

"Yes, he is below in the court-yard, at the bottom of the stairs: he is receiving the Governor's instructions; then he will come up here."

"The Governor's instructions!"

"Listen, and I will try to tell you all about it in two words. The Stadtholder has a country-house, a league from Leyden, a large farm-dairy to be exact; his nurse, who is my aunt, has charge of all the animals on the farm. As soon as I received your letter, which unfortunately I could not read, but which your nurse read to me, I went at once to my aunt's house. There I stayed till the Prince paid a visit to the dairy, and when he came, I asked him to allow my father to exchange the post of chief jailer of the prison at The Hague for that of jailer at the fortress of Loevestein. He did not suspect my object; if he had known it, very likely he would have refused my request. But, as it was, he granted the favour."

"And so you are now here!"

"As you see."

"So that I shall see you every day?"

"As often as ever I can."

"Oh! Rosa, my own dear Rosa!" said Cornelius, "you love me a little, then?"

"A little!" said she. "Oh! you are not exacting enough, M. Cornelius."

Cornelius stretched out his hands to her eagerly,

but he only succeeded in touching her fingers through the grating.

" Here is my father," said Rosa.

And hastily leaving the dor, she ran towards old Gryphus, who was just appearing at the top of the staircase.

XV

THE WICKET IN THE CELL DOOR

GRYPHUS was followed by the watch-dog.

He was taking him round in order that, in case of need, he might recognise the prisoners again.

"Father," said Rosa, "here is the famous cell from which M. Grotius escaped. M. Grotius, you know?"

"Yes, yes, that rascally Grotius: a friend of the scoundrel Barneveldt, whom I saw executed when I was a boy. Grotius! ha! ha! so it was from this cell he escaped, was it? Well, I will answer for it that no one will escape from it after him."

And opening the door, he began in the dark to speak to the prisoner.

As for the dog, he went over to the prisoner and began to growl and sniff at his legs, as though to ask him by what right he was still alive, considering that he had seen him go out between the Recorder and the executioner.

But Rosa called him off, and the dog went to her.

"Sir," said Gryphus, raising the lantern in order to try and throw a little light round him, "you see in me your new jailer. I am chief warden and have charge of the cells. I am not at all spiteful, but in everything that regards discipline I am inflexible."

"Oh! I know you very well, my dear M. Gryphus," said the prisoner, entering the ring of light cast by the lantern.

"Well, well, it's you, M. van Baerle," said Gryphus, "it's you. Well, well, well, how people do meet again!"

"Yes, and it is with great pleasure, my dear M. Gryphus, that I see your arm is all right now, since you are holding a lantern with it."

Gryphus frowned.

"That's how it is," he said. "In politics people always make mistakes. His Highness granted you your life. I would not have done that."

"Bah!" said Cornelius, "why not?"

"Because you are just the man to conspire again. You learned men have dealings with the devil!"

"Ah! Master Gryphus, are you dissatisfied, then, with the way in which I set your arm, or with the fee I asked?" said Cornelius laughing.

"No, by Jove, no, quite the opposite," growled the jailer; "you set my arm very well; there was some sorcery in that, too; at the end of six weeks I could use it as if nothing had happened; so much so that the doctor at the Buitenhof, who knows his business, wanted to break it again, so as to set it in the recognised way, and he promised that this time I should be three months without being able to use it."

The Wicket in the Cell Door

" And you would not agree? "

" I said, ' No, as long as I can make the sign of the cross with this arm ' "—Gryphus was a Catholic— " ' as long as I can make the sign of the cross with this arm, I laugh at the devil.' "

" But if you laugh at the devil, M. Gryphus, with much more reason ought you to laugh at learned men."

" Oh! learned men, learned men! " cried Gryphus without answering the argument, " I would rather have ten soldiers to guard than one learned man. Soldiers smoke, and drink, and get drunk: they are as quiet as sheep, if you give them some brandy or some Moselle. But for a learned man to drink, and smoke, and get drunk, oh, no! They are sober, they spend nothing, they keep their heads clear, so as to be able to conspire. But I may as well tell you at once, you won't find it an easy thing to conspire. To begin with, no books, no paper, no works on magic. It was by means of books that M. Grotius escaped."

" I assure you, Master Gryphus," replied Van Baerle, " that though I had perhaps at one time the idea of escaping, I no longer have any intention of doing so."

" That's well, that's well," said Gryphus; " keep a strict watch over yourself. I will do the like. All the same, his Highness has made a great mistake."

" In not having my head cut off? Thank you, M. Gryphus, thank you! "

The Black Tulip

"Certainly; you see that the De Witts are quite calm and tranquil now."

"That is an abominable thing to say, M. Gryphus," said Van Baerle, turning his head away to hide his disgust. "You forget that one of those unfortunate men was my friend, and the other—the other was a second father to me."

"Yes, but I remember that both of them were conspirators. Besides, it is philanthropy that makes me speak thus."

"Indeed! Explain that a little, my dear M. Gryphus. I don't very well understand it."

"Yes, if your head had remained on M. Harbruck's block . . ."

"Well?"

"Well, you would not be suffering now. Whereas, I do not conceal from you that here I shall give you a very hard time of it."

"Thank you for the promise, Master Gryphus."

And the prisoner smiled ironically at the old jailer, while Rosa, from behind the door, answered him with a sweet smile of consolation.

Gryphus went towards the window.

There was still enough daylight to enable one to see indistinctly an immense horizon, lost in a grayish mist.

"What sort of view is there from here?" asked the jailer.

"Oh! a very fine one," said Cornelius, looking at Rosa.

164

The Wicket in the Cell Door

" Yes, yes, too much of a view."

At that moment the two pigeons, scared by the sight, and above all by the voice, of one whom they did not know, flew out of their nest and disappeared in alarm into the mist.

" Ho! ho! what is this? " asked the jailer.

" My pigeons," replied Cornelius.

" My pigeons! " cried the jailer, " *my* pigeons? Can a prisoner have anything of his own, then? "

" Well," said Cornelius, " the pigeons which God in his goodness has lent me, then."

" Here is a breach of the regulations already," replied Gryphus. " Ah! young man, young man, I warn you of something, and that is that by to-morrow those pigeons will be boiled in my pot."

" You'll have to catch them first, Master Gryphus," said Van Baerle. " You won't allow that those pigeons are mine, but I swear they are still less yours."

" What is put off is not necessarily lost," growled the jailer, " and to-morow, at the latest, I will wring their necks."

And as he made this spiteful promise Gryphus leant out of the window to examine the structure of the nest. This gave Cornelius time to run to the door and press Rosa's hand.

" At nine this evening," she said to him.

Gryphus, quite engrossed with his idea of catching the pigeons the next day as he had promised, saw and heard nothing of this; and as he had now closed the window, he took his daughter by the arm, went out, gave the key a double turn in the lock, pushed the bolts, and went away to make similar promises to another prisoner.

Scarcely had he disappeared when Cornelius ran to the door to lisen to the sound of his retreating steps, and when it had died away, he went to the window and totally demolished the nest of the two pigeons.

He preferred to drive them from his presence forever, rather than expose to the risk of death the gentle messengers to whom he owed the happiness of seeing Rosa again.

This visit of the jailer, his brutal threats, and the gloomy prospect of being subject to the guardianship of one whose brutality he well knew, could not deprive Cornelius of the sweet thoughts, and especially of the sweet hopes, which the presence of Rosa had just reawakened in his mind.

He waited impatiently for the prison clock to strike nine.

Rosa had said, " At nine o'clock, expect me."

The last stroke of the bell was still ringing in the air, when Cornelius heard on the staircase the light step and the swaying dress of the fair Frisian, and soon the shutter was thrown back and the grating in the door, on which Cornelius had fixed his eager gaze, was lighted up.

" Here I am," said Rosa, still breathless with hurrying up the stairs, " here I am."

" Oh, my good Rosa! "

The Wicket in the Cell Door

" You are pleased to see me, then? "

" Can you ask me that? But how did you manage to come? tell me."

" Listen: my father goes to sleep every evening immediately after supper: I make him lie down, a little stupefied with gin. Do not say a word about it to any one, for thanks to this habit of his, I shall be able to come every evening and talk to you for an hour."

" Oh! thank you, Rosa, dear Rosa."

And, as he said this, Cornelius brought his face so close to the bars that Rosa withdrew hers a little.

" I have brought you your tulip-bulbs," she said.

The heart of Cornelius leapt within him. He had not dared, so far, to ask Rosa what she had done with the precious treasure that he had intrusted to her.

" Ah! you have preserved them, then? "

" Did you not give them to me as something that was dear to you? "

" Yes, but as I gave them to you, it seems to me that they are yours."

" They were to be mine after your death, and happily you are alive. Oh, how I have blessed his Highness! If God grants to Prince William all the happiness which I have wished him, King William will certainly be not only the happiest man in his kingdom, but the happiest man in the whole world. Your life was spared, I say, and I resolved, while still keeping the Bible of your godfather Cornelius, to bring back your bulbs to you. Only, I did not know how to do it. I had already made up my mind to go and ask the Stadtholder to give my father the post of jailer at Gorcum, when the nurse brought me your letter. Ah! we wept over it together, I assure you. But your letter only strengthened my resolution. It was then that I set out for Leyden; the rest you know."

"What! dear Rosa," replied Cornelius, "before you received my letter you were thinking of coming to rejoin me?"

"Was I thinking of it?" replied Rosa, allowing her love to get the better of her shyness, "why, I thought of nothing else!"

As she said this, Rosa became so beautiful that for the second time Cornelius placed his forehead and his lips against the bars, no doubt to thank the beautiful young woman.

Rosa drew back as she had done before.

"In truth," she said, with that coquetry which is to be found in the heart of every girl, "in truth, I have often regretted that I could not read; but never so much, or in the same way, as when your nurse brought me your letter. I held in my hand a letter which spoke to others, but conveyed nothing to me, poor ignorant creature that I am."

"You have often regretted that you could not read?" said Cornelius, "and why did you want to read at those times?"

"Why," said the young woman laughing, "so as to understand all the letters that were written to me."

The Wicket in the Cell Door

" Did you receive letters, then, Rosa? "

" Hundreds."

" But who wrote to you? "

" Who wrote to me? Why, first of all, all the students who passed the Buitenhof, all the officers who went to the parade ground, all the clerks, and even the merchants who saw me at my little window."

" And all those notes, my dear Rosa, what did you do with them? "

" Formerly," said Rosa, " I got some friend to read them to me, and that used to amuse me extremely, but since a certain date, what was the use of wasting one's time in listening to all that rubbish? since a certain date I have burnt them all."

" Since a certain date! " cried Cornelius, with a look in which love and joy showed themselves together.

Rosa blushed, and lowered her eyes.

Thus she did not notice the near approach of Cornelius's lips, which unfortunately encountered nothing but the grating, though they were able to communicate through it to Rosa the breath of a tender kiss.

At this Rosa became as pale as she had been at the Buitenhof on the day of the execution, or perhaps even paler. She uttered a plaintive sigh, shut her eyes and fled, striving in vain to repress with her hand the violent beating of her heart. Rosa fled so precipitately that she forgot to return to Cornelius the three bulbs of the black tulip.

XVI

MASTER AND SCHOLAR

THE excellent Gryphus, as will have been noticed, was far from sharing the goodwill felt by his daughter towards the godson of Cornelius de Witt.

There were only five prisoners at Loevestein; the task of looking after them was, therefore, not a heavy one, and the post had been given to Gryphus as a sort of sinecure in his old age.

But in his zeal the worthy jailer had exaggerated with all the powers of his imagination the task imposed on him. In his eyes Cornelius had assumed gigantic proportions, and was a criminal of the first class. Consequently he had become the most dangerous of all the prisoners. The jailer watched every step he took, and never spoke to him without scowling, in order to punish him for what he called his frightful rebellion against the merciful Stadtholder.

Three times every day he entered Van Baerle's cell, thinking to surprise him in some offence; but Cornelius had given up letter-writing now that he had his correspondent at hand.

It was even probable that had Cornelius obtained

full liberty, and permission to retire to any place he chose, he would have preferred to stay in prison with Rosa and his bulbs, rather than to live anywhere else without his bulbs and without Rosa.

Rosa had promised to come every evening at nine o'clock and talk to the prisoner, and from the first evening, Rosa, as we have seen, kept her word.

The next day she came up as she had done the day before, with the same secrecy and the same precautions. Only, she had promised herself that she would not put her face too near the grating. Moreover, in order to begin at once a conversation which would arouse Van Baerle's serious attention, she began by handing to him through the grating the three bulbs, still wrapped in the same paper.

But, to her great surprise, Van Baerle pushed back her white hand with the tips of his fingers.

The young man had been reflecting.

" Listen to me," he said; " we risk too much, I think, in placing all our eggs in the same basket. Remember, my dear Rosa, that what we have to accomplish is something which up till now has been regarded as impossible. The one thing is to make the black tulip flower. Let us take every precaution, so that if we fail we may have nothing to reproach ourselves with. Now, this is how I think we shall be able to succeed in our efforts."

Rosa gave her whole attention to what the prisoner was going to say, rather because of the importance which the unfortunate tulip-fancier attached to it, than because of the importance which she attached to it herself.

"This," continued Cornelius, "is how I have arranged our co-operation in this important affair."

"I am listening," said Rosa.

"You must have in this fortress a little garden; or, in default of a garden, a court-yard; or, in default of a court-yard, a terrace."

"We have a very good garden," said Rosa; "it lies by the side of the Waal, and is full of fine old trees."

"Could you, dear Rosa, bring me a little of the mould from this garden, that I may see what it is like?"

"Yes, to-morrow."

"You must take some in the shade and some in the sun, so that I may judge of its qualities, under varying conditions of dryness and dampness."

"Yes, you may rely upon me for that."

"When I have chosen the mould, and modified it as may be necessary, we will divide our bulbs into three lots: you will take one bulb, and on a day which I will fix you must plant it in the soil which I shall then have decided upon; it will certainly flower, if you take care of it according to my directions."

"I will devote every moment of my time to it."

"The second bulb you will give to me and I will try to raise it here in my cell. This will help me to pass the long days during which I do not see you. I have very little hope, I confess, for this second bulb, and I regard it as already sacrificed to my egotism. Still, the sun does sometimes visit me. I will turn everything to account, even the heat and the ashes from my pipe. Finally, we will keep, or rather you will keep, in reserve, the third bulb, our last resource in case the first two experiments fail. In this way, my dear Rosa, we shall be sure to obtain the hundred thousand florins for our dowry, and to have besides the supreme happiness of seeing our labours crowned with success."

"I quite understand," said Rosa. "I will bring you some mould to-morrow; you will choose yours and mine; as to yours, it will require several journeys, for I can only bring you a little at a time."

"Oh, we are not pressed for time, dear Rosa; our tulips ought not to be put in the ground for a month at least. So you see, we have all that time before us. Only, in planting your bulb you will follow all my directions, will you not?"

"I promise you I will."

"And once planted, you will tell me everything that can affect our treasure, such as changes in the weather, marks on the walks, and marks on the flower-beds. You must listen at night and find out whether your garden is frequented by cats. Two of those wretched animals once nearly ruined two of my flower-beds at Dort."

"I will listen."

"On nights when the moon is up—can you see into your garden at night, my dear child?"

The Black Tulip

" The window of my bed-room looks on to it."

" Good! On nights when the moon is up, you must notice whether rats do not come out of the holes in the walls. Rats are given to gnawing, and are very much to be feared. I have heard unfortunate tulip-growers complain bitterly of Noah for having put a pair of rats into the ark."

" I will look out, and if there are cats or rats . . ."

" Well, it will be necessary to decide what is to be done in that case. Then," continued Van Baerle, who had become suspicious since he had been arrested, " then, there is an animal much more to be feared than the cat or the rat."

" And what animal is it? "

" Man. You know, my dear Rosa, that persons will steal a florin, and risk the galleys for a wretched thing like that. Much more would they steal a bulb worth a hundred thousand florins."

" No one but myself shall enter the garden."

" You promise that? "

" I swear it."

" That is well, Rosa. Thank you, dear Rosa. All the joy in my life is to come to me through you."

And as the lips of Van Baerle approached the grating with the same eagerness as on the evening before, and as, moreover, the hour for retiring had arrived, Rosa drew back her head, and put out her hand.

In this pretty hand, of which the coquettish young woman took particular care, was the bulb. Cornelius tenderly kissed the tips of the fingers of this hand. Was it because the hand held one of the bulbs of the famous black tulip? Or was it because the hand was Rosa's? Others, cleverer than we are, must decide.

Rosa retired, holding the other two bulbs close to her heart. Did she hold them close to her heart because they were the bulbs of the black tulip, or because they had been given to her by Cornelius?

This point will, we think, be more easily decided than the other.

However that may be, from this moment life became once more sweet and full of hope to the prisoner.

Rosa, as we have seen, had given him one of the bulbs.

Every evening she brought him, handful by handful, mould from that portion of the garden which he had fixed upon as the best, and which was, in fact, excellent.

A large pitcher, which Cornelius had cleverly contrived to break, served as a very good substitute for a flower-pot. Cornelius half filled it with the mould which Rosa brought, and added to the latter a little dried river mud, which made an excellent compost.

Then, towards the beginning of April, he planted the first bulb.

To describe the care, the skill, the artifices, which Cornelius used in concealing from the watchful Gryphus the labours which afforded him so much pleasure, is quite beyond us. For a prisoner who is also a philosopher, half an hour is long enough for the thoughts and sensations of a hundred years.

No day passed without Rosa coming to talk to Cornelius.

The tulips—a subject on which Rosa had a full course of instruction—furnished the basis of their conversation, but interesting as the topic was, they did not always talk of tulips.

They sometimes spoke of other things, and then the tulip-fancier discovered, to his astonishment, how greatly the range of conversation can be extended.

But Rosa had adopted a new rule for these occasions: she invariably kept her face six inches from the grating, for she doubtless felt mistrustful of herself, when she remembered what had occurred on a previous occasion.

At this time there was one thing which troubled Cornelius very much, almost as much indeed as his tulips did: this was the thought, which continually recurred to his mind, that Rosa was entirely dependent on her father.

The life of Van Baerle, the learned doctor, the skilful artist, the remarkable man, of Van Baerle who was in all probability the first discoverer of that masterpiece of the creation, which was to be called, as had already been arranged, the *Rosa Baerlensis*, the life, and still more the happiness, of this man depended on the mere caprice of another man, a man of inferior type and of the lowest cast, a jailer, something less intelligent than the locks and bolts which he fastened. There was in the relations between the two something that reminded one of Caliban in *The Tempest.*

The happiness of Van Baerle depended on this man; some fine day the jailer might grow weary of Loevestein, might find that the air there was bad or that the gin was not good, and might leave the fortress, taking his daughter with him—and once more Cornelius and Rosa would be separated. God might not reunite them a second time.

"And what good would carrier-pigeons be then?" said Cornelius to the young girl, "for you, my dear Rosa, could neither read what I wrote to you, nor write to me any of your own thoughts."

"Well," replied Rosa, who in her heart feared the separation as much as Cornelius did, "we have an hour every evening, let us make a good use of it."

"But it seems to me," replied Cornelius, "that we do not make a bad use of it, as it is."

"Let us employ it still better," said Rosa smiling. "Show me how to read and write. I shall make the most of your lessons, believe me, and in this way we shall be secure against ever being separated again except by our own will."

"Oh! then," cried Cornelius, "we have eternity before us."

Rosa smiled and shrugged her shoulders slightly.

"Will you always remain in prison?" replied

she. "After having given you your life, will not his Highness give you your liberty? Will you not then have your property again? Will you not be rich? Once free and rich, will you condescend to look, as you pass in your carriage or on horseback, at little Rosa, the daughter of a jailer, of an executioner almost?"

Cornelius was about to protest, and certainly he would have done it with all his heart and with the simplicity and directness of an ardent lover, but the young girl interrupted him.

"How is your tulip going on?" she asked smiling.

To speak to Cornelius about his tulip was a method Rosa had of making Cornelius forget everything else, even Rosa herself.

"Oh! very well," he answered; "the outer skin is growing darker, the work of fermentation has begun, the veins of the bulbs are becoming heated and swelling out; in eight days from now, perhaps sooner, we shall be able to distinguish the first signs of the coming stem. And yours, Rosa?"

"Oh! I have done things in fine style, and exactly according to your directions."

"Tell me, then, Rosa, what you have done," said Cornelius, his eyes almost as eager and his breath coming almost as quickly as on the evening when he had so startled Rosa once before.

"I have," said the young girl, smiling—for she could not help studying this double love of the prisoner for herself and for the black tulip—" I have done things in fine style. In a vacant space in the garden, far from the trees and the walls, in mould slightly sandy and rather damp than dry, without a pebble or a single particle of stone, I have prepared a bed such as you described."

" Excellent, Rosa, excellent! "

" The site so prepared now only awaits a word from you. On the first fine day you will tell me to plant my bulb, and I shall plant it; you know, I ought to begin later than you do, since I have all the advantages afforded by good air, sunlight, and an abundant supply of earth."

" That is true, that is true," cried Cornelius, clapping his hands with joy; " you are a capital pupil, Rosa, and will certainly gain your hundred thousand florins."

" Do not forget," said Rosa, " that your pupil, as you call me, has yet another thing to learn besides the cultivation of tulips."

" Yes, yes, I am as much interested as yourself, my dear Rosa, in your learning to read."

" When shall we begin? "

" At once."

" No, to-morrow."

" Why to-morrow? "

" Because our time for to-day is over, and I must leave you."

" What! already? But stay, what book shall we read in? "

The Black Tulip

"Oh!" said Rosa, "I have a book—one which I hope will bring us good fortune."

"To-morrow, then?"

"To-morrow."

The next day Rosa returned, bringing with her the Bible that had belonged to Cornelius de Witt.

XVII

THE FIRST BULB

THE next day, as we said, Rosa returned, bringing the Bible of Cornelius de Witt.

Then began between master and pupil one of those charming scenes which are the delight of the novelist when he is fortunate enough to have to describe them.

For persons who had hitherto been content to read in each other's faces all that they had wished to read, the grating, the only opening through which the lovers could communicate, was now much too high. It was impossible to read with comfort the book which Rosa had brought.

Consequently the young girl had to lean against the grating, with her head turned to one side, holding up the book at the height of the lamp which she carried in her right hand; to rest her a little Cornelius thought of fastening the lamp with a handkerchief to the iron bars. Rosa could then follow with her finger the letters and syllables which Cornelius made her spell out. Cornelius himself, with a piece of straw passed through an aperture in the grating, indicated the letters to his attentive pupil.

The Black Tulip

The light of the lamp lit up Rosa's beautiful face, her dark blue eyes, and her fair hair, which was confined by the cap of dark cloth of gold, which, as we have said, was used as a head-dress by Frisian maidens. From her raised fingers the blood receded, leaving them of a pale rosy colour, which shone in the light of the lamp, and showed the circulation of the mysterious life-giving fluid beneath the flesh.

Rosa's intelligence developed rapidly under the vivifying contact of Cornelius's mind; and when the difficulties appeared too hard, their eyes which sought each other, their eye-lashes which almost touched, and their hair which intermingled, generated, as it were, electric sparks capable of lighting up the darkness of idiocy itself.

And Rosa, alone in her room again, went over once more in her mind the lessons in reading, and at the same time in her heart the unavowed lessons of love.

One evening she arrived half an hour later than usual. Half an hour's delay was so serious a matter to Cornelius that before doing anything else he inquired what was the cause of it.

" Oh! do not scold me," said the young girl, " it is not my fault. My father has renewed his acquaintance at Loevestein with a worthy man who often came to him at The Hague to ask if he might see the prison. He was a jovial soul, who loved his glass and told amusing stories; he was, besides, a good payer, who did not shrink from meeting his share of the reckoning."

"You did not know him except in this way?" asked Cornelius surprised.

"No," replied Rosa. "It is about a fortnight since my father began to be taken up with this new-comer, who is so assiduous in visiting him."

"Oh!" said Cornelius, shaking his head uneasily, for this new event presaged some calamity, "probably some spy such as they send into prisons to keep an eye on both prisoners and jailers."

"I think," said Rosa laughing, "that if this good man spies on any one, it is not on my father."

"Who is it, then?"

"Why, me!"

"You?"

"Why not?" said Rosa laughing.

"Ah, it is true," said Cornelius with a sigh; "you will not always have suitors in vain, Rosa; this man may become your husband."

"I do not say he may not."

"And on what do you base this hope?"

"Say this fear, M. Cornelius."

"Thank you, Rosa; you are right: this fear, then?"

"I base it on this . . ."

"Yes, I am listening; tell me."

"This man has already been to the Buitenhof, and to The Hague, on several occasions, just at the very times, too, when you were at those places.

The Black Tulip

When I left, he left; when I came here, he came. At The Hague he used to pretend that he wanted to see you."

" To see me? "

" Oh! it was evidently only a pretence, for now when he could give the same reason for coming, since you have again become one of my father's prisoners, or rather since my father has again become your jailer, he no longer takes any interest in you. Quite the contrary, in fact, for I heard him say yesterday to my father that he did not know you."

" Go on, Rosa, I pray, so that I may try to guess who this man is, and what he wants."

" You are sure, M. Cornelius, that none of your friends could be interesting themselves on your behalf? "

" I have no friends, Rosa. I had only my nurse, whom you know and who knows you. Alas! poor Zug, she would come herself and would make use of no trickery; she would begin to cry, and would say to you or your father, ' Sir, or miss, my child is here: you see how wretched I am: let me see him for an hour only, and I will pray for you all the rest of my life.' Oh, no," continued Cornelius, " except my good Zug, I have no friends."

" I come back, then, to what I thought at first, and the more so because yesterday at sunset, as I was arranging the flower-bed in which I am to plant your bulb, I saw a shadow which slipped through the door by which I had entered, and glided behind the elders and the aspen-trees. I pretended not to see it, but it was our friend. He hid himself and watched me raking the mould. I am certain it was I whom he had followed, and whom he was spying upon. I did not give a stroke with the rake, I did not touch an atom of soil, of which he did not take account."

"Yes, yes, he is a lover," said Cornelius. "Is he young? is he handsome?"

And he looked anxiously at Rosa, impatiently awaiting her answer.

"Young! handsome!" cried Rosa, with a burst of laughter. "He is a perfect fright. His body is bent over, he is nearly fifty years old, and he does not dare to look me in the face, or to speak out loud."

"And he is called?"

"Jacob Gisels."

"I do not know him."

"You see, then, that it is not on your account that he comes."

"In any case, Rosa, if he loves you—which is very likely, for to see you is to love you—you do not love him?"

"Oh! certainly not."

"You wish me to be quite easy on that point?"

"I implore you to be so."

"Well, now that you begin to know how to read, Rosa, you will read all that I write to you, will you not, about the torments of jealousy and of absence?"

"I will, if you write very large."

The Black Tulip

Then, as the turn of the conversation began to disquiet Rosa, she said:

"By the way, how is your tulip?"

"Rosa, imagine my joy: this morning I was looking at it in the sunlight, after having carefully lifted the layer of earth which covers the bulb, and I saw the point of a shoot beginning to appear. Ah! Rosa, my heart was filled with joy; this pale, almost imperceptible bud, which a fly's wing would injure if it brushed against it, this first faint sign of what was coming, moved me more than the reading of that order of his Highness which arrested the sword of the executioner and gave me my life again, on the scaffold of the Buitenhof."

"You hope, then," said Rosa smiling.

"Yes, yes, I hope."

"And I, when shall I plant my bulb?"

"On the first favourable day I will give the word; but remember, above all, not to let any one help you in the work; do not confide your secret to a single soul; a connoisseur, you know, would be able at the first glance to recognise its value; above all, my dearest Rosa, put carefully away the third bulb which is left."

"It is still in the same paper in which you wrapped it, and is just as it was when you gave it to me, M. Cornelius; it is hidden away quite at the bottom of my clothes-press, under some lace, which keeps it dry without weighing upon it. But, good-bye, poor prisoner."

The First Bulb

" Already! "

" It is absolutely necessary."

" To come so late and go away so early? "

" My father might be impatient at not seeing me come back; the lover, too, might suspect that he had a rival."

And she listened uneasily.

" What is the matter? " asked Van Baerle.

" I thought I heard something."

" What was it? "

" Something like the sound of a foot on the stairs."

" That could not be Gryphus, certainly; one can hear him a long way off."

" No, it is not my father, I am sure, but . . ."

" But what? "

" But it might be M. Jacob."

Rosa flew towards the staircase, and a door was heard to shut quickly before the young girl had descended the first ten steps. Cornelius remained very uneasy, but this was only a prelude to what was still to happen to him.

Fate, on beginning some evil work, is usually charitable enough to forewarn the victim, as a hired bravo does his adversary, to give him time to place himself on guard.

Nearly always these warnings come from a man's own instincts, or from inanimate objects, which are often less inanimate than they are commonly supposed to be; nearly always, too, these warnings are neglected. The blow whistles through the air, and falls on the head which ought to have taken warning from the sound and protected itself.

The next day passed without anything remarkable occurring. Gryphus made his three visits. He discovered nothing. When he heard the jailer coming —and, in the hope of surprising the secrets of his prisoner, Gryphus never came at the same hours— when he heard the jailer coming, Van Baerle, by the aid of a mechanical contrivance which he had invented and which was like that by which corn is raised and lowered in farm-yards, managed to let down his pitcher below the entablature, first of the tiles, and then of the stones, which ran below his window. As for the strings by means of which this operation was carried out, our mechanician had discovered a way of hiding them with the moss which grew on the tiles and in the crevices of the stones.

Gryphus suspected nothing.

During eight days this arrangement was successful. But one morning, when it was very windy and everything in the tower was creaking, Cornelius, absorbed in the contemplation of his bulb, from which a sprout was beginning to emerge, did not hear old Gryphus coming up. Suddenly the door opened, and Cornelius was surprised with his pitcher in his hands.

Gryphus, seeing an unknown, and consequently a forbidden, object in the prisoner's hand, darted upon it more rapidly than a falcon darts on its prey.

Chance, or that fatal skill which the evil spirit sometimes accords to evildoers, directed his coarse

The First Bulb

and heavy hand—for the power of using which he was indebted to Cornelius—right into the middle of the pitcher, on that part of the mould which covered the precious bulb.

"What have you got there?" he cried. "Ah! I have caught you at it!" and he thrust his hand into the mould.

"I? Nothing, nothing!" cried Cornelius, greatly agitated.

"Ah! I have caught you. A pitcher? Earth? There is some guilty secret in this."

"My dear M. Gryphus," begged Van Baerle, as disturbed as a partridge from whom the reaper has just taken her brood.

Gryphus began to dig into the mould with his crooked fingers.

"Sir, sir, take care!" cried Cornelius, growing pale.

"What of? What of?" shouted the jailer.

"Take care, I tell you! you will kill it."

And with a rapid and almost desperate movement he snatched the pitcher from the jailer's hands, and hid it like a treasure beneath his two arms.

But Gryphus, with all the obstinacy of an old man, and more and more convinced that he was on the point of discovering some conspiracy against the Prince of Orange, Gryphus rushed upon the prisoner with his stick raised in the air; but seeing the resolute determination of the captive to protect his flower, he felt that Cornelius trembled much less on account of his head than on account of his pitcher.

He tried, therefore, to take the pitcher from him by brute force.

"Ah!" said the jailer furiously, "you know well that this is mutiny."

"Leave me my tulip," cried Van Baerle.

"Oh, yes! your tulip," replied the old man. "I know the tricks of prisoners."

"But I swear to you . . ."

"Let go!" repeated Gryphus, stamping his foot. "Let go, or I will call the guard."

"Call any one you like, but you shall not have this poor flower except with my life."

The exasperated Gryphus drove his fingers again into the mould, and this time he drew out the bulb, which was quite black; and while Van Baerle, delighted at having saved the receptacle, was quite unaware that his adversary had obtained possession of what had been in it, Gryphus flung down the softened bulb on the ground, where it was broken to pieces on the flag-stones, and almost immediately disappeared, crushed to a pulp beneath the heavy boot of the jailer.

Van Baerle saw the murder, caught sight of the crushed fragments on the floor, understood Gryphus's ferocious joy, and uttered a cry of despair which would have softened the heart even of that jailer-assassin who some years earlier had killed the spider of Pelisson.

The idea of killing this wicked man passed like a flash through the tulip-fancier's brain. Fire and blood mounted together to his brain and blinded him. He

The First Bulb

raised in his two hands the pitcher weighted with all the useless mould that remained in it. A moment more and he would have let it fall on the bald head of old Gryphus. A cry stopped him, a cry full of tears and anguish, uttered behind the grating in the door by poor Rosa, who, pale, trembling, and with her arms raised to heaven, had thus intervened between her father and her friend.

Cornelius dropped the pitcher, and it broke, with a frightful crash, into a thousand pieces.

Then Gryphus understood the dangerous position which he had been in, and broke out into terrible threats.

"Oh!" said Cornelius to him, "what a coward, what a low blackguard you must be, to take from a poor prisoner his only consolation, the bulb of a tulip!"

"For shame, father," added Rosa; "you have committed a crime."

"Ah! it is you, you minx," cried he, turning towards his daughter in a furious rage. "Mind your own business, and go downstairs at once."

"Unfortunate man that I am!" continued the despairing Cornelius.

"After all, it is only a tulip," added Gryphus, a little ashamed of himself. "You can have as many tulips as you like. I have three hundred of them in the loft."

"To the devil with your tulips!" cried Cornelius. "They are worthy of you, and you of them. Oh! a hundred thousand millions of millions, if I had them,

The Black Tulip

I would give them all for the one you have crushed there!"

"Ha! ha!" said Gryphus triumphantly. "It is not the tulip you are concerned about, that's clear. Evidently there was some sorcery about this sham tulip, perhaps some means of correspondence with the enemies of his Highness, who pardoned you. I say again they made a great mistake in not cutting your throat."

"Father! Father!" cried Rosa.

"Well, all the better! all the better!" repeated Gryphus, becoming excited again. "I have destroyed it; I have destroyed it. It will be the same as often as you begin again. Ah! I warned you, my fine fellow, that I would give you a bad time of it."

"Accursed wretch!" shouted Cornelius, in despair, turning over with trembling fingers the last vestiges of the bulb, the dead body of so many joys and hopes.

"We will plant the other to-morrow, dear M. Cornelius," said Rosa, in a low voice. She understood the intense sorrow of the tulip-fancier, and in this way she tried, sweet soul that she was, to assuage the pain of the wound that had been inflicted on Cornelius's heart.

XVIII

ROSA'S LOVER

ROSA had scarcely said these consoling words to Cornelius, when a voice was heard on the stairs asking Gryphus what had happened.

"Father," said Rosa, "do you hear?"

"What?"

"M. Jacob is calling you. He is alarmed."

"There has been such a disturbance," said Gryphus. "One would have thought that this learned man was murdering me. What trouble one always has with these learned men!"

And pointing with his finger to the staircase, he said to Rosa, "Go in front, miss."

Then shutting the door, he added:

"I am coming down to you, friend Jacob."

And Gryphus went away again, taking Rosa with him, and leaving to his solitude and bitter grief the poor tulip-fancier, who murmured:

"Oh! it is you who have murdered me, old hangman. I shall never survive it."

And indeed the poor prisoner would have fallen ill, had it not been for the counteracting effect which Providence had supplied in the person of Rosa.

The Black Tulip

In the evening the young girl returned.

Her first words announced to Cornelius that for the future her father would not any longer prevent his cultivating flowers.

" And how do you know that? " said the prisoner sadly to the girl.

" I know it because he has said so."

" Only to deceive me, perhaps."

" No, he has repented."

" Yes, but it is too late."

" This repentance was not his own idea."

" Where did he get the idea, then? "

" If you only knew how his friend abuses him."

" Ah! M. Jacob; he has not left you, then—M. Jacob? "

" He never does, except when he is obliged."

And she smiled in such a way that the little cloud of jealousy which had darkened the brow of Cornelius was dispersed.

" How did this come about? " asked the prisoner.

" Well, at supper, in answer to his friend's questions, my father related the history of the tulip, or I should say of the bulb, and his fine exploit in crushing it."

Cornelius gave a sigh which was almost a groan.

" If you had seen M. Jacob at that moment! " continued Rosa. " Really, I thought he was about to burn down the fortress; his eyes were blazing torches, his hair stood on end, he clenched his fists; for a moment I thought he was going to strangle my father. 'You did that?' he cried; 'you crushed the bulb?' 'Certainly,' said my father. 'Infamous! odious!' he continued; 'you have committed a crime!' My father was dumb with astonishment. 'Have you gone mad, too?' he asked his friend."

"Oh, what a worthy man is this M. Jacob!" murmured Cornelius; "he is an honest soul, a choice spirit."

"The fact is, no one could be more harshly treated than my father was by him," added Rosa; "he was really in despair; he repeated incessantly, 'Crushed, the bulb crushed! My God, crushed!' Then turning to me, he asked: 'But it was not the only one, was it?'"

"He asked that?" said Cornelius, looking up in surprise.

"'You think it was not the only one?' asked my father. 'Good; I will look for the others.' 'You will look for the others!' cried M. Jacob, taking my father by the collar; but immediately he let go and turned to me, asking, 'And what did the poor young man say?'

"I did not know what to answer, as you had warned me never to let slip any sign of the interest which you took in the bulb. Happily, my father saved me from further embarrassment:

"'What did he say?—he raved.'

"I interrupted him. 'How could he be anything but furious?' I said to him. 'You were so unjust

The Black Tulip

and brutal.' 'Ah! you must be mad,' cried my father; 'a dreadful misfortune, truly, to crush a tulip-bulb; one can get them by hundreds for a florin in Gorcum market.' 'But perhaps not such precious ones as this,' I unluckily answered."

"And what did Jacob do, when you said that?" asked Cornelius.

"At the words, I must say, it seemed to me that his eyes flashed."

"Yes, but that was not all," said Cornelius; "he said something, did he not?"

"'So, fair Rosa,' he said in a honeyed tone, 'you think this bulb was very valuable?' I saw that I had made a mistake. 'How do I know?' I replied carelessly: 'do I understand tulips? Unfortunately, however, I do know, since we are condemned to live with the prisoners, that for a prisoner every pastime is valuable. This poor M. van Baerle amused himself with that bulb. Well, I say it was cruel to deprive him of the amusement.'

"'But first of all,' said my father, 'how did he get this bulb? It would be a good thing to find that out, I think.'

"I turned my head away, to avoid my father's eye, but I met the eye of M. Jacob. He looked as if he wished to follow my thoughts down to the bottom of my heart. A pretence of ill-humour often does for an answer. I shrugged my shoulders, turned my back, and went towards the door. But I was stopped by a word which I caught, though it was uttered in a very

low voice. Jacob said to my father: ' It is easy to settle that point.'

" ' We could search him, and if he has other bulbs
we should find them.'

" ' Yes, generally there are three.' "

" There are three!" cried Cornelius; " he said I
had three bulbs!"

" You will understand that the word struck me as
it has struck you. I turned round again. They
were both so occupied that they did not notice my
movement. ' But,' said my father, ' perhaps he has
not his bulbs on him.' ' Then get him down here on
some pretext or other, and during the time I will
search his cell.' "

" Ho, ho!" said Cornelius, " he is a scoundrel, this
M. Jacob."

" I am afraid so."

" Tell me, Rosa . . ." said Cornelius, thought-
fully.

" What?"

" Did you not say that on the day on which you
prepared your flower-bed this man followed you?"

" Yes."

" And that he glided like a shadow behind the
elders?"

" Certainly."

" And that he did not lose a single stroke of your
rake?"

" Not one!"

" Rosa . . ." said Cornelius, turning pale.

" Well? "

" It was not you that he followed."

" What was he following, then? "

" It was not you that he was in love with."

" Who was it, then? "

" It was my bulb he was following; it was my tulip that he was in love with."

" Yes, certainly that might be so," cried Rosa.

" Will you make sure of it? "

" How? "

" Oh, that is very easy."

" Tell me how."

" Go to-morrow to the garden; manage to let Jacob know, as he did before, that you are going there; let him follow you, as he did the first time; pretend to plant the bulb, and then go out of the garden, but look through the gate and you will see what he will do."

" Very well; but after that? "

" After that we will act according to what he does."

" Ah! " said Rosa, sighing, " you are very fond of your bulbs, M. Cornelius."

" The fact is," said the prisoner, with a sigh, " that since your father crushed the unfortunate bulb, part of my life seems to have gone out from me."

" Come," said Rosa, " will you try something else? "

" What? "

" Will you accept my father's proposal? "

Rosa's Lover

" What proposal? "

" He has offered you bulbs by the hundred."

" That is so."

" Accept two or three, and among them you will be able to raise the third bulb."

" Yes, that would do very well," said Cornelius, frowning, " if your father were alone; but this other man, this Jacob, who spies on us . . ."

" Ah! that's true; but still, just think! You are depriving yourself of a great amusement, I can see."

And she pronounced these words with a smile which was not altogether free from irony.

Cornelius did indeed think for a moment; it was easy to see that he was struggling against a very strong desire.

" Well, no! " he cried, with a stoicism worthy of the ancients; " no, it would be weak, it would be foolish, it would be cowardly. I should only be exposing to all the dangers arising from malice and envy the last resource left to us; it would be unpardonable to do so. No, Rosa, no; to-morrow we will make up our minds with regard to your tulip; you will grow it according to my instructions; as for the third bulb "—Cornelius sighed heavily—" keep it in your drawer, watch over it as a miser does over his first, or his last, piece of gold, as the mother watches over her child, as the wounded man watches over the least drop of blood in his veins; watch over it, Rosa! Something tells me that it will prove our salvation and the source of our riches— watch over it! And if fire falls from heaven upon

199

The Black Tulip

Loevestein, swear to me, Rosa, that, instead of your rings, instead of your jewels, instead of your beautiful golden cap, which frames your face so well, you will carry off in safety the last bulb, which holds within itself my black tulip."

"Do not be uneasy, M. Cornelius," said Rosa, sadly and solemnly; "do not be uneasy; to me your wishes are commands."

"And even," continued the young man, becoming more and more excited, "if you perceive that you are followed, that your actions are spied upon, that your conversation arouses the suspicions of your father or of this abominable Jacob, whom I hate—well, Rosa, sacrifice me at once, though I live only through you and have no one but you in the world, sacrifice me, too; do not come to see me any more."

Rosa felt her heart shrink within her; tears sprang to her eyes.

"Alas!" said she.

"What?" asked Cornelius.

"I see one thing."

"What do you see?"

"I see," said the young girl, bursting into sobs, "I see that you love your tulips so much that there is no place in your heart for any other love."

And she fled.

After Rosa's departure Cornelius passed one of the worst nights he had ever passed in his life.

Rosa was angry with him, and she had good reason to be so. Very likely she would not come to see him any more, and he would have no more news either of Rosa or of his tulips.

How are we to explain this strange character to the enthusiastic tulip-fanciers who still exist in the world?

We confess, to the shame of our hero and of florists in general, that of his two loves, Cornelius felt more inclined to regret Rosa; and when, towards three o'clock in the morning, he fell asleep, worn out with fatigue, harassed with fears, and overcome with remorse, he dreamt, not of the great black tulip, but of the sweet blue eyes of the fair Frisian maid.

XIX

A WOMAN AND A FLOWER

But poor Rosa, shut up in her room, had no means of knowing whom or what Cornelius was dreaming of.

And so, after what he had said to her, she was much more inclined to believe that he was dreaming of his tulip than that he was dreaming of her; and yet Rosa was mistaken.

But as there was no one there to tell her that she was mistaken, and as the imprudent words of Cornelius had sunk into her heart like drops of poison, Rosa did not dream; she wept.

Thanks to her elevation of mind and her strong and keen common sense, Rosa quite understood her position, not in respect of moral or physical qualities, but in respect of social rank.

Cornelius was learned, Cornelius was rich, or at least had been so before the confiscation of his property. He belonged to that commercial middle class which was prouder of its emblazoned shop-signs than the nobility of birth had ever been of its armorial bearings. Cornelius might, indeed, amuse himself for

A Woman and a Flower

a time with Rosa, but certainly when it became a question of giving his heart away, it would be rather to a tulip, that is, to the noblest and proudest of flowers, that he would give it, than to Rosa, the lowly daughter of a jailer.

Rosa thus understood the preference of Cornelius for the tulip, and was all the more wretched because she understood it.

And in consequence, during the terrible sleepless night which she passed, she took a resolution.

This resolution was that she would go back no more to the grated window.

But as she knew how anxious Cornelius was to receive news of his tulip; as she desired not to expose herself to the danger of again seeing a man for whom she felt her pity growing to such an extent that it was rapidly on the way to becoming love; and as she did not wish to drive this man to despair, she resolved to continue alone those lessons in reading and writing which she had begun. Luckily, she had arrived at a point in her studies at which a master would no longer have been necessary had he not been named Cornelius.

Rosa therefore set to work with great ardour to read the Bible of poor Cornelius de Witt, on the second leaf of which—the first, really, since the other had been torn out—on the second leaf of which was written the will of Cornelius van Baerle.

" Ah! " she murmured, as she read the will, a thing she never did without letting one tear, a pearl of love, fall from her bright eyes on to her pale cheek—" ah!

at that time I really believed for a moment that he loved me."

Poor Rosa! she was mistaken. The love of the prisoner had never been real until the moment at which we have arrived, when, as we have already said with embarrassment, in the struggle between the great black tulip and Rosa, the great black tulip finally succumbed. But Rosa, we repeat, was quite unaware of the defeat of the great black tulip.

Accordingly, having finished her reading, in which she had made great progress, Rosa took up her pen, and set herself with equally laudable determination to the work of writing, which she found much more difficult.

But as she could already write almost legibly on the day on which Cornelius had so imprudently allowed his heart to speak, Rosa did not despair of making such progress as to be able, in eight days at the latest, to give the prisoner some news of his tulip.

She had not forgotten one word of the directions which Cornelius had given her. Indeed, Rosa did not forget any word of Cornelius's, even when what he said did not take the form of directions.

Cornelius himself awoke more in love than ever. The tulip was still vividly present to his mind, but now he regarded it no longer as a treasure to which he ought to sacrifice everything, even Rosa, but as a precious flower, a marvelous combination of nature and art, which Providence had given him as an ornament for the bosom of his queen.

A Woman and a Flower

During the whole of the day a vague uneasiness troubled him. He was like one of those men who have the strength of mind to forget for a time that a great danger threatens to overtake them during the next night or on the following morning. Having once conquered the thought, they live their life as usual. Only, from time to time the forgotten danger suddenly gnaws at their hearts with its sharp tooth. They shudder, and ask themselves why they have shuddered; then, recollecting what they had banished from their minds, they say with a sigh, " Ah! yes, that is it."

In the case of Cornelius this haunting fear was that Rosa could not come in the evening as she had been accustomed to do. And in proportion as night approached, his anxiety became more and more acute, until at last it took entire possession of him and he was conscious of nothing else.

It was with a fast-beating heart, therefore, that he welcomed the darkness; as the darkness increased, the words which he had spoken to Rosa, and which had so pained the poor child, became more and more present to his mind, and he asked himself how he could have told his consoler to sacrifice him to the tulip—that is, to give up seeing him, when, as a matter of fact, the sight of her had become for him a necessary of life.

From Cornelius's cell one could hear the clock of the fortress strike the hours. Seven o'clock struck, then eight, then nine. Never before had the sound of the bell vibrated so strongly in any one's heart as did that which followed the ninth stroke of the hammer at nine o'clock that evening.

Then all was silent once more. Cornelius pressed his hand to his heart to restrain its beating, and listened.

The sound of Rosa's footstep, the rustle of her dress on the stairs, were so familiar to him that from the very first step she mounted he had been accustomed to say, " Ah! here comes Rosa."

That evening no sound disturbed the silence of the corridor. The clock struck a quarter past nine; then, with two different notes, half past nine; then a quarter to ten; then, finally, its deep voice announced not only to those in the fortress, but also to the inhabitants of Loevestein, that it was ten o'clock.

It was the hour at which Rosa used to leave Cornelius. The hour struck, and Rosa had not yet come.

So then, his forebodings had been correct. Rosa was angry, and remained in her room; she had abandoned him.

" Oh! I have richly deserved what has happened to me," said Cornelius. " She will never come again, and she will be right not to come. Certainly, in her case I would do the same."

And yet, in spite of this, Cornelius continued to listen, to wait, and to hope. He listened and waited till midnight; but at midnight he ceased to hope, and threw himself, dressed as he was, upon his bed. The night was long and sad; then day came ; but day brought no hope to the prisoner.

A Woman and a Flower

At eight o'clock his door opened, but Cornelius did not even turn his head; he had heard the heavy step of Gryphus in the corridor; but he knew perfectly well that that step was the only one.

He did not even cast a side glance at the jailer.

And yet he would have liked very much to ask him for some news of Rosa. In fact, he was on the point of asking the question, strange as it would have appeared to the jailer. He hoped, egotist that he was, that Gryphus would say his daughter was ill.

Except under extraordinary circumstances, Rosa never came during the daytime. Cornelius, as long as daylight lasted, did not really expect her. Still, from his sudden starts, his listening near the door, and the quick glances which he frequently directed towards the grating, it was evident that the prisoner had a half-hearted hope that Rosa would break her usual rule.

At the second visit of the jailer, Cornelius, contrary to all precedent, asked Gryphus, in his sweetest voice, how he was. But Gryphus, with Spartan brevity, confined his reply to the words, " I'm all right."

At the third visit Cornelius changed the form of his question.

" No one is ill at Loevestein? " he asked.

" No one," replied Gryphus, still more laconically than before, shutting the door in the prisoner's face.

Gryphus was so little accustomed to such polite speeches on the part of Cornelius that he saw in them the beginnings of an attempt at corruption.

The Black Tulip

Cornelius found himself alone again; it was seven in the evening. Then began once more, in a still greater degree than on the previous evening, the anguish which we have attempted to describe.

But, as before, the hours rolled by without bringing the sweet vision which, through the grating, had formerly lit up the cell of poor Cornelius with a brightness that lingered even after the vision had disappeared.

Van Baerle passed the night in a condition of despair. The next day Gryphus seemed to him more ugly, more brutal, and more irritating, even than usual. It had occurred to his mind, or rather to his heart, that it was Gryphus who prevented Rosa from coming. He was seized with a ferocious desire to strangle the jailer; but he reflected that if Gryphus were to be strangled by Cornelius, every law, human and divine, would forbid Rosa ever to see Cornelius again.

The jailer thus escaped, without knowing it, the greatest danger that had ever threatened him in his life.

The night came, and despair was turned into melancholy, and the melancholy became the deeper because, in spite of his efforts, memories of his poor tulip mingled themselves with Van Baerle's other sorrows. The precise period of the month had arrived which the most experienced gardeners had fixed upon for the planting of tulips. He had said to Rosa, " I will tell you the day on which you ought to put the bulb into the earth!" On the next day he ought to give directions that the bulb should be planted the following evening. The weather was good; the air, though a little damp, began to be tempered by the pale rays of the April sun, which, as they come first, seem so delightful in spite of their paleness. "What if Rosa was going to let the time for planting pass by—if to the sorrow of not seeing the young girl was to be added that of seeing the bulb fail, through having been planted too late, or even through not having been planted at all!"

These two sorrows together were enough to make him lose all desire to eat or drink.

And that, indeed, is what happened on the fourth day.

It was pitiable to see Cornelius, dumb with grief and pale from want of food, leaning out of his barred window, at the risk of being unable to draw his head back from between the bars, trying to see on the left the little garden of which Rosa had spoken, the parapet of which, as she had told him, overlooked the river. He hoped in this way to catch a glimpse of the young girl or of the tulip, his two lost loves.

In the evening, Gryphus took away Cornelius's breakfast and dinner, which had scarcely been tasted.

The next day Cornelius ate nothing at all, and Gryphus took down the food intended for those two meals quite untouched.

That day Cornelius did not even get up.

"Good!" said Gryphus, when he went downstairs

after the last visit. "I think we shall soon be quit of our learned man."

Rosa started.

"Bah!" said Jacob, "how do you make that out?"

"He no longer eats, nor drinks, nor gets up," said Gryphus; "like M. Grotius, he will go out of here in a box, but the box will be a coffin."

Rosa became as pale as death.

"Oh!" she murmured, "I understand. He is worried about his tulip."

And getting up from her chair, she returned to her room, where she took a pen and paper, and spent the whole night in forming letters.

The next day, Cornelius, on rising to drag himself to the window, perceived a paper which had been pushed under his door.

He darted to the paper, opened it, and read, in writing which he scarcely recognised as Rosa's, so much had she improved during her seven days' absence:

"Do not be uneasy, your tulip is going on well."

Although these few words of Rosa's partially relieved the grief of Cornelius, he was not the less sensible of the irony in them.

So, that was it; Rosa was not ill, Rosa was hurt; it was not force that had kept Rosa from coming again; it was by her own will that she remained away from Cornelius. Rosa was free, then, and Rosa had enough strength of will to remain away from him, al-

A Woman and a Flower

though he was dying of mortification at not seeing her.

Cornelius had a pencil and paper, which Rosa had brought him. He understood that the young girl would expect an answer, but that she would not come to get it till the evening. He wrote therefore on a piece of paper like that which he had received:

" It is not uneasiness about my tulip that is making me ill; it is the disappointment I feel at not seeing you."

Then, when Gryphus had gone, and evening was come, he slipped the paper under the door, and listened.

But, though he listened most carefully, he heard neither the step nor the rustle of the dress. He only heard a voice, gentle as a breath of wind and soft as a caress, which whispered, through the grating, the word:

" To-morrow."

To-morrow! it was the eighth day. For eight days Cornelius and Rosa had not seen each other.

XX

WHAT HAD HAPPENED DURING THE EIGHT DAYS

THE next day, at the usual hour, Van Baerle heard a tap on the shutter of the grating such as Rosa had been accustomed to give during the happy days of their friendship.

Cornelius, as will be imagined, was not far from the door, through the grating of which he was at last to see again the charming face which had so long disappeared.

Rosa, who was waiting with her lamp in her hand, could not restrain a start when she saw the prisoner looking so sad and so pale.

" Are you ill, M. Cornelius? " she asked.

" Yes, miss, ill in body and mind," replied Cornelius.

" I saw, sir, that you did not eat; my father told me that you did not get up, so I wrote to ease your mind with regard to the fate of the precious object of all your anxieties."

" And I," said Cornelius, " I answered you. I thought on seeing you here again, dear Rosa, that you had received my letter."

What Had Happened in Eight Days

"Yes, I have received it."

"You will not give as an excuse this time that you cannot read. Not only do you read easily, but you have also made wonderful progress in writing."

"I not only received but also read your note. That is why I have come to see whether there is not some means of restoring your health."

"Restoring my health!" cried Cornelius. "You have, then, some good news to tell me?"

And so saying the young man fixed his eyes hopefully on Rosa.

Whether she did not, or would not, understand the look, the young woman replied gravely:

"I have only to speak to you of your tulip, which is, I know, the greatest anxiety you have."

Rosa pronounced these words in an icy tone which greatly affected Cornelius.

The eager tulip-fancier did not understand all that was concealed under this veil of indifference by the poor girl, who was always on the defensive against her rival, the black tulip.

"Ah! again! Rosa, again! Good heavens! have I not told you that I thought only of you, that it was you alone that I regretted, you alone that I wanted, that it was your absence that was depriving me of air, of sunlight, of warmth, of light and of life?"

Rosa smiled in a melancholy fashion.

"Ah!" said she, "your tulip has been in such danger."

The Black Tulip

In spite of himself Cornelius started, and fell into the trap, if trap it was.

"Such danger?" he cried, trembling. "Good gracious! what was it?"

Rosa looked at him with sweet compassion; she felt that what she wished for was beyond his strength, and that she would have to be content with him as he was, in spite of his little weakness.

"Yes," she said, "you guessed aright: this suitor, this lover, Jacob, did not come on my account."

"And what did he come for, then?" asked Cornelius anxiously.

"He came for the tulip."

"Oh!" said Cornelius, growing paler at this news than he had done when Rosa, a fortnight earlier, had told him, by mistake, that Jacob came to see her.

Rosa perceived his alarm, and Cornelius saw, from the look on her face, that she was thinking just what we have mentioned.

"Oh! forgive me, Rosa," said he; "I know you: I know the goodness and the uprightness of your heart. God has endowed you with thought, judgment, strength, and power of movement, with which to defend yourself, but he has not given my poor threatened tulip any of these things."

Rosa made no reply to this excuse of the prisoner's, but continued:

"From the moment when you became anxious about this man, who had followed me and whom I had recognised as Jacob, I became more anxious still.

What Had Happened in Eight Days

I therefore followed the advice you gave me, and on the day after that on which I last saw you, when you said . . ."

Cornelius interrupted her.

" Once more, forgive me, Rosa," he said. " I was wrong to say to you what I did. I have already asked your forgiveness for those unhappy words. Will it always be in vain? "

" The day after that day," replied Rosa, " remembering what you had said to me about the trick by which I was to make sure whether it was after me, or after the tulip, that this odious man . . ."

" Yes, odious! . . . You hate the man very much, do you not? "

" Yes, I do," said Rosa, " for he has made me suffer very much during the last eight days."

" Ah! you also have suffered, have you? Thank you for those words, Rosa."

" The day after that miserable day," continued Rosa, " I went to the garden and walked towards the flower-bed in which I was to plant my tulip, looking round to see whether I was followed this time, as I had been before."

" Well? " asked Cornelius.

" Well, the same shadow glided between the gate and the wall, and again disappeared behind the elders."

" You pretended not to notice it, did you not? " asked Cornelius, remembering all the details of the advice he had given Rosa.

"Yes, and I bent over the flower-bed and dug a hole in it with a spade, as though I were planting the bulb."

"And he . . . he . . . during this time?"

"I saw his eyes glittering like those of a tiger through the branches of the trees."

"There, you see, you see!" said Cornelius.

"Then, having finished my pretended work, I retired."

"But only behind the door of the garden, was it not? so that through a chink, or through the key-hole of the door, you could see what he did after you had gone."

"He waited for a moment, no doubt to make sure that I was not coming back, then he came out like a wolf from his hiding-place, and approached the flower-bed by a circuitous path; when he arrived opposite the place where the earth had been freshly dug up, he stopped with an air of indifference, looked round on all sides, examined every corner of the garden, and every window of the neighbouring houses, as well as the earth, the air, and the sky; and then, believing that he was quite alone, and isolated, and out of sight of every one, he threw himself upon the flower-bed, thrust his two hands into the soft mould, lifted a portion of it and broke it up gently between his hands to see if the bulb was there. This he did three times over, each time more eagerly than before, until at last, beginning to understand that he had been duped, he repressed the agitation which was devouring him, took up the rake, smoothed over the earth so as to leave it on his departure just as it had been before he dug into it, and quite ashamed, and sheepish, went back along the path to the gate, affecting the innocent air of one who was merely taking a walk."

"Oh! the wretch!" muttered Cornelius, wiping away the moisture which bedewed his forehead. "Oh! the wretch! I guessed it. But the bulb, Rosa, what have you really done with it? Alas! it is already a little late to plant it."

"The bulb has already been six days in the ground."

"Where? how?" cried Cornelius. "Good heavens! what imprudence! Where is it? In what sort of soil is it? Is it well, or ill, exposed? Does it not run the risk of being stolen from us by this abominable Jacob?"

"It is in no danger of being stolen, unless Master Jacob should force the door of my room."

"Ah! it is in your room, then, Rosa?" said Cornelius, slightly relieved. "But in what mould, and in what sort of receptacle? You do not make it grow in water, I hope, like the good wives of Haarlem and Dort, who will persist in believing that water can take the place of earth, as if water, which is composed of thirty-three parts of oxygen and sixty-six parts of hydrogen, could take the place of . . . But what am I saying to you, Rosa?"

"Yes, that is rather too learned for me," replied

the young girl smiling. "I shall content myself, therefore, with telling you, in order to allay your fears, that your bulb is not in water."

"Ah! I breathe again."

"It is in a good stone pot, of the same size as the pitcher in which you placed your bulb. The earth is composed of three parts of ordinary mould and one part of street-dust. Oh! I have so often heard you and the infamous Jacob, as you call him, say in what kind of soil a tulip should be grown, that I know it as well as the best gardener at Haarlem."

"And now there remains the exposure. What exposure has it, Rosa?"

"Now, it has the sun all day, on days when there is any sun. But when it comes out of the ground, and when the sun is hotter, I shall do as you did here, dear M. Cornelius. I shall expose it on the sill of one of my windows to the rising sun from eight o'clock till eleven, and again on the sill of my other window to the declining sun from three o'clock in the afternoon until five."

"Oh, that's it! that's it!" cried Cornelius. "You are a perfect gardener, my dear Rosa. But I think the care of my tulip will take up all your time."

"Yes, that is true," said Rosa. "But what does it matter! It is your tulip: and it is my daughter. I will devote as much time to it as I should to my child, if I were a mother. It is only by becoming its mother that I can cease to be its rival," said Rosa smiling.

"Good and dear Rosa!" murmured Cornelius,

What Had Happened in Eight Days

casting on the young girl a glance in which there was more of the lover than of the gardener, and which therefore consoled Rosa a little.

Then, after a moment's silence, during which Cornelius tried, though in vain, to clasp Rosa's hand through the grating, he said:

"And so the bulb has been six days in the earth already?"

"Yes, six days, M. Cornelius," replied the young girl.

"And it has not yet shown itself at the surface?"

"No, but I think it will to-morrow."

"Very well, to-morrow you will bring me news of it, when you bring me news of yourself, will you not, Rosa? I am very anxious about the daughter, as you called it just now; but I am much more interested in the mother."

"To-morrow?" said Rosa, taking a side look at Cornelius, "to-morrow, I do not know if I shall be able."

"Oh, good heavens!" said Cornelius, "why won't you be able to to-morrow?"

"M. Cornelius, I have a thousand things to do."

"While I have only one," murmured Cornelius.

"Yes," replied Rosa, "to love your tulip."

"To love you, Rosa."

Rosa shook her head.

Another silence followed.

"Well," continued Van Baerle, breaking the silence, "everything in Nature changes. To the flow-

The Black Tulip

ers of spring there succeed other flowers, and the bees which tenderly caressed violets and stocks, devote themselves later on with equal love to honeysuckles, roses, jessamines, chrysanthemums, and geraniums."

" What is the meaning of that? " asked Rosa.

" The meaning is that you liked at one time to hear the recital of my joys and sorrows; you were pleased with the flower of our common youth. But mine is fading in the gloom. The garden of a prisoner's hopes and pleasures has but one season. It is not like those beautiful gardens which enjoy the sun and the fresh air. Once the harvest of May has been gathered in, once the spoil has been collected, bees like yourself, Rosa, bees with delicate frames, with golden antennæ and diaphanous wings, pass through the barriers, desert the cold, the sadness and the solitude, and seek elsewhere for flowers and sweet-scented breezes, that is to say, for happiness."

Rosa looked at Cornelius with a smile, which he did not see; he was looking up to the heavens.

With a sigh he continued:

" You have abandoned me, Rosa, to have your own season of pleasure. You have done rightly. I do not complain. What right have I to claim your fidelity? "

" My fidelity! " cried Rosa, all in tears and not even trying to conceal from Cornelius the shower of pearls which rolled down her cheeks, " my fidelity! Have I not been faithful to you? "

What Had Happened in Eight Days

"Alas!" cried Cornelius, "is it being faithful to me to go away, to leave me here to die?"

"But, M. Cornelius," said Rosa, "do I not do everything I can to please you, in occupying myself with your tulip?"

"You are bitter, Rosa; you reproach me with the one unalloyed pleasure which I have had in this world."

"I reproach you with nothing, M. Cornelius, except with the one great grief which I have felt since they told me at the Buitenhof that you were to be put to death."

"You are displeased, Rosa, my sweet Rosa, you are displeased because I love flowers."

"I am not displeased because you love them, sir, but it makes me sad to find that you love them more than you love me."

"Ah! dear, dear sweetheart," cried Cornelius, "do you not see how my hand shakes and how pale I am? Can you not hear how my heart beats? Well, it is not because my black tulip smiles at me and calls me; no, it is because you smile at me, it is because you are near me; it is because—I do not know whether this is so or not—it is because it seems to me that your hands, though they avoid mine, are nevertheless inclined to stretch forth towards them; it is because I feel the warmth of your fair cheeks behind the cold grating. Rosa, my love, destroy the black tulip, destroy the hope of this flower, put out the light of this charming dream which I have grown

The Black Tulip

so accustomed to. Be it so: no more beautiful flowers with their elegant grace and their divine caprices!—deprive me of all that, flower jealous of other flowers, deprive me of all that, but do not prevent me from hearing and seeing you, and from listening to your footstep on the dull staircase; do not deprive me of the light of your eyes in this gloomy corridor, or of the assurance of your love which unceasingly soothes my heart. Love me, Rosa, for I know well that I love you alone."

"Next to the black tulip," said the young girl, whose soft and yielding hands at last consented to submit themselves through the iron grating to the lips of Cornelius.

"No, before everything, Rosa . . ."

"Ought I believe you?"

"As you believe in heaven."

"Be it so; but that does not bind you very much."

"Too little, alas! dear Rosa, but it binds you."

"Me! To what does it bind me?"

"Not to marry, first of all."

She smiled. "Ah! that's how it is," she said, "with you tyrants. You adore a beauty, you think only of her, you dream only of her. You are condemned to death and on your way to the scaffold you devote your last sigh to her, and you exact from me, poor girl, the sacrifice of my dreams and my ambition."

"But what beauty are you talking about, Rosa?"

222

asked Cornelius, seeking in vain to recollect a woman to whom Rosa could be alluding.

" Why, the black beauty, sir; the black beauty with elegant figure, small feet, and noble head. I am speaking of your flower, in fact."

Cornelius smiled.

"An imaginary sweetheart, my good Rosa; whereas you, without counting your, or rather my, lover, Jacob, you are surrounded by gallants who pay court to you. You remember, Rosa, what you said to me about the students and officers and clerks at The Hague? Well, are there no clerks, or officers, or students, at Loevestein? "

" Oh! indeed there are, and plenty of them," said Rosa.

" Who write? "

" Yes, who write."

" And now that you know how to read . . ."

And Cornelius sighed to think that it was to him, the poor prisoner, that Rosa owed the privilege of reading the love-letters she received.

" Well, but," said Rosa, " it seems to me, M. Cornelius, that in reading the letters which are written to me and in taking notice of the lovers who present themselves, I am only following your instructions."

" What! my instructions? "

" Yes, your instructions; do you forget," continued Rosa, sighing in her turn, " do you forget the will you wrote in the Bible of M. Cornelius de Witt? I do not forget it, for now that I can read, I read it every day, and oftener twice in the day than once. Well, in that will you order me to love and marry a handsome young man of twenty-six or twenty-eight. I am looking for this handsome young man, and as all my day is taken up with your tulip, you must leave me the evening in which to find him!"

"Ah! Rosa, the will was made in view of my death, and, thanks be to Heaven, I am still alive."

"Well, then, I will not look for this handsome young man of twenty-six or twenty-eight, but I will come to see you."

"Oh! yes, Rosa, come, do come!"

"But on one condition."

"It is accepted beforehand."

"It is that for three days there shall not be a word about the black tulip."

"There shall never be any mention of it again, Rosa, if you require it."

"Oh!" said the young girl, "one must not ask for impossibilities."

And as though by inadvertence she placed her fair cheek so close to the grating that Cornelius was able to touch it with his lips.

Rosa uttered a little cry, full of love, and disappeared.

XXI

THE SECOND BULB

THE night was fine, and the morning of the next day finer still.

On the preceding days the prison had been heavy, gloomy, and depressing; it had weighed with full force on the poor prisoner; the walls were black, the air cold, the bars seemed so close together as hardly to let in the daylight.

But when Cornelius awoke, a ray of morning sunshine was playing between the bars; outside, pigeons cleaved the air with extended wings, or cooed lovingly on the roof near the still-closed window.

Cornelius ran to the window and opened it; it seemed to him that life, joy, liberty almost, entered along with this ray of sunshine into the gloomy room.

This was because love flowered there, and made everything else do the same; love, which is a flower of heaven, far more radiant and more fragrant than any flower of earth.

When Gryphus entered the prisoner's cell, instead of finding him, as on previous days, morose and still lying in bed, he found him already up and singing

The Black Tulip

softly to himself. Gryphus scowled at him, and said:

" Halloa? "

" How are we this morning? "

Gryphus scowled at him.

" The dog, and M. Jacob, and our fair Rosa, how are they all? "

Gryphus ground his teeth.

" Here is your breakfast," said he.

" Thank you, friend Cerberus," said the prisoner. " It has come at the right time, for I am very hungry."

" Ah! you are very hungry, are you? " said Gryphus.

" Well, why not? " asked Van Baerle.

" It seems that the conspiracy is getting on? "

" What conspiracy? " asked Cornelius.

" Oh! all right, I know what I am talking about; but we shall keep our eyes open, Mr. Scholar. Make your mind easy, we shall keep our eyes open."

" Keep them open as much as you like," said Van Baerle; " my conspiracy, like my person, is quite at your service."

" We shall see that at midday," said Gryphus, as he went out.

" At midday? " said Cornelius; " what does he mean by that? Well, let us wait till midday, and then we shall see."

It was easy for Cornelius to wait for midday; he was already waiting for nine o'clock.

Twelve o'clock struck, and Cornelius heard on the

The Second Bulb

stairs not only Gryphus's step, but also the steps of three or four soldiers, who were coming up with him.

The door opened, Gryphus came in, brought in his men and shut the door behind them.

" There he is—search him."

They turned out Cornelius's pockets, looked between his coat and his waistcoat, between his waistcoat and his shirt, between his shirt and his skin; they found nothing. Then they looked among the bedclothes, in the mattress, in the paillasse; again they found nothing.

Then indeed Cornelius congratulated himself on not having accepted the third bulb. Gryphus, during this examination, would certainly have found it, however well it might have been hidden, and would have treated it as he treated the first one.

As it was, no prisoner ever assisted with greater calmness at a search made in his dwelling.

Gryphus retired with the pencil and the three or four pieces of paper which Rosa had brought Cornelius: these were the sole trophies of his expedition.

At six o'clock Gryphus returned, but alone. Cornelius tried to pacify him, but Gryphus growled, showed a tusk which he had in the corner of his jaw, and went out backwards, as though he was afraid of being forcibly assisted.

Cornelius burst out laughing.

This made Gryphus, who was of a literary turn, call back through the grating, " All right! all right! he laughs best who laughs last."

The Black Tulip

He who laughed last, that night at any rate, was Cornelius, for he was expecting Rosa.

Rosa came at nine o'clock, but she came without her lantern; she had no longer any need of a light, she could read. Then, too, the light might betray her, for she was now spied upon by Jacob more than ever.

Finally, in the light, Rosa's blushes, when she did blush, would be too easily seen.

What did the two young people talk about that evening? They spoke of things which lovers speak of on a door-step in France, from either side of a balcony in Spain, from above and below a flat roof in the East.

They spoke of things which made the hours fly, which added feathers to the wings of time. They spoke of everything except the black tulip. Then, at ten o'clock, they parted as usual.

Cornelius was happy, as completely happy as any tulip-fancier could be when no one had spoken to him about his tulip. He found Rosa as beautiful as all the other women in the world put together; he found her good, gracious, charming. But why did Rosa forbid him to speak of the black tulip?

It was a great defect, that, in Rosa.

Cornelius said to himself with a sigh that woman was not perfect.

During a part of the night he thought about this imperfection, which is the same thing as saying that as long as he was awake he thought of Rosa.

The Second Bulb

When he fell asleep he dreamt of her.

But the Rosa of his dreams was much more perfect than the real Rosa. Not only did she speak of the tulip, but she also brought to Cornelius a magnificent black tulip in a china vase.

Cornelius awoke trembling with excitement and joy, murmuring, " Rosa, I love you."

And as it was daylight Cornelius thought it well not to go to sleep again. He remained, therefore, all day thinking of the idea which had possessed him when he woke.

Ah! if Rosa had only spoken of the tulip, Cornelius would have preferred her to Semiramis, or Cleopatra, or Queen Elizabeth, or Anne of Austria—that is to say, to the greatest or most beautiful queens that had ever lived.

But Rosa, under penalty of his not seeing her again, had forbidden him to say anything about the tulip for three days.

True, this was seventy-two hours given to the lover; but then, it was seventy-two hours taken from the tulip-fancier.

It was true also that of these seventy-two hours thirty-six had already passed.

The other thirty-six would pass very quickly, eighteen in expectation, and eighteen in remembrance.

Rosa returned at the usual hour. Cornelius endured his punishment heroically. Cornelius would have made a very good Pythagorean, and, provided he had been allowed to ask once a day for news of his tulip, would easily have remained five years, according to the rules of the order, without speaking of anything else.

Moreover, the fair visitor understood that when one gives orders on one side, one must yield something on the other. Rosa allowed Cornelius to draw her fingers through the grating, and to impress a kiss on her fair tresses through the iron bars.

It would have been much safer for the poor child to have been talking about the black tulip; and this she recognised after she had returned, with fast-beating heart, to her own room.

Accordingly, the next evening, after they had exchanged their first words and endearments, she looked at Cornelius through the grating in the dark, with the look which one has when one does not see.

" Well," said she, " it has come up."

" Come up—what? who? " asked Cornelius, hardly venturing to believe that Rosa herself was cutting short the period of his probation.

" The tulip," said Rosa.

" What! " cried Cornelius, " you will allow me then? "

" Well, yes," replied Rosa, like a mother granting some little pleasure to her child.

" Ah, Rosa! " cried Cornelius, suddenly putting his lips to the grating in the hope of meeting a cheek, a hand, a forehead—anything, in fact.

The Second Bulb

He met something better; he met two half-opened lips.

Rosa gave a little scream.

Cornelius saw that he must hasten to keep up the conversation: this unexpected kiss had evidently startled Rosa very much.

" Come up quite straight? " he asked.

" Straight as a Frisian spindle," said Rosa.

" And it is a good height? "

" Two inches high at least."

" Oh, Rosa! take great care of it; you will see how quickly it grows."

" Can I take more care of it than I do? " said Rosa; " I think of nothing else."

" Of nothing else, Rosa? Be careful, or you will make me jealous in my turn."

" But you know well that to think of it is to think of you. I do not let it go out of my sight. I can see it from my bed; when I awake, it is the first thing I look at, and when I go to sleep, the last thing I lose sight of. During the day I sit and work near it, for since it has been in my room I do not leave the room."

" You are right, Rosa; it is your dowry, you know."

" Yes, and, thanks to it, I shall be able to marry a young man of twenty-six or twenty-eight, whom I shall love."

" Be quiet, you bad girl."

And here Cornelius succeeded in his design of

catching hold of the young girl's fingers, which, if it did not turn the conversation, at any rate caused silence to follow on the dialogue.

That evening Cornelius was the happiest of men. Rosa allowed him to hold her hand as long as he pleased, and he spoke quite freely about his tulip.

From this moment, every day brought an increase to the tulip, and to the love of the two young people. At one time it was the leaves which had opened, at another the bud itself which had formed.

At this news the delight of Cornelius was extreme, and the rapidity with which his questions succeeded each other showed their importance.

" Formed! " cried Cornelius, " it has formed? "

" Yes, it has formed," repeated Rosa.

Cornelius was ready to faint with joy, and was obliged to support himself by holding the grating.

" Ah! " he exclaimed.

Then, again addressing Rosa, he asked, " Is the oval perfect?—is the volute full?—are the tips quite green? "

" The oval is about an inch long, and comes to a point like a needle, the volute is swelling out, the tips are ready to open."

That night Cornelius slept little; the moment when the tips opened was a supreme one.

Two days later Rosa announced that they had opened.

" Open? " cried Cornelius, " the involucrum is

The Second Bulb

open! Then one can see, one can distinguish already . . ."

The prisoner paused breathlessly.

" Yes," replied Rosa, " it is possible to distinguish a line of a different colour, as fine as a hair."

" And the colour? " asked Cornelius, trembling.

" Ah! " replied Rosa, " it is very dark."

" Brown? "

" Oh! darker than that."

" Darker, my good Rosa, darker? Oh, thank you! As dark as ebony, as dark as . . ."

" As dark as the ink with which I wrote to you."

Cornelius uttered a wild cry of joy.

Then, suddenly stopping and clasping his hands, he said, " Oh, there is not an angel to be compared to you, Rosa! "

" Really! " said Rosa, smiling at his excitement.

" Rosa, you have worked so hard, you have done so much for me, Rosa; my tulip is going to flower, and it will flower black. Rosa, you are the most perfect thing in God's creation."

" After the black tulip."

" Be quiet, you bad girl, be quiet: for pity's sake, do not lessen my delight. But tell me, Rosa, if the tulip has got to this point, in two or three days more it will flower."

" To-morrow or the day after, yes."

" Oh! and I shall not see it! " cried Cornelius, starting back, " and I shall not be able to kiss it, as a marvel made by God to be worshipped, as I kiss your hand, and your hair, Rosa, and your cheek, when they happen to be near enough to the grating."

Rosa placed her cheek there, not by accident but on purpose, and the lips of the young man touched it.

" I will pluck it, if you wish," said Rosa.

" Oh, no! As soon as it is open, put it in the shade, Rosa, and on the very instant send word to the President of the Horticultural Society of Haarlem that the great black tulip has flowered. It is a long way to Haarlem, I know, but with money you will find a messenger. Have you any money, Rosa? "

Rosa smiled. " Oh, yes," said she.

" Enough? " asked Cornelius.

" I have three hundred florins."

" Oh, if you have three hundred florins you must not send a messenger, you must go to Haarlem yourself."

" But during this time what will happen to the tulip? "

" Oh, the flower! you must take it with you. You understand, you must not be separated from it for a moment."

" But in remaining with the flower I shall be separating from you, M. Cornelius," said Rosa sadly.

" Ah! that is true, my dear, my sweet Rosa. Oh! how wicked men are! What have I done? Why should they deprive me of liberty? You are right, Rosa. I could not live without you. Well, you will send some one to Haarlem, that will be the way. My word! the miracle is great enough to send the president out of his mind; he will come himself to fetch the tulip."

Then stopping short, he murmured in a trembling voice, "Rosa, Rosa, if it should turn out not to be black!"

"Well, you will know to-morrow, or the day after, in the evening."

"Wait till evening to know, Rosa? Why, I should die of impatience. Could we not arrange a signal?"

"I will do better than that."

"What will you do?"

"If it opens at night I will come myself to tell you. If it opens in the daytime I will pass by the door and slip a note in to you, either under the door or through the grating, between the first and second of my father's visits."

"Oh, Rosa, that is it—a word from you telling me the news; that will be a double happiness."

"There is ten o'clock," said Rosa; "I must go."

"Yes, yes!" said Cornelius, "yes! go, Rosa, go!"

Rosa retired almost sad.

Cornelius had almost sent her away.

It is true that it was to watch over the black tulip.

XXII

THE OPENING OF THE FLOWER

THE night slipped away, sweet indeed, but at the same time full of anxiety for Cornelius. Every moment he seemed to hear the soft voice of Rosa calling him. He awoke with a start, went to the door, and put his face close to the grating; but there was no one there, the corridor was empty.

Doubtless, Rosa too was watching. But, happier than he, she was watching over the tulip; she had before her eyes the splendid flower, the marvel of marvels, hitherto not merely unknown, but considered an impossibility.

What would the world say when it learned that the black tulip had been discovered, that it was actually in existence, and that it was the prisoner Van Baerle who had produced it?

If any one had come to offer Cornelius freedom in exchange for his tulip, how indignantly he would have driven him away!

The day came, but no news; the tulip had not yet flowered.

The day passed like the night.

236

The Opening of the Flower

The night came, and with it Rosa, joyful and light as a bird.

" Well? " asked Cornelius.

" Well, everything is going beautifully. To-night, without a doubt, your tulip will flower."

" And flower black? "

" Black as jet."

" Without a single spot of any other colour? "

" Without a single spot."

" Oh, how good God is to me! Rosa, I passed the night in dreams; first of all about you, . . ."

Rosa signified that she could not believe it.

" Then about what we must do."

" Well? "

" Well, this is what I have decided on. As soon as the tulip flowers, and it is quite clear that it is black, perfectly black, you must find a messenger."

" If that is all, I have found one already."

" A safe messenger? "

" A messenger whom I can answer for; he is one of my lovers."

" It is not Jacob, I hope? "

" No, don't imagine that. It is the ferryman of Loevestein, a fine young man of about twenty-five or twenty-six . . ."

" Oh, the devil! "

" Don't be uneasy," said Rosa, laughing; " he has not reached the age yet; you fixed the age yourself at between twenty-six and twenty-eight."

The Black Tulip

"Well, then, you think you can count on this young man?"

"As I could on myself. He would throw himself from his boat into the Waal, or into the Maas, whichever I chose, if I told him to."

"Well, Rosa, in ten hours this young man can be in Haarlem. You must give me a pencil and paper, or better still, a pen and ink, and I will write, or rather, you write yourself. I am a poor prisoner, and perhaps they might, like your father, see a conspiracy in it, if I wrote. You must write to the President of the Haarlem Society, and I am sure the president will come."

"But if he should delay?"

"Suppose he does delay for a day, or even two days—but that is impossible; a tulip-fancier like the president would not delay an hour, not a minute, not a second, in setting out to see the eighth wonder of the world. But, as I was saying, even if he delays a day, or two days, the tulip will still be in full splendour. Once he has seen the tulip, and an official account of it has been drawn up, the thing is done. You must keep a copy of the account, Rosa, and you must intrust the tulip to him. Ah! if we could carry it ourselves, Rosa, it should not leave my arms except for yours; but that is a dream which we must not indulge in," continued Cornelius, with a sigh. "Other eyes will see it fade. Above all, Rosa, before the president sees it, do not let any one see it. The black tulip! Good gracious! if any one saw the black tulip, he would steal it."

The Opening of the Flower

" Oh! "

" Did you not say yourself that you were afraid of what your lover Jacob might do? People will steal one florin; why would they not steal a hundred thousand? "

" I will keep a good watch, depend on it."

" If it were to open while you are here? "

" The capricious creature is quite capable of it."

" If you find it open when you go back? "

" Well, what then? "

" Ah! Rosa, from the moment it opens, remember there is not an instant to be lost in informing the president."

" And you also. Oh, yes, I quite understand."

Rosa sighed, not bitterly, but rather like a woman who begins to understand a weakness, if not to grow accustomed to it.

" I will return to the tulip, M. van Baerle, and as soon as it opens you shall be told; and as soon as you are told, the messenger shall set out."

" Rosa, Rosa, I do not know what wonder of heaven to compare you to."

" Compare me to the black tulip, M. Cornelius, and I shall be very much flattered, I assure you. Let us say good-bye, then, M. Cornelius."

" Say ' good-bye, my friend.' "

" Good-bye, my friend," said Rosa, a little consoled.

" Say ' my dearest friend.' "

" Oh, my . . ."

239

"Dearest friend, Rosa, I beg of you—dearest, am I not?"

"Dearest, yes, dearest," said Rosa, breathless and full of joy.

"And now, Rosa, that you have said 'dearest,' say also 'happiest'; say 'as happy as any man ever was in this world and as fortunate.' There is only one thing more that I want."

"What is that?"

"Your cheek, Rosa, your fresh, rosy cheek; but willingly, Rosa, not by surprise or by accident. Ah!"

The prisoner ended his request in a sigh; he had touched the lips of the young girl, and not by accident or by surprise, as a hundred years later St. Preux was to touch those of Julie.

Rosa ran away.

Cornelius remained, with his soul on his lips, standing by the door.

He was almost choking with joy and happiness. He opened his window, and for a long time, with a heart filled with gratitude, he contemplated the cloudless blue sky, and the moon, which lit up the two rivers and the hills beyond. He drew into his lungs the strong pure air, the inspirer of good thoughts and the source of religious recognition and admiration.

"Oh! thou art ever there above, my God," he said, almost on his knees, and with his eyes turned towards the stars; "forgive me for having almost doubted thee during these last days. Thou didst hide thyself behind clouds, and for a moment I ceased to

The Opening of the Flower

see thee, O good, eternal, and merciful God. But to-day, this evening, this night, I see thee plainly in the mirror of the sky, and above all in the mirror of my own heart."

The poor sick man was cured, the poor prisoner was free.

During part of the night Cornelius remained holding the bars of his window, his ear directed towards the grating, concentrating his five senses in one, or rather in two only. He looked and he listened. He looked at the sky, he listened to the earth.

Turning his eyes from time to time towards the corridor, he said:

"Down there, Rosa, like myself, is watching and waiting from moment to moment. Down there, under the eyes of Rosa, is the mysterious flower, which lives, which begins to open, which opens. Perhaps at this moment Rosa is holding the stem of the tulip between her warm soft fingers. Touch the stem gently, Rosa. Perhaps she is touching with her lips the half-open calyx. Touch it lightly, Rosa, or your lips will injure it. Perhaps at this moment the two objects of my love are caressing each other . . ."

At that instant a star flamed in the south, passed across the whole space between the horizon and the fortress, and fell over Loevestein.

Cornelius trembled.

"Ah!" said he, "God is sending a soul into my flower."

And, as though he had guessed rightly, almost at

the same instant the prisoner heard in the corridor a
light sylph-like step, and the rustling of a dress which
seemed like the beating of wings, and a well-known
voice saying to him:

" Cornelius, my friend, my dearest and most happy
friend, come, come quickly."

Cornelius made but one bound from the window to
the grating; this time again his lips met those of
Rosa, who murmured as she kissed him:

" It is open, it is black; here it is."

" What! It is here? " cried Cornelius.

" Yes, yes; one must risk a small danger to give
a great joy. Here it is, take it."

And with one hand she raised to the height of the
grating a little dark lantern, which she had just un-
covered, while with the other she lifted to the same
height the miraculous tulip.

Cornelius uttered a cry of joy, and felt as though
he would faint.

" Oh! " he murmured. " My God, my God, thou
repayest me for my innocence and my captivity, since
thou hast made these two flowers bloom at the grating of my prison door."

" Kiss it," said Rosa, " as I have just done."

Cornelius, holding his breath, touched with his lips
the tip of the flower, and never was a kiss given to
any one, even to Rosa, which so profoundly affected
the heart of the giver.

The tulip was beautiful, splendid, magnificent; its
stem was more than eighteen inches high; it rose from

The Opening of the Flower

the bosom of four green leaves, smooth and straight as lance-heads; its flower was entirely black and as brilliant as jet.

"Rosa," said Cornelius breathlessly, "Rosa, not a moment is to be lost; the letter must be written."

"It is written already, my dearest Cornelius," said Rosa.

"Really?"

"As you did not wish a moment to be lost, I wrote it myself while the tulip was opening. Here is the letter; tell me if you think it will do."

Cornelius took the letter and read, in writing which had still further improved since he had received Rosa's note:

"To the President of the Horticultural Society.

"SIR: The black tulip will open in about ten minutes. As soon as it is open, I will send a messenger to ask you to come in person to fetch it from the fortress of Loevestein. I am the daughter of the jailer Gryphus, and almost as much a prisoner as those whom my father has charge of. I cannot therefore bring you this marvel. That is why I venture to ask you to come for it yourself.

"I wish it to be called the *Rosa Baerlensis*.

"It has just opened; it is perfectly black.

"Come, sir, come.

"I have the honour to be,

"Your humble servant,

"ROSA GRYPHUS."

The Black Tulip

"That will do, dear Rosa; that will do. The letter is excellent. I could never have written it with such charming simplicity. At the meeting of the committee you must give them all the information they ask for. They must be told how the tulip was produced, what cares and watchings and fears it has caused; but just now there is not a moment to be lost, Rosa. The messenger, the messenger!"

"What is the name of the president?"

"Give it me; I will address it. Oh, he is well known. He is Mynheer van Systens, Burgomaster of Haarlem. Give it me, Rosa, give it me."

And with a trembling hand Cornelius wrote on the letter, "To Mynheer Peters van Systens, Burgomaster, and President of the Horticultural Society of Haarlem."

"And now, go, Rosa, go," said Cornelius, "and let us place ourselves under the protection of God, who has up to now taken such care of us."

XXIII

THE JEALOUS MAN

INDEED, the poor young people had great need of the direct protection of God.

Never had they been so near to despair as at the moment when they thought themselves certain of happiness.

We have no doubt that the intelligence of our readers will, before now, have recognised in Jacob our old friend, or rather our old enemy, Isaac Boxtel.

The reader has guessed, then, that Boxtel had followed, from the Buitenhof to Loevestein, the object of his love and the object of his hatred—the black tulip and Cornelius van Baerle.

What no one but a tulip-grower, and a jealous one, could have discovered—that is to say, the existence of the bulbs and the ambition of the prisoner—that Boxtel, urged on by jealousy, had been able to find out, or at least to guess.

We have seen him, more successful under the name of Jacob than under that of Isaac, become friends with Gryphus, whose gratitude and hospitality he had fostered during several months with the best gin ever distilled between the Texel and Antwerp. He quieted his mistrust—for, as we have seen, old Gryphus was naturally mistrustful—he quieted his mistrust by flattering him with the idea of a marriage with Rosa.

After having flattered his pride as a father, he gratified also his jailer's instincts, by painting in the darkest colours the character of the learned prisoner whom Gryphus had under his charge, and who, to believe the so-called Jacob had made a compact with Satan to injure his Highness the Prince of Orange.

He had at first been fairly successful also with Rosa, not by inspiring her with friendly feelings—for Rosa had always disliked Mynheer Jacob—but by dissipating, through his wild talk of love and marriage, all the suspicions which she might have had with regard to him. We have seen how his imprudence in following Rosa in the garden had at last shown him in his true colours to the young girl, and how the instinctive fears of Cornelius had put the two young people on their guard against him.

What had mainly inspired the prisoner with uneasiness was, as our readers will remember, the great anger which Jacob showed when Gryphus crushed the first bulb.

At that moment Boxtel's rage was the greater because, though he very strongly suspected that Cornelius had a second bulb, he was not by any means sure of it.

It was then that he spied upon Rosa and followed

The Jealous Man

her about, not only to the garden, but also along the passages.

Only, as he now followed her at night and with his shoes off, he was neither seen nor heard, except, indeed, on that occasion when Rosa thought she saw something passing on the staircase like a shadow.

But it was then too late. Boxtel, from the mouth of the prisoner himself, had learnt of the existence of the second bulb.

Duped by Rosa's trick of pretending to plant it in the flower-bed, and having no doubt but that the little comedy had been played to make him betray himself, he redoubled his precautions, and brought into play every trick he could devise, in order to continue to spy upon the others without being noticed himself.

He saw Rosa carry a large earthenware pot from her father's kitchen to her own room. He saw her carefully washing from her beautiful hands the earth with which they had become incrusted while she was kneading the mould in order to prepare the best possible bed for the tulip.

Finally, he hired in a neighbouring house a little room just in front of Rosa's, far enough off to escape recognition himself with the naked eye, but near enough to enable him to follow, through his telescope, everything that was done in the young girl's chamber, just as he had followed everything that was done in Cornelius's drying-room.

He had not been installed three days in his new

abode, when all his doubts were removed. In the morning, at sunrise, the earthenware pot was on the window-sill, and Rosa, like those charming women of Mieris and Metzu, appeared at the window which was framed by the first green shoots of the creeper and the honeysuckle that grew round it.

Rosa looked at the earthenware vessel in a manner which proved to Boxtel the true value of the object contained in it.

What the earthenware pot contained was evidently the second bulb, that is to say, the supreme hope of the prisoner.

When the nights threatened to be too cold Rosa took in the pot. Clearly, she was following the instructions of Cornelius, who feared that the bulb might be frost-bitten.

When the risen sun became too strong, Rosa took in the pot between eleven o'clock and two o'clock. Evidently, again, Cornelius feared that the mould would become too dry.

But when the stem of the flower rose above the mould, Boxtel was quite convinced. It was not more than an inch high when the jealous man's doubts entirely disappeared.

Cornelius had two bulbs, then, and the second was intrusted to the love and the care of Rosa.

For, as may be imagined, the love of the two young people had not escaped Boxtel's notice.

The thing to be done, then, was to find some way of removing the second bulb from the care of Rosa and the love of Cornelius. Only, this was not an easy thing to do.

Rosa watched over her tulip as a mother watches over her child; more than that, as a dove broods over her eggs.

Rosa did not leave her room during the day; what was stranger still, Rosa did not leave her room in the evening.

For seven days Boxtel spied upon Rosa without any result. Rosa did not leave her room.

This was during the seven days of misunderstanding, which made Cornelius so unhappy, by depriving him at the same time of all news of Rosa and of all news of his tulip.

Was Rosa going to sulk forever? That would have made the theft much more difficult than M. Isaac had at first thought. We say the theft, for Isaac had quite made up his mind to steal the tulip; and, as it was grown in complete secrecy; as the two young people hid its existence from everybody; as he, a known tulip-fancier, would be much more readily believed than a young girl ignorant of every detail of horticulture, or than a prisoner condemned for high treason, and guarded, watched and spied upon, who would find it difficult from inside his prison to bring forward a claim; as, moreover, he would be the possessor of the tulip, and as, in the case of movable property and things which can be carried about, possession gives rise to a presumption of ownership, he would certainly gain the prize, he would certainly be crowned instead of Cornelius, and the tulip, instead of being called the *tulipa nigra Baerlensis*, would be called the *tulipa nigra Boxtellensis* or *Boxtellea*.

M. Boxtel had not decided which of these names to give to the black tulip; but as the two signified the same thing, that was a minor point. The chief point was to steal the tulip.

But for Boxtel to be able to steal the tulip, Rosa must leave her room. It was therefore with veritable delight that Jacob, or Isaac, which you choose, saw the usual meetings recommence.

He began by taking advantage of Rosa's absence to examine her door. The door closed tightly and was fastened with a double turn of the key; the lock was a simple one, but Rosa alone had a key to it.

Boxtel thought of stealing the key from Rosa, but, in the first place, it would not be easy to take it from the young girl's pocket; and in the second, if he did, Rosa, on finding that she had lost the key, would have the lock changed, and would stay in her room till a new one was put on, and thus Boxtel would have committed a crime for nothing.

It would be better, then, to use some other means.

Boxtel collected all the keys he could find, and while Cornelius and Rosa were passing one of their happy hours at the grating, he tried them all.

Two would go into the lock; one of the two went round once, and only stopped at the second turn.

Very little, then, needed to be done to this key.

The Jealous Man

Boxtel covered it with a thin coating of wax, and renewed his experiment.

The obstacle which the key met with at the second turn left its imprint on the wax.

Boxtel had only to work upon this imprint with the sharp edge of a very fine file.

After two days of labour Boxtel brought his key to perfection. Rosa's door opened noiselessly, without effort, and Boxtel found himself in the young girl's room, alone with the tulip.

The first evil act of Boxtel's had been to climb over a wall, in order to dig up the tulip; the second had been to get into Cornelius's drying-room through an open window; the third was to get into Rosa's room by means of a false key.

Thus we see that jealousy caused Boxtel to advance rapidly in a career of crime.

Boxtel, then, found himself alone with the tulip.

An ordinary thief would have put the pot under his arm, and walked off with it. But Boxtel was not an ordinary thief, and he deliberated.

Looking at the tulip by the aid of his dark-lantern, he reflected that it was not yet sufficiently advanced for him to be certain that it would flower black, although appearances showed that there was every probability of its doing so. He reflected that if it did not flower black, or if it flowered with some spot on it, he would have committed a useless theft. He reflected that the report of the theft would be spread about; that, after what had happened in the garden, the real thief would be suspected; that search would be made, and that, however carefully he might hide it, the tulip might possibly be discovered. He reflected that even if he hid it so well that it was not discovered, still it might be injured in being moved from place to place.

Finally, he reflected that, since he had the key of Rosa's room and could enter it whenever he pleased, it would be better to await the flowering of the tulip; to take it an hour before it opened, or an hour after, and to set out, without a moment's delay, for Haarlem, where, before any one could reclaim it, he would bring it before the judges.

Then it would be the person who claimed it that Boxtel would accuse of theft.

It was a well-conceived plan, and worthy in all respects of its contriver.

Accordingly, every day, during that delightful hour which the young people passed at the cell-door, Boxtel entered the young girl's room to follow the progress which the black tulip made towards flowering.

On the evening at which we have arrived, he was going to enter as on other evenings, but, as we saw, the young people had exchanged only a few words, when Cornelius sent Rosa to look after the black tulip. And, seeing Rosa re-enter her room ten minutes after having left it, Boxtel understood that the tulip had flowered, or was about to do so.

This was the night, then, during which his project

was to be carried out. Boxtel therefore presented himself at Gryphus's with a double supply of gin—that is to say, with a bottle in each pocket.

If Gryphus was once fuddled, Boxtel would be almost master of the house.

At eleven o'clock, Gryphus was dead drunk. At two o'clock in the morning, Boxtel saw Rosa leave her room, but evidently she was carrying something very carefully in her arms.

This object was, without doubt, the black tulip which had just flowered.

But what was she going to do with it? Was she going on the instant to set off with it to Haarlem? It was impossible that a young girl should undertake such a journey alone and in the night-time.

Was she merely going to show the tulip to Cornelius? It was probable.

He followed her with bare feet, and on tip-toe.

He saw her approach the grating. He heard her call Cornelius.

By the light of her dark-lantern he saw the tulip, open, and black as the night which surrounded it.

He heard all the arrangements made between Cornelius and Rosa for sending a messenger to Haarlem. He saw the lips of the two young people meet; then he heard Cornelius send Rosa away.

He saw Rosa put out her dark-lantern and make her way back to her room.

He saw her go into the room; then, ten minutes

later, he saw her go out again, carefully shutting and double-locking the door.

Why did she shut the door so carefully? Evidently because inside the door she had left the black tulip.

Boxtel, who saw all this from a hiding-place on the landing above Rosa's room, descended step by step from his story as Rosa descended from hers; so that when Rosa touched the last step of the staircase with her light foot, Boxtel, with a hand still lighter, touched the lock of Rosa's room; and in his hand, it must be understood, was the false key which opened Rosa's door as easily as the true one.

That is why we said, at the beginning of this chapter, that the young people were in great need of the immediate protection of God.

XXIV

IN WHICH THE BLACK TULIP CHANGES ITS MASTER

CORNELIUS remained on the spot where Rosa had left him, hardly able to summon up strength enough to sustain his twofold burden of happiness.

Half an hour passed away.

Already the first rays of daylight, bluish and fresh, were coming through the bars of Cornelius's window, when he started suddenly at the sound of steps ascending the stairs, and cries coming nearer and nearer.

Almost at the same instant he was confronted by the pale and distressed face of Rosa.

He started back, pale himself with fright.

"Cornelius! Cornelius!" she cried breathlessly.

"Good heavens, what is it?" asked the prisoner.

"Cornelius, the tulip . . ."

"Well?"

"How can I tell you?"

"Tell me, Rosa, tell me!"

"It has been taken from us—stolen from us . . ."

"It has been taken? Stolen?" cried Cornelius.

"Yes," said Rosa, leaning against the door to prevent herself falling. "Yes, taken, stolen!" and, in

255

spite of herself, her limbs failing her, she slipped down, and fell on her knees.

"But how?" asked Cornelius; "tell me, explain to me."

"Oh! it is not my fault, my friend."

Poor Rosa, she no longer dared to say "my dearest friend."

"You left it alone, then!" cried Cornelius, sorrowfully.

"Only for one moment, to go and tell our messenger, who lives barely fifty yards off, on the banks of the Waal."

"And during that time, in spite of my warnings, you left the key in the door, unhappy girl!"

"No! no! no! That is what I cannot understand. I have not let go of the key. I held it in my hand all the time, clutching it tightly, as if I were afraid it would escape from me."

"But how was it done, then?"

"I do not know. I had given the letter to the messenger; the messenger had set out before my eyes. I came in again, the door was shut, everything was in its place in my room, except the black tulip; that had disappeared. Some one must have got hold of a key to my room, or made a false one."

She was almost choking; her tears cut short her speech.

Cornelius, motionless and with a distracted air, heard almost without understanding, murmuring only:

"Stolen, stolen, stolen! I am ruined!"

The Black Tulip Changes its Master

" Oh, M. Cornelius, forgive me! forgive me! It will kill me."

At this threat of Rosa's, Cornelius seized the bars of the grating, and, shaking them furiously, exclaimed:

" Rosa, it is true they have stolen it from us, but need we be in despair on that account? No; the misfortune is great, but perhaps it can be remedied; we know the thief."

" Alas! I cannot really be positive even about that."

" I tell you, it is that infamous Jacob. Shall we let him carry off to Haarlem the fruit of our labours, the child of our love? Rosa, he must be pursued and overtaken."

" But how can we do that, my friend, without my father finding out that we have been communicating with each other? How can I, a woman, with so little liberty and so little experience, how can I do all this, which you yourself might not perhaps be able to achieve? "

" Rosa, Rosa, open this door for me, and you shall see whether I will achieve it. You shall see whether I will not discover the thief, whether I will not make him confess his crime and beg for mercy."

" Alas! " said Rosa, bursting into sobs, " how can I open the door? Have I the keys here? If I had, you would have been free long since."

" Your father has them, your infamous father,

the hangman who crushed my first bulb. Oh!
the wretch! the wretch! he is the accomplice of
Jacob."

" Not so loud, not so loud, for heaven's sake! "

" Oh! if you do not open this door for me, Rosa,"
cried Cornelius, in a paroxysm of fury, " I will smash
down the grating, and kill everything I find alive in
the prison."

" My friend, for pity's sake! "

" I tell you, Rosa, I will pull down the cell, stone
by stone."

And the unfortunate man, with his two hands, the
strength of which was doubled by his fury, shook the
door with a great noise, regardless of the fact that
the sound of his voice was already re-echoing to the
bottom of the spiral staircase.

Rosa was terror-stricken, and tried in vain to calm
the furious tempest.

" I tell you I will kill the infamous Gryphus! "
shouted Van Baerle; " I tell you I will shed his blood,
as he shed that of my black tulip! "

The unfortunate man was beginning to lose his
reason.

" Well, yes," said Rosa, trembling with excitement, " yes, only be calm; yes, I will take his keys;
I will open the door for you, only be calm, my Cornelius, be . . ."

She did not finish, for a furious voice, close by
her, cut short the sentence.

" My father! " cried Rosa.

The Black Tulip Changes its Master

"Gryphus!" yelled Van Baerle. "Ah! the scoundrel!"

Old Gryphus, in the midst of the disturbance, had come up without being heard.

He seized his daughter roughly by the wrist.

"Ah! you will take my keys!" he said, in a voice choked by rage. "Ah! this infamous monster, this conspirator, fit to be hanged, is 'your Cornelius,' is he? Ah! we have relations with prisoners of state! Very good!"

Rosa wrung her hands despairingly.

"So," continued Gryphus, passing from the feverish accents of anger to the cold irony of triumph, "so, my innocent tulip-fancier, my gentle scholar, you will murder me, you will drink my blood! Only that! Very good! And my daughter is your accomplice. Good heavens! am I in a cave of brigands here? in a den of thieves? Oh! the governor shall hear of this in the morning, and his Highness, the Stadtholder, shall hear of it the day after. We know the law: 'Whoever shall revolt in the prison . . . Article 6.' We shall give you a second edition of the Buitenhof, Mr. Scholar, and a good edition, too. Yes, that's right! gnaw your fists like a bear in a cage; and you, my beauty, devour your Cornelius with your eyes. I warn you, my lambs, you will not have any more chances of conspiring together. There, go downstairs, unnatural daughter! And you, Mr. Scholar, good-bye—till we meet again!"

Rosa, wild with terror and despair, threw a kiss to

Cornelius; then, suddenly struck by an idea, she flew towards the staircase, calling out as she did so, "All is not yet lost. Count upon me, my Cornelius."

Her father followed her, growling.

As for the poor tulip-fancier, he relaxed by degrees his grasp on the iron bars, which his fingers had been convulsively clutching; his head grew heavy, his eyes rolled in their sockets, and he fell heavily on the floor of his cell, muttering:

"Stolen! they have stolen it from me!"

In the meantime Boxtel had left the fortress by the door which Rosa herself had opened. He took with him the black tulip wrapped in a large cloak, flung himself into a light carriage which was awaiting him at Gorcum, and disappeared, without giving any notice to his friend Gryphus of his precipitate departure.

And now that we have seen him mounted in his carriage, we will follow him, with the reader's permission, to the end of his journey. He went slowly, for one cannot with impunity go at a gallop when one is carrying a black tulip.

But Boxtel, fearing that he would not arrive soon enough, obtained, at Delft, a box lined with fine fresh moss, in which he packed the tulip, in such a way that the flower was equally and softly supported on all sides, and had a supply of air from above. Then the carriage was able to proceed at full speed, without any risk of injury to the tulip.

He arrived the next morning at Haarlem, worn out but triumphant; changed the earthenware pot

The Black Tulip Changes its Master

which held the tulip, in order to do away with every trace of the theft; broke up the pot and threw the pieces into a canal; wrote to the President of the Horticultural Society, announcing that he had just arrived in Haarlem with a perfectly black tulip; installed himself in a good hotel, with his flower still safe and sound, and there, waited.

XXV

PRESIDENT VAN SYSTENS

ROSA, on leaving Cornelius, had made up her mind what to do. She determined either to restore to him the black tulip, which Boxtel had stolen, or never to see him again.

She had seen the despair of the poor prisoner, a double and incurable despair. On the one hand was an inevitable separation, Gryphus having discovered the secret both of their love and of their meeting-place; on the other was the overthrow of all the ambitious hopes of Cornelius van Baerle, hopes which he had been entertaining for seven years.

Rosa was one of those whom a trifle will stop, but who, in the presence of a supreme misfortune, are full of strength, and find in the misfortune itself energy with which to combat it, or resources by which to remedy it.

The young girl returned to her room, threw a last look round it to see whether she had not made a mistake, and whether the tulip was not, after all, in some corner where it had escaped her notice. But Rosa sought in vain—the tulip was still missing, still stolen.

President Van Systens

Rosa made up a small parcel of things she would require, took the three hundred florins which she had saved, and which were her whole fortune, felt among her lace for the third bulb, hid it carefully in her bosom, shut her door and double-locked it, so as to gain the time which it would take to open it and discover her flight, descended the staircase, went out of the door through which Boxtel had passed an hour earlier, went to the livery-stable, and asked whether she could have a light carriage on hire.

The job-master had but one carriage, which Boxtel had hired the evening before, and in which he was now on his way to Delft.

We say, to Delft, for it was necessary in going from Loevestein to Haarlem to make an enormous detour; as the crow flies, the distance would have been less than half.

But it is only birds that can travel in that way in Holland, a country which is more cut up by rivers, streams, rivulets, canals, and lakes, than any other country in the world.

Rosa was therefore obliged to take a horse; the owner made no difficulty about supplying it, as he knew that Rosa was the daughter of the jailer at the fortress.

Rosa hoped to be able to rejoin the worthy young man who was acting as her messenger, and to take him along with her, both as guide and as protector.

She had not gone a league when she saw him striding along one of the shaded sidewalks of a charming road which ran by the river side.

Putting her horse to a trot, she joined him.

The young man did not know the importance of his message; nevertheless, he was making as much haste as he could. Already, in less than an hour, he had gone a league and a half.

Rosa took from him the letter which was now useless, and explained to him the need which she had of his assistance. The ferryman placed himself at her disposal, promising to go as fast as the horse, provided Rosa would allow him to hold on, either to the crupper or to the front of her saddle.

The young girl said that he might hold on in any way he pleased, as long as he did not delay her.

The two travellers had already been on the road five hours, and had travelled more than eight leagues, before Gryphus suspected that the young girl had left the fortress.

Moreover, the jailer, a very malicious man at heart, was quite delighted at having, as he thought, terrified his daughter so thoroughly. But while he was congratulating himself on having such a fine story to tell his friend Jacob, Jacob himself was also on his way to Delft.

Only, thanks to his carriage, he was already four leagues ahead of Rosa and the ferryman.

While he was thinking of Rosa as trembling or sulking in her room, the young woman was gradually gaining on him. Thus the prisoner was the only person who was where Gryphus thought him to be.

Rosa had appeared so little in her father's presence since she had taken charge of the tulip, that it was only at dinner-time, that is at midday, that Gryphus perceived, through the medium of his appetite, that his daughter had been sulking rather too long. He told one of his assistants to call her; then, as the man came down and reported that he had searched and called in vain, he determined to seek and call her himself.

He began by going straight to her room, but, hard as he knocked, Rosa did not answer.

The locksmith of the fortress was sent for; he opened the door, but Gryphus did not find Rosa, any more than Rosa had found the tulip.

Rosa at that moment had just entered Rotterdam.

Hence Gryphus found no more sign of her in the kitchen than in her room, in the garden than in the kitchen.

One can imagine the anger of the jailer when, after searching the whole neighbourhood, he learnt that his daughter had hired a horse and, like Brada-mante or Chlorinda, had set out like a veritable lady knight-errant, without saying where she was going.

Gryphus went up again to Van Baerle in a fury; abused him, threatened him, overturned all his miser-able furniture, promised him the secret cell, the dun-geon, starvation, and beating.

Cornelius, without even hearing what the jailer

said, allowed himself to be maltreated, abused, and threatened, remaining all the time mournful, motionless, and impassive, insensible to every emotion, dead to all fear.

After having sought for Rosa on all sides, Gryphus sought for Jacob, and as he did not find him, any more than he had found his daughter, he at once began to suspect that Jacob had run away with her.

The young girl, however, after having halted for two hours at Rotterdam, had resumed her journey. The same evening she slept at Delft, and the next day reached Haarlem, four hours only after Boxtel himself had arrived there.

Rosa went first of all to the President of the Horticultural Society, Master van Systens.

She found the worthy citizen in a situation which we must describe, if we are not to be wanting in our duty as historians.

The president was drawing up a report for the committee of the society.

This report was inscribed on full-sized paper, in the best handwriting of the president.

Rosa had herself announced under the simple name of Rosa Gryphus; but this name, though it sounded very well, was evidently unknown to the president, for Rosa was refused admission. It is difficult to force one's self past outposts in Holland, a country of dikes and sluices.

But Rosa was not disheartened; she had undertaken a mission, and had sworn to herself that she would not be defeated by rebuffs, or brutalities, or insults.

"Tell the president," she said, "that I have come to speak to him on behalf of the black tulip."

These words, not less magical than the famous "open, Sesame" of the Arabian Nights, served as a passport. Thanks to them, she was able to enter the office of President van Systens, who came forward politely to meet her.

He was a worthy little man, with a frail body which closely resembled the stalk of a flower, his head forming the calyx, and his two arms, which hung loosely down, representing the double oblong leaf of the tulip; a curious swinging motion with which he walked completed his resemblance to the flower as it looks when bending over under a breeze. His name, as we have said, was Van Systens.

"You come, miss," he said, "you come, you say, on behalf of the black tulip?"

In the eyes of the President of the Horticultural Society, the *tulipa nigra* was a first-class power, which, in its character of queen of tulips, might well send ambassadors.

"Yes, sir," replied Rosa; "at least I come to speak to you about it."

"Is it going on well?" asked Van Systens, with a smile of tender veneration.

"Alas! sir, I do not know," replied Rosa.

"What! can any misfortune have happened to it?"

"A very great misfortune has happened, sir, not to it, but to me."

"What is that?"

"They have stolen it from me."

"They have stolen the black tulip from you?"

"Yes, sir."

"Do you know who has done it?"

"Oh! I suspect, but I do not dare to accuse the person."

"But it will be easy to find out the truth."

"How so?"

"As they have stolen it from you, the thief cannot be far off."

"Why not?"

"Because I have seen it within the last two hours."

"You have seen the black tulip?" cried Rosa, running towards M. Van Systens.

"As I see you, miss."

"Where?"

"At your master's."

"At my master's?"

"Yes; are you not in the service of M. Isaac Boxtel?"

"I?"

"Yes, you."

"But for whom do you take me, sir?"

"For whom do you take me?"

"Sir, I take you, I hope, for what you are, that is to say, for the Honourable M. van Systens, Burgomaster of Haarlem, and President of the Horticultural Society."

" And you have come to tell me . . . ? "

" I have come to tell you, sir, that they have stolen my tulip from me."

" Then your tulip is M. Boxtel's. You explain yourself very badly, my child. It is not from you, but from M. Boxtel, that they have stolen the tulip."

" I tell you, sir, that I do not know who this M. Boxtel is, and that this is the first time I ever heard his name."

" You do not know who M. Boxtel is, and you, too, have a black tulip? "

" Is there another, then? " said Rosa, trembling.

" There is M. Boxtel's, yes."

" What is it like? "

" Why, black, of course."

" Without a spot? "

" Without a single spot, without the least mark upon it."

" And you have this tulip? It is here now? "

" No, but it will be, for I must show it to the committee before the prize is awarded."

" Sir," cried Rosa, " this Boxtel, this Isaac Boxtel, who says he is the owner of the black tulip . . ."

" Who is the owner."

" Sir, is he not a thin man? "

" Yes."

" Bald? "

" Yes."

"With haggard eyes?"

"I think so."

"Restless, stooping, bow-legged?"

"Indeed, you have given a very correct portrait of M. Boxtel."

"Sir, is the tulip in a blue-and-white earthenware pot, with yellow flowers and a basket on three sides of the pot?"

"As to that I am not sure. I took more notice of the man than of the pot."

"Sir, it is my tulip. It is the one that was stolen from me. Sir, it is my property. I come here to claim it before you, from you."

"Oh, oh!" said M. van Systens, looking at Rosa, "what! you come here to claim M. Boxtel's tulip? My word, but you are a bold baggage!"

"Sir," said Rosa, a little confused at this mode of address, "I did not say I came to claim M. Boxtel's tulip. I say I have come to claim my own."

"Yours?"

"Yes, the one I planted and raised myself."

"Well, go and find M. Boxtel at the White Swan Inn; you can settle the matter with him. As for me, the case seems as difficult to decide as the one which was brought before King Solomon, and as I have no pretensions to his wisdom, I shall content myself with making my report, establishing the existence of the black tulip, and ordering the hundred thousand florins to be given to the discoverer of it."

"Oh! sir, sir! . . ." insisted Rosa.

President Van Systens

"Only, my child," continued Van Systens, "as you are young and pretty, and not as yet wholly perverted, take my advice. Be very careful how you act in this matter, for we have a court and a prison at Haarlem. Moreover, we are extremely sensitive with regard to the honour of tulips. Go away, my child, go away. M. Isaac Boxtel, White Swan Inn."

And M. van Systens, taking up his fine pen, continued his interrupted report.

XXVI

A MEMBER OF THE HORTICULTURAL SOCIETY

Rosa, perplexed, and almost distracted with joy and with fear, at the thought that the black tulip was found again, took the road to the White Swan Inn, still followed by the ferryman, a well-built son of Friesland, who was match for ten Boxtels at least.

During the journey, he had been told how matters stood; he did not shrink from the prospect of a struggle, in case it should come to that; only, he had orders, if it did, to be very careful of the tulip.

But Rosa, when she reached the Groote-Markt, suddenly stopped; a thought struck her, like that Minerva in Homer, who seized Achilles by the hair, at the moment when he was about to be carried away by his rage.

" Good heavens!" she murmured, " I have made a dreadful mistake; I have very likely ruined Cornelius, and the tulip, and myself. I have given the alarm, I have awakened suspicion. I am only a woman, and these men may league themselves against me, and then I am undone. If I am ruined, it is nothing; but Cornelius! and the tulip!"

She thought for a moment.

" If I go to Boxtel's and do not recognise him, if this Boxtel is not Jacob, if he is another tulip-grower who has also discovered the black tulip, or if my tulip has been stolen by some one whom I do not suspect, if it has already passed into other hands, if I do not recognise the man but only the tulip, how shall I prove that the tulip is mine?

" On the other hand, if I recognise, in this Boxtel, the pretended Jacob, who knows what will happen? While we are disputing, the tulip will die. O holy Virgin, inspire me! My whole future is in question, and so is that of the poor prisoner, who is perhaps expiring at this moment."

Having offered this prayer, Rosa piously awaited the inspiration she had asked for from heaven.

Meanwhile, at the end of the Groote-Markt, a great hubbub had arisen. Men were running about, doors were being opened. Rosa alone was unconscious of all this excitement among the populace.

" We must go back to the president," she murmured.

" Very well, let us go, then," said the ferryman.

They went along the little street called La Paille, which led straight to the house of M. van Systens, who, with his best pen and in his best handwriting, continued to work at his report.

Everywhere, on the way, Rosa heard people speaking of the black tulip and the hundred thousand florins; the news had already spread through the town.

The Black Tulip

Rosa had considerable difficulty in gaining admission to M. van Systens' house; nevertheless the president was again influenced by the magic words " black tulip." But when he recognised Rosa, whom he had set down in his mind as mad, or worse, he was very angry, and wanted to send her away.

But Rosa clasped her hands and, with that accent of honest truth which reaches the heart, said:

" Sir, in the name of Heaven, do not drive me away, but listen to what I am going to say to you; and if you cannot do me justice, you will at least not have to reproach yourself some day, before God, with having been an accomplice in a crime."

Van Systens stamped his foot with impatience. This was the second time that Rosa had disturbed him in the midst of a work which appealed to his vanity both as Burgomaster and as President of the Haarlem Society.

" But my report! " he cried, " my report on the black tulip! "

" Sir," resumed Rosa, with all the firmness of innocence and truth, " your report on the black tulip will be based, if you do not listen to me, on a crime or a deception. I beg of you, sir, to make this M. Boxtel come here, before you and before me: this M. Boxtel, who I maintain is M. Jacob, and I swear to you that I will not dispute his ownership of the tulip, if I do not recognise both the tulip and the man himself."

" My word! that would carry us a long way, wouldn't it? "

" What do you mean?"

" I ask you, what will it prove even if you do recognise them?"

" Sir," said Rosa in desperation, " you are an honourable man. Well, not only are you going to give a man a prize for something which he has not done, but you are going to give it him for something which he has stolen."

Perhaps Rosa's earnestness had some effect on the mind of Van Systens, for he was about to reply more gently to the unfortunate young woman, when a great noise was heard in the street; it appeared to be merely a continuation of the noise which Rosa had already heard in the Groote-Markt, without attaching any importance to it and without being disturbed by it in her fervent prayer.

Vociferous cheers shook the house.

M. van Systens listened intently to these cheers, which Rosa had at first not noticed, and which she did not now take to be anything very unusual.

" What is that?" cried the burgomaster. " Is it possible? did I hear aright?"

And without paying any further attention to Rosa, he left her where she was, and ran into the anteroom.

Scarcely had he reached it, when he cried out at the sight of his staircase, crowded with people almost up to the landing.

Accompanied, or rather followed, by the crowd, a young man, simply dressed, in a coat of violet velvet, embroidered with silver, was ascending, with dignified slowness, the beautifully clean and white stone steps.

Behind him walked two officers, one belonging to a cavalry regiment, the other to the navy.

Van Systens, making his way through his excited domestics, bowed and almost prostrated himself before the newcomer, who was the cause of all this commotion.

"My Lord!" he exclaimed, "my Lord! Your Highness in my house! This is an honour which will make my humble abode famous forever."

"My dear M. van Systens," said William of Orange, with that serenity which, with him, took the place of a smile, "I am a true Hollander. I love water, and beer, and flowers, and sometimes even the cheese which the French are fond of. Among flowers, those which I prefer are, of course, tulips. I heard it stated at Leyden that the city of Haarlem at last possessed the black tulip, and having made sure that the news was true, though incredible, I have come to ask the president of the Horticultural Society for more information about it."

"Oh, my Lord!" said Van Systens, delighted, "what an honour for the society should its labours please your Highness!"

"Have you the flower here?" said the Prince, who no doubt already repented of having spoken too much.

"Alas! no, my Lord, I have not got it here."

Member of the Horticultural Society

" And where is it? "

" At the owner's."

" Who is the owner? "

" A worthy tulip-grower of Dort."

" Of Dort? "

" Yes."

" And what is his name? "

" Boxtel."

" Where is he staying? "

" At the White Swan. I will send for him, and if, while waiting, your Highness will do me the honour of coming into my sitting-room, he will hasten, knowing that your Highness is here, to bring his tulip for your Highness to see."

" Very well, send for him."

" Yes, your Highness, only . . ."

" What? "

" Oh, nothing of any importance, my Lord."

" Everything is of importance in this world, M. van Systens."

" Well, my lord, a difficulty has arisen."

" What is it? "

" The tulip has already been claimed by pretenders. It is true, it is worth a hundred thousand florins."

" Is this really so? "

" Yes, my Lord, by pretenders, by swindlers."

" That is a criminal offence, M. van Systens."

" Yes, your Highness."

" And have you any proofs of this crime? "

The Black Tulip

"No, my Lord, the guilty woman . . ."

"The guilty woman, sir?"

"I mean the woman who claims the tulip, my Lord, is here, in the next room."

"Here! And what do you think about the matter, M. van Systens?"

"I think, my Lord, that the prospect of the hundred thousand florins has tempted her."

"And she claims the tulip?"

"Yes, my Lord."

"And what does she say, on her side, by way of proof?"

"I was about to question her when your Highness arrived."

"Let us hear what she has to say, M. van Systens. I am the chief magistrate in the country. I will hear the case, and see that justice is done."

"Here is my King Solomon found already," said Van Systens, bowing, and showing the way to the Prince.

The latter was going to pass in front of the burgomaster, but he suddenly stopped and said:

"Go first, and call me simply Mynheer."

They entered the president's office.

Rosa was still in the same place, leaning against the window, and looking through the glass into the garden.

"Ah! a Frisian girl," said the Prince, perceiving Rosa's cap of cloth-of-gold, and her red skirts.

Rosa turned round on hearing their steps, but

scarcely saw the Prince, who had seated himself in the darkest corner of the room.

All her attention was devoted, as we may well imagine, to the important personage called Van Systens, and not to the unpretending stranger who followed the master of the house, and who was probably no one of any consequence.

The quiet stranger took a book from the bookcase, and made a sign to Van Systens to commence the examination.

Van Systens, on a further sign from the young man in the velvet coat, sat down and, quite delighted and proud of his newly acquired importance, said to Rosa:

" Young woman, do you promise to tell me the truth, and the whole truth, with regard to this tulip? "

" I promise."

" You may speak before this gentleman; he is one of the members of the Horticultural Society."

" Sir," said Rosa, " what can I say to you that I have not said already? "

" Well, what then? "

" Then I come back to the request which I made to you."

" What to do? "

" To make M. Boxtel come here with his tulip. If I do not recognise it as mine, I will say so frankly; but if I recognise it, I will claim it, even if I have to go to his Highness the Stadtholder with my proofs in my hand."

The Black Tulip

" You have some proofs, then, my child? "

" God, who knows I am in the right, will provide them."

Van Systens exchanged a look with the Prince, who, from the moment when Rosa began to speak, had apparently been trying to recollect something, as though this was not the first time that he had heard her voice.

An official went to fetch Boxtel. Van Systens continued the examination.

" And on what do you base your assertion that you are the owner of the black tulip? " he said.

" On the very simple fact that I planted it, and raised it, in my own room."

" In your own room? And where is your room? "

" At Loevestein."

" You come from Loevestein, then? "

" I am the daughter of the jailer at the fortress there."

The Prince made a slight gesture, which signi-fied, " Ah! that is it, I remember now."

And still pretending to read, he looked at Rosa with more attention than ever.

" And you love flowers? " continued Van Systens.

" Yes, sir."

" Then you are an experienced flower-grower? "

Rosa hesitated a moment; then, speaking from the very bottom of her heart, she said:

" Gentlemen, I am speaking to men of honour? "

There was such earnestness and sincerity in her

voice, that Van Systens and the Prince both replied at the same moment by a gesture of assent.

"Well, then, I am not an experienced flower-grower. No, I am only a poor girl, a daughter of the people, a poor peasant from Friesland, who, three months ago, did not even know how to read and write. No, the black tulip was not discovered by me."

"By whom was it discovered, then?"

"By a poor prisoner of Loevestein."

"By a political prisoner, then," said the Prince.

At the sound of his voice Rosa started in her turn.

"By a political prisoner," continued the Prince, "for at Loevestein there are only political prisoners."

And he began to read again, or at least pretended to do so.

"Yes," replied Rosa, trembling, "yes, by a political prisoner."

Van Systens turned pale at hearing such a confession before such a witness.

"Continue," said William coldly to the president of the Horticultural Society.

"Oh! sir," said Rosa, addressing herself to him whom she thought her real judge, "I am going to make a grave accusation against myself."

"Yes, indeed," said Van Systens, "for the political prisoners at Loevestein ought to be in solitary confinement."

"Alas! sir."

"And, according to what you have said, it would

281

The Black Tulip

seem that you have taken advantage of your position as the jailer's daughter, and have been in communication with this prisoner, in order to cultivate flowers."

"Yes, sir," murmured Rosa, "yes, I am obliged to confess it. I used to see him every day."

"Unhappy girl!" cried M. van Systens.

Observing Rosa's terror and the president's paleness, the Prince raised his head, and in the clear and precise tone which was characteristic of him, said:

"That has nothing to do with the members of the Horticultural Society. They have to judge the black tulip, and have nothing to do with political offences. Go on, young woman, go on."

By an eloquent look Van Systens, in the name of tulips, thanked the new member of the Horticultural Society.

Rosa, reassured by this slight encouragement which she had received from the stranger, related all that had happened during the preceding three months, all she had done, all she had suffered. She described the harshness of Gryphus, the destruction of the first bulb, the grief of the prisoner, the precautions taken to secure the success of the second bulb, the patience of the prisoner, his anguish at their separation, how he no longer ate or drank, because he could no longer hear any news of his tulip, his joy at their reunion, and, lastly, the despair which had fallen on both, when they saw that the tulip which had just flowered had been stolen from them an hour after it opened.

Member of the Horticultural Society

All this was related with an air of truthfulness which, though it left the Prince apparently unmoved, did not fail to have its effect on M. van Systens.

"But," said the Prince, "you have not known this prisoner long, have you?"

Rosa opened her large eyes and looked at the stranger, who drew back into the shadow as though he did not wish her to see him.

"Why so, sir?" she asked.

"Because the jailer Gryphus and his daughter have only been at Loevestein four months."

"That is so, sir."

"And unless you asked for your father to be moved, in order to follow some prisoner, who had been transferred from The Hague to Loevestein . . ."

"Sir!" said Rosa, blushing.

"Finish your story," said William.

"I confess it: I did know the prisoner at The Hague."

"Happy prisoner!" said William, with a smile.

At this moment, the official who had been sent to Boxtel's returned, and informed the Prince that the man whom he had been sent to fetch was following close behind with his tulip.

XXVII

THE THIRD BULB

Scarcely had Boxtel's approach been announced, when Boxtel in person entered the president's sitting-room; he was followed by two men, who carried their precious burden in a box, and deposited it on a table.

The Prince, being informed of this, left the president's office, passed into the sitting-room, admired the tulip without saying anything, and returned silently to his seat in the obscure corner where he himself had placed his chair.

Rosa, pale, breathless, and terrified, waited for them to invite her to go and look at the tulip.

She heard Boxtel's voice.

" It is he! " she cried.

The Prince signed to her to go and look into the sitting-room through the half-open door.

" It is my tulip! " cried Rosa, " yes, I recognise it! Oh, my poor Cornelius! "

And she burst into tears.

The Prince rose, went to the door, and stood there for a moment in the light.

The Third Bulb

Rosa's eyes were fixed on him. She felt more certain than ever that this was not the first time she had seen him.

" M. Boxtel," said the Prince, " come in here."

Boxtel hurried forward, and found himself face to face with William of Orange.

" His Highness! " he cried out, drawing back.

" His Highness? " repeated Rosa, quite amazed.

At this exclamation on his left, Boxtel turned and recognised Rosa.

At the sight of her the jealous man shook from head to foot, as though he had touched a galvanic battery.

" Ah! " said the Prince to himself, " he is disconcerted."

But Boxtel, by a powerful effort, had already recovered himself.

" M. Boxtel," said William, " it seems that you have discovered the secret of the black tulip."

" Yes, my Lord," replied Boxtel in a rather unsteady voice.

His agitation might, it is true, have been caused by the emotion which the tulip-fancier had experienced on first recognising William.

" But," continued the Prince, " here is a young woman who also claims to have discovered it."

Boxtel smiled disdainfully, and shrugged his shoulders.

William followed all his movements with singular interest and curiosity.

The Black Tulip

"You do not know this young girl, then?" said the Prince.

"No, my Lord."

"And you, young woman, do you know M. Boxtel?"

"No, I do not know M. Boxtel, but I know M. Jacob."

"What do you mean?"

"I mean that, at Loevestein, the man who now calls himself Isaac Boxtel used to call himself M. Jacob."

"What do you say to that, M. Boxtel?"

"I say that this girl is telling lies, my Lord."

"You say you have never been at Loevestein?"

Boxtel hesitated; the imperious and searching gaze of the Prince prevented him from lying.

"I do not deny that I have been at Loevestein, but I deny having stolen the tulip."

"You stole it from me, out of my own room," cried Rosa indignantly.

"I deny it."

"Listen to me. Do you deny having followed me into the garden, on the day when I was preparing the flower-bed in which I intended to plant it? Do you deny having followed me in the garden, on the day on which I pretended to plant it? Do you deny that, on that evening, after I had gone out again, you flung yourself on the spot where you hoped to find the bulb? Do you deny having rummaged in the ground with your hands, though in vain, thank God! for it was only

286

a trick to learn your intentions? Answer, do you deny all that? "

Boxtel did not think it advisable to answer these different questions. Taking no notice of Rosa's argument, he turned to the Prince and said:

" My Lord, for twenty years I have cultivated tulips at Dordrecht. I have even acquired a certain reputation in the art: one of my hybrids is known in the catalogues by an illustrious name. I dedicated it to the King of Portugal. Now, this is the truth of the matter. This young woman knew that I had found the black tulip, and, in concert with a lover she has in the fortress of Loevestein, she formed a plan to ruin me by appropriating the prize of a hundred thousand florins, which I hope that, thanks to your justice, I shall still obtain."

" Oh! " cried Rosa, furiously.

" Silence! " said the Prince.

Then, turning to Boxtel, he added:

" And what sort of person is this prisoner, who, you say, is the lover of this young girl? "

Rosa nearly fainted away, for the prisoner had been placed in confinement as a great criminal, by the Prince's own order.

Nothing could have suited Boxtel better than this question.

" What sort of man is the prisoner? " he repeated.

" Yes."

" The prisoner, your Highness, is a man whose name alone will be enough to show your Highness how much faith you can have in his honesty. The prisoner is a political criminal, once condemned to death."

"And what is his name?"

Rosa, with a gesture of despair, hid her face in her hands.

"His name is Cornelius van Baerle," said Boxtel, "and he is the godson of that scoundrel, Cornelius de Witt."

The Prince started. His dark eyes flashed, and a deathlike coldness spread itself over his impassive countenance.

He went to Rosa, and with his finger made her a sign to remove her hands from her face.

Rosa obeyed, as a mesmerized person would have done, without seeing.

"It was, then, in order to follow this man, that you came to me at Leyden to ask for the transfer of your father?"

Rosa bowed her head, and sinking down as though crushed, murmured:

"Yes, my Lord."

"Go on," said the Prince to Boxtel.

"I have no more to say," resumed the latter. "Your Highness knows all. But what I did not wish to say, because it will make this girl blush for her ingratitude, is this: I went to Loevestein because business took me to that town. I there made the acquaintance of old Gryphus, and I fell in love with his daughter. I asked her in marriage, and as I was not

The Third Bulb

rich, I imprudently confided to him my hopes of obtaining the hundred thousand florins; and to justify these hopes, I showed him the black tulip. This girl's lover had pretended, when at Dordrecht, to cultivate tulips, in order to have a cloak for the political plots he was engaged in, and now he and she together plotted my ruin.

" On the day before that on which the tulip would flower, it was carried off from my house by this young girl, and taken to her room, from which, however, I was fortunate enough to recover it, at the moment when she had impudently sent a messenger to announce to the members of the Horticultural Society that she had discovered the black tulip; but even that did not put her out of countenance. No doubt, during the few hours that she had it in her room, she will have shown it to some persons, whom she will call as witnesses. But, happily, your Highness has now been forewarned against this adventuress and her witnesses."

" Oh! my God, what infamy! " cried Rosa, throwing herself in tears at the feet of the Stadtholder, who, although he believed her guilty, could not help taking pity on her terrible anguish.

" You have done wrong, young woman," he said, " and your lover shall be punished for having given you such advice. For you are so young and have such an honest look, that I am inclined to believe that the wickedness is not yours, but his."

" Sir! sir! " cried Rosa, " Cornelius is not guilty."
William started.

The Black Tulip

"Not guilty of having advised you—that is what you mean, is it not?"

"I mean, my Lord, that Cornelius is no more guilty of the second crime imputed to him than he was of the first."

"Of the first? and do you know what the first crime was? Do you know what he was accused and convicted of? Of having, as the accomplice of Cornelius de Witt, hidden the correspondence of the Grand Pensionary with the Marquis of Louvois."

"Well, my Lord, he was not aware that he was keeping that correspondence: he knew nothing about it. If he had known, he would have told me. Would so transparent a soul have kept a secret from me? No, no, my Lord, I repeat, even though I incur your anger by so doing, Cornelius is no more guilty of the first crime than of the second, or of the second than of the first. Oh, if you only knew my Cornelius!"

"A De Witt!" cried Boxtel. "Ah! my Lord knows him only too well: he has already once granted him his life."

"Silence!" said the Prince. "All these political matters, I have already observed, have nothing to do with the Horticultural Society of Haarlem." Then, knitting his brow, he added:

"As for the tulip, M. Boxtel, make your mind easy. Justice will be done."

Boxtel, with joy in his heart, bowed to the Prince, and received the congratulations of the president.

"You, young woman," continued William of

Orange, "have been very near committing a crime. I shall not punish you for it, but the real criminal shall pay the penalty for both of you. A man of his name may conspire, may even commit treason, . . . but he should not be a thief."

"A thief!" cried Rosa, "a thief! my Cornelius? Oh! my Lord, be careful; it would kill him to hear you say so; your words would kill him more surely than the executioner's axe on the Buitenhof would have done. If there has been a theft, my Lord, I swear it is this man who has committed it."

"Prove it," said Boxtel, coldly.

"Well, yes, then, with the help of God I will prove it," said Rosa, with great animation.

Then, turning to Boxtel:

"The tulip was yours?" she said.

"Yes."

"How many bulbs had it?"

Boxtel hesitated a moment; but he felt that the young girl would not ask this question, if the two known bulbs were the only ones in existence.

"Three," said he.

"What has become of these bulbs?" asked Rosa.

"What has become of them? . . . One was a failure, the other produced the black tulip . . ."

"And the third?"

"The third?"

"Yes, the third, where is it?"

"The third is in my house," said Boxtel, quite confused.

The Black Tulip

"At your house—where? at Loevestein, or at Dordrecht?"

"At Dordrecht," said Boxtel.

"You lie," said Rosa. "My Lord," she added, turning towards the Prince, "I will tell you the true history of these three bulbs. The first was crushed by my father in the prisoner's cell, and this man knows it, for he hoped to get possession of the bulb, and when he saw his hope of doing so disappointed, he nearly fell out with my father for having deprived him of it. The second, cared for by me, has produced the black tulip; and the third, the last "—the young girl drew it from her bosom—"the third is here, in the same paper in which it was wrapped with the two others, at the moment when Cornelius van Baerle, on the point of mounting the scaffold, gave me all three of them."

And Rosa, taking the bulb out of the paper in which it was wrapped, held it out to the Prince, who took it in his hand and examined it.

"But, my Lord," muttered Boxtel, "this girl may have stolen it, as she did the tulip."

He was alarmed at the attention with which the Prince was examining the bulb, and still more at the eagerness with which Rosa was reading some lines written on the paper which remained in her hands.

Suddenly her eyes brightened; with breathless haste she reread the mysterious paper and, uttering a cry, handed it to the Prince, saying:

"Oh! read this, my Lord—in Heaven's name, read this!"

The Third Bulb

William handed the third bulb to the president, took the paper, and began to read.

Scarcely had he cast his eyes on the sheet when he staggered, his hand shook as if it would let the paper fall, and there came into his face a dreadful expression of sorrow and of pity.

The sheet of paper which Rosa had given him was the leaf of the Bible, which Cornelius de Witt had sent to Van Baerle at Dordrecht, by the hand of Craeke, his brother John's servant, begging him to burn the correspondence of the Grand Pensionary with Louvois.

The message, it may be remembered, was as follows:

"DEAR GODSON: Burn the packet which I intrusted to you; burn it without looking into it, without opening it, so that you may remain quite ignorant of its contents. Secrets of the kind which it contains are fatal to those with whom they are deposited. Burn it, and you will have saved John and Cornelius. Farewell, and love me.

"CORNELIUS DE WITT.

"August 20, 1672."

This sheet of paper was the proof, both of Van Baerle's innocence, and of his right to the ownership of the bulbs of the black tulip.

Rosa and the Stadtholder exchanged one look.

Rosa's meant, "Now, you see."

The Stadtholder's signified, "Keep silence and wait."

The Black Tulip

The Prince wiped away a drop of cold sweat, which had fallen from his forehead to his cheek.

He folded the paper slowly, allowing his eyes to follow his thoughts into that bottomless and irremediable abyss, which is called remorse and shame for the past.

In a short time he recovered himself with an effort, and said:

"Go, M. Boxtel, justice shall be done, I promise you."

Then to the president he added:

"You, my dear M. van Systens, take charge of this young woman and of the tulip, and keep them safe here. Farewell."

Every one bowed, and the Prince left the house, bending beneath the storm of popular acclamations which greeted him.

Boxtel returned to the White Swan in a painful state of mind. The paper which William had received from Rosa's hands, and had read and folded up and placed so carefully in his pocket, troubled him extremely.

Rosa approached the tulip, kissed its leaves reverently, and, with absolute confidence in God, murmured:

"My God, didst thou know to what end my good Cornelius taught me to read?"

Yes, God knew, for he it is, who punishes and rewards men, according to their deserts.

XXVIII

THE SONG OF THE FLOWERS

WHILE the events which we have just recorded were taking place, the unhappy Van Baerle, forgotten in his cell in the fortress of Loevestein, was suffering, at the hands of Gryphus, everything that a prisoner can suffer, when his jailer has made up his mind to become an executioner.

Gryphus, finding that he could obtain no news of Rosa, or of Jacob, persuaded himself that everything that had happened to him was the work of the devil, and that Dr. Cornelius van Baerle was the agent of the devil on earth.

The result was, that one fine morning—it was the third after the disappearance of Jacob and Rosa—he went up to Cornelius's cell, more furious even than usual.

Cornelius, with his elbows resting on the window, his head supported by his hands, and his looks lost in the mists of the horizon, which the mills of Dordrecht were beating with their wings, was trying to refresh himself with the pure air, in order to be better able to keep back his tears and prevent all his philosophy from evaporating.

The Black Tulip

The pigeons were still there; but hope was absent, and the future was as dark as the present.

Alas! Rosa was too closely watched to be able to come. Would she be able to write to him? and if she did write, would she be able to send him her letters?

No! He had seen on the previous evening, and on the evening before that, too much fury and malignity in the eyes of old Gryphus to believe that his vigilance would be relaxed for a moment; and then, besides confinement, besides absence, had she not perhaps to suffer still worse torments? Would not this brutal and worthless drunkard avenge himself after the fashion of the fathers in the Greek drama? when the Hollands got into his head, would not his arm, too well mended by Cornelius, have the strength of two arms? and had he not a stick?

This idea, that perhaps Rosa was being maltreated, made Cornelius wild.

He then felt how useless, and powerless, and helpless he was. He asked himself whether God had been just in so afflicting two innocent creatures. And certainly at that moment he began to doubt. Misery does not assist belief.

Van Baerle had determined to write to Rosa. But where was Rosa? He had also had the idea of writing to The Hague to forestall Gryphus, who would certainly try, by making a complaint against him, to bring down new storms upon his head.

But what was he to write with? Gryphus had

The Song of the Flowers

taken away his pencils and his paper. Besides, even if he had had both, Gryphus would certainly not take charge of the letter.

Then Cornelius turned over in his mind, again and again, all the pitiful shifts adopted by prisoners.

He thought, too, of escaping, a thing he had not dreamt of when he could see Rosa every day. But the more he thought the more impossible escape appeared. He was one of those choice spirits who have a horror of the commonplace, and who often miss all the best opportunities in life, through not following the common track, that great high-road of the ordinary man, which leads to everything.

"How would it be possible," said Cornelius to himself, "for me to escape from Loevestein from which Grotius has escaped before me? Since his escape, has not every precaution been taken? Are not the windows strongly barred? Are not the doors double or triple? Are not the sentinels ten times more watchful?

"Then, besides the barred windows, the double doors, the sentinels more vigilant than ever, have I not in Gryphus an ever-watchful Argus, an Argus all the more dangerous because he has the keen eyes of hatred? Finally, am I not paralyzed by one single circumstance—the absence of Rosa? Even if I were to use up ten years of my life in making a file to cut through the bars, or in platting ropes to let myself down from the window, or in fastening wings to my shoulders so as to fly away like Dædalus . . . but fortune has entirely deserted me; the file will lose its edge, the rope will break, my wings will melt in the sun. I shall fall and die miserably. They will pick me up lame, one-armed, or with my legs broken off short. They will put me in the museum at The Hague, between the blood-stained doublet of William the Silent and the mermaid caught at Stavesen, and my enterprise will have no result, except to obtain for me the honour of being one of the curiosities of Holland.

"No—and this will be better—some fine day Gryphus will play me some dirty trick. I have lost all my patience since I lost the joy and the companionship of Rosa, and especially since I lost my tulips. There is no doubt of it, some day or other Gryphus will attack me in a manner which will be offensive to my self-respect, or insulting to my love, or dangerous to my personal security. I feel, since I have been in prison, a strange, irrepressible, and aggressive energy. I long for a struggle, for a fight, for blows. I shall spring at the old scoundrel's throat, and strangle him."

At these last words, Cornelius stopped for a moment, with his eyes fixed and his lips drawn tight.

He turned over in his mind a pleasing idea which had occurred to him.

"But," he continued, "when Gryphus is once strangled, why not take his keys? Why not go down the staircase as if I had just done a most virtuous action? Why not go and find Rosa in her room? Why not explain to her what had happened, and leap with her from her window into the Waal? I can swim well enough for the two of us . . .

"Rosa—but, good heavens! this Gryphus is her father. Much as she loves me, she would never approve of my strangling her father, brutal as he is, and malicious as he has been. An argument will be required, and just as I am coming to the end of it, some assistant or turnkey will arrive, who will have found Gryphus still breathing, or quite dead, and he will place his hand on my shoulder. I shall then see the Buitenhof again, and the flash of that villainous sword, which this time will not stop on its way, but will make acquaintance with my neck. No more of that, Cornelius, my friend. It is a bad plan.

"But, then, what is to become of me? and how am I to find Rosa?"

Such were the reflections of Cornelius on the third day after the sad scene of separation between Rosa and her father, at the moment when he was standing at the window in the attitude we have described.

It was at this moment that Gryphus entered.

He held in his hand a heavy stick, his eyes gleamed with malice, an evil smile curled his lips, his very walk showed his malevolence, and his whole person, though he said not a word, breathed hatred.

Cornelius, restrained by the necessity of patience, a necessity which reason had almost turned into conviction, heard him come in and guessed that it was

The Black Tulip

he, but did not even turn round. He knew that this time Rosa would not come with him.

Nothing is more irritating to persons who are angry than indifference on the part of the person against whom their anger is directed. They have had the trouble of working themselves up, and they do not like to have had it for nothing. It is not worth doing, if one cannot have the satisfaction of at least causing a little disturbance. Every honest rascal who has excited his evil inclinations wishes at the very least to make some one feel the painful effects of them.

Accordingly, Gryphus, seeing that Cornelius did not stir, tried by a vigorous " Hem! hem! " to attract his attention.

Cornelius hummed between his teeth the sad but charming Song of the Flowers.

> " Children are we of secret fire,
>   That warms the veins of Earth ;
>   Children are we of dawn and dew,
>   Of air and fruitful showers ;
>   But above all are children of
>   The sky, for we are flowers."

This song, the quiet sadness of which was heightened by the softness and sweetness of the melody, exasperated Gryphus.

He struck the flags with his stick, calling out:

" Eh! master singer, don't you hear me? "

" Good-day," said Cornelius; and he resumed his song:

The Song of the Flowers

> " Men love us well, but in their love
> Our lives they take, or spoil;
> We hold to earth but by a thread,
> Our root beneath the soil;
> But to the sky our arms we raise . . ."

" Ah! you accursed sorcerer, you are trying to make game of me, I believe," cried Gryphus.

Cornelius continued:

> " And this we do because we know
> The sky for our true home;
> Thence came our souls—our perfumes these,
> And thither they return."

Gryphus approached the prisoner.

" But don't you see, then, that I have found a very good way of bringing you to reason and forcing you to confess your crimes to me? "

" Have you gone mad, my dear M. Gryphus? " asked Cornelius, turning round.

As he did so, he observed the distorted features, the glittering eyes, and the foaming mouth of the old jailer.

" The devil! " he said, " it seems we are worse than mad, we are raving lunatics."

Gryphus flourished his stick.

But, without moving, Van Baerle crossed his arms and said:

" Ah! master Gryphus, you appear to be threatening me."

" Oh, yes! I do threaten you," cried the jailer.

" And with what? "

The Black Tulip

"First of all, look at what I have in my hand."

"I fancy that is a stick," said Cornelius calmly, "and a big stick too, but I do not suppose that's what you are threatening me with."

"Oh! you don't suppose so! and why not?"

"Because every jailer who strikes a prisoner is liable to a twofold punishment. The first, Article 9 of the Regulations of Loevestein:

"'Any jailer, inspector, or warder, who lays hands on a political prisoner, will be dismissed.'"

"'Hands!'" shouted Gryphus furiously, "but the stick? Ah! the regulations say nothing about sticks."

"The second," continued Cornelius, "is not included in the regulations, but will be found in the New Testament; the second is this:

"'He that takes the sword shall perish with the sword.'

"He that strikes with the stick shall be thrashed with the stick."

Gryphus, more and more exasperated by the calm and sententious tone of Cornelius, brandished his cudgel; but at the moment when he raised it, Cornelius darted towards him, snatched it from his hand, and put it under his own arm.

Gryphus yelled with rage.

"There, there, my good man, do not run the risk of losing your place."

"Ah! you sorcerer, I will pay you out for this in another way, you'll see."

"Just as you please."

The Song of the Flowers

" You see that my hand is empty."

" Yes, I see that, and I am very well satisfied to see it so."

" You know that it is not usually empty when I come upstairs in the morning."

" Ah! that is true, you generally bring me the worst soup and the most miserable rations that can possibly be imagined. But that is no punishment to me. I eat only bread, and the worse the bread is to your taste, the better it is to mine, M, Gryphus."

" The better it is to yours? "

" Yes."

" And why so? "

" Oh! the reason is very simple."

" Tell it me, then."

" With pleasure. I know you think that by giving me bad bread you make me suffer."

" As a matter of fact, I do not give it you in order to please you, you brigand."

" Well, I, who am a sorcerer, as you know, I change your bad bread into very good bread, which I enjoy more than I should cakes, and thus I have a double pleasure: first, that of eating what I like, and second, that of making you furiously angry."

Gryphus almost howled with rage.

" Ah! you admit that you are a sorcerer, then? "

" My word, I should think I am. I don't tell everybody so, because it might bring me to the stake, like Gaufredy. or Urbain Grandier; but when we are by ourselves, I don't see why I should not tell you."

The Black Tulip

" Very good, very good," said Gryphus, " but if a sorcerer makes white bread out of black, will not the sorcerer die of hunger if he has no bread at all? "

" Eh? " said Cornelius.

" Very well, then, I won't bring you any bread at all in future, and at the end of eight days we shall see."

Cornelius turned pale.

" And this," continued Gryphus, " we will begin from to-day. Since you are such a wonderful sorcerer, let us see you change the furniture in your cell into bread. As for me, I shall get the eighteen halfpence a day which I am paid for your food."

" But this is murder! " cried Cornelius, overcome by the sudden feeling of terror with which this horrible kind of death inspired him.

" Oh, well," continued Gryphus jeeringly, " since you are a sorcerer, you will live in spite of everything."

Cornelius resumed his laughing air, and shrugging his shoulders, said:

" Did you not see me make pigeons come here from Dordrecht? "

" Well, what of that? " said Gryphus.

" Well, a pigeon is very nice, roasted; a man who eats a pigeon every day will not starve, I fancy."

" And what about the fire? "

" Fire? Why, you know well that I have made a compact with the devil. Do you think the devil will leave me without fire, when fire is his own particular element? "

The Song of the Flowers

" A man, however strong, cannot eat a pigeon every day. Bets have been made about that, and those who made them have always failed."

" Well, but when I am tired of pigeons," said Cornelius, " I will make the fish from the Waal and the Meuse come up here."

Gryphus opened his big eyes in a fright.

" I am rather fond of fish," continued Cornelius; " you never give me any. Well, I will take advantage of the fact that you want to starve me to death, and will regale myself with fish."

Gryphus was nearly fainting with fright and rage combined; but pulling himself together, he said:

" Very well, since you force me to it," and he drew a knife from his pocket and opened it.

" Ah! a knife! " said Cornelius, making ready to defend himself with his stick.

XXIX

The Song of the Flowers

IN WHICH VAN BAERLE, BEFORE QUITTING LOEVE-
STEIN, SETTLES HIS ACCOUNTS WITH GRYPHUS

THEY remained thus for a moment, Gryphus on the offensive, and Van Baerle ready to meet the attack.

Then, as the situation seemed likely to be indefinitely prolonged, Cornelius, not understanding the reasons for this renewed outbreak of anger on the part of his antagonist, asked:

" Well, what more do you want? "

" I will tell you what I want," replied Gryphus, " I want you to give me back my daughter."

" Your daughter? " cried Cornelius.

" Yes, Rosa, Rosa whom you have spirited away by your devilish arts. Come now, will you tell me where she is? "

And the attitude of the jailer became more and more threatening.

" Is Rosa not at Loevestein? " cried Van Baerle.

" You know well she is not. Once more, will you give me back Rosa? "

" Ah! " said Cornelius, " this is a trap you are laying for me."

Van Baerle Settles with Gryphus

" Once more, and for the last time, will you tell me where my daughter is? "

" Oh, guess it, you scoundrel, if you don't know."

" Wait a moment," muttered Gryphus, whose trembling lips showed the madness that was beginning to turn his brain. " Ah! you won't say anything! Well, I will open your mouth for you."

He made a step towards Cornelius, showing him the weapon which glittered in his hand.

" Do you see this knife? " said he; " well, I have killed more than fifty black cocks with it. I will kill their master, the devil, too, just as I killed them; do you understand that? "

" But, you ruffian," said Cornelius, " you mean to murder me, then? "

" I mean to open your heart, so as to discover where you have hidden my daughter."

And saying these words with delirious fury, Gryphus rushed upon Cornelius, who had only just time to spring behind his table so as to escape the first blow.

Gryphus brandished his huge knife, uttering the most horrible threats.

Cornelius saw that, if he was out of reach of the hand, he was not out of reach of the weapon: the knife, thrown from a distance, could easily traverse the space between them and bury itself in his heart. He therefore lost not a moment, but, with the stick, which he had fortunately kept, struck Gryphus a violent blow on the wrist just above the knife.

The Black Tulip

The knife fell to the ground, and Cornelius put his foot on it.

Then, as Gryphus seemed bent on a struggle, which the pain of the blow from the stick, and the shame of having been twice disarmed, would render desperate, Cornelius took a decisive step.

He thrashed the jailer with the most matter-of-fact coolness, choosing at each blow the particular spot on which the terrible cudgel was to fall.

Gryphus soon begged for mercy.

But before doing so he had howled, and that very loudly: his cries had been heard, and had alarmed all the officials in the prison. Two warders, an inspector, and three or four guards, suddenly appeared, and surprised Cornelius in the midst of his labours with the stick, with the knife still under his foot.

At the sight of these witnesses of his offence, of which the extenuating circumstances, as they would now be called, were quite unknown, Cornelius felt that he was hopelessly lost.

All the appearances, in fact, were against him.

In the twinkling of an eye Cornelius was disarmed; and Gryphus, surrounded, lifted up, and supported, was able to count the bruises which were already swelling up on his shoulders and back, like so many hillocks on a rough mountain-side.

An offical report regarding the violent assault made by the prisoner on his jailer was drawn up on the spot, and as the account was prompted by Gryphus, it could not be accused of lukewarmness; the case was one of nothing less than open rebellion and the attempted murder of a jailer, long premeditated and prepared for.

While the document was being drawn up Gryphus, whose presence was not required after he had made his statement, was assisted downstairs by the two warders, groaning as he went.

During this time, the guards who had seized Cornelius occupied themselves in charitably instructing him in the usages and customs of Loevestein, which, as a matter of fact, he knew as well as they did, for the rules had been read to him on his arrival at the prison, and certain articles in the regulations had impressed themselves firmly on his mind.

Moreover, they described to him how the rules had been applied in the case of a prisoner named Mathias, who, in 1668, that is to say about five years before, had been guilty of an act of rebellion much less serious than that which Cornelius had committed. He had found his soup too hot, and had thrown it at the head of the chief warder, who, in wiping his face after this ablution, had been so unfortunate as to remove some of the skin.

Within twelve hours Mathias had been taken from his cell; then been conducted to the jailer's office, where he was registered as quitting Loevestein; then been taken to the Esplanade, from which there is a very fine view over eleven leagues of country. There they had tied his hands, bandaged his eyes, and recited three prayers. Then they had invited him to kneel down, and the guards of Loevestein, to the number of twelve, had, at a sign made by a sergeant, very skilfully lodged twelve musket-balls in his body.

Upon which Mathias had incontinently died.

Cornelius listened to this disagreeable story with great attention. Then, having heard the end of it, he said:

" Ah! within twelve hours, you say? "

" Yes, the twelfth hour had not even struck, I believe," said the narrator of the story.

" Thank you," said Cornelius.

There still lingered on the guard's lips the pleasant smile which had served as a full stop to his recital, when a loud step was heard on the stairs.

Spurs jingled on the worn edges of the steps.

The guards separated to allow an officer to pass.

The latter entered the cell of Cornelius while the clerk of the prison was still writing out the report.

" Is this number eleven? " he asked.

" Yes, captain," replied a non-commissioned officer.

" Then this is the cell of Cornelius van Baerle? "

" Precisely so, captain."

" Where is the prisoner? "

" Here, sir," replied Cornelius, growing rather pale in spite of his courage.

" Are you M. Cornelius van Baerle? " asked the officer, addressing himself this time to the prisoner.

" Yes, sir."

" Then follow me."

Van Baerle Settles with Gryphus

"Oh! oh!" said Cornelius, whose heart sank at the near approach of death, "how quickly they do their business in the fortress of Loevestein, and the fellow spoke of twelve hours!"

"Eh! what did I tell you?" said the guard-historian in Cornelius's ear.

"A lie."

"How is that?"

"You promised me twelve hours."

"Ah! yes, but then they have sent you an aide-de-camp of his Highness, one of his most intimate friends, even. The deuce! they did not pay such honour to poor Mathias."

"Come, come," said Cornelius, taking as deep a breath as he could, "come, let us show these people that a burgher, the godson of Cornelius de Witt, can, without making faces over it, receive as many musket-balls as a fellow named Mathias."

And he passed proudly before the registrar, who, on being interrupted in the performance of his duties, ventured to say to the officer:

"But, Captain van Deken, the official report is not yet finished."

"It is not worth while finishing it," replied the officer.

"Very good," replied the clerk philosophically, putting away his paper and pen in a worn and greasy writing-case.

"It was decreed by fate," thought poor Cornelius, "that I should not give my name in this world to a child, or to a flower, or to a book, the three things one, at least, of which God, so they say, expects from every moderately gifted man whom he deigns to intrust on this earth with the ownership of a soul and the use of a body."

And he followed the officer with resolute heart and uplifted head.

Cornelius counted the steps which lead to the Esplanade, regretting that he had not asked the guard how many there were, a thing which the soldier, in his officious affability, would certainly not have failed to tell him.

Cornelius regarded this journey as the last he would ever make in this life: but the only thing about it that he dreaded was that he would see Gryphus, and not see Rosa. What satisfaction he would see in the face of the father, and what grief in that of the young woman! How Gryphus would applaud this punishment, which was a ferocious vengeance on an act eminently just, which Cornelius felt in his conscience he had performed as a duty!

But Rosa, poor girl! was he not to see her? was he to die without having given her a last kiss, or, at the very least, a last farewell? Was he to die, too, without having any news of the great black tulip, and to awake on high, without knowing whither to turn his eyes in order to find it again?

Indeed, not to weep at such a moment, the poor tulip-fancier must have had around his heart more of the *æs triplex* than Horace attributes to the sailor who

Van Baerle Settles with Gryphus

was the first to visit the " ill-omened Acroceraunian rocks."

In vain Cornelius looked to the right, in vain he looked to the left; he arrived at the Esplanade without having seen Rosa, and without having seen Gryphus. The absence of the one almost compensated for that of the other.

Cornelius, on reaching the Esplanade, looked bravely about for the guards who were to be his executioners, and saw, indeed, a dozen soldiers standing together talking.

But they were standing together and talking, without muskets and without being drawn up in line. Indeed, they were rather whispering than talking, conduct which seemed to Cornelius not in accordance with the solemnity which usually reigns over such events.

Suddenly Gryphus, limping, staggering, and leaning on a crutch, appeared at the door of his office. He had concentrated in a last look of hatred all the fire of his old catlike gray eyes. He began to pour out against Cornelius such a torrent of curses and abuse that Cornelius, addressing the officer, said:

" Sir, I do not think it at all proper on your part to allow me to be so insulted by this man, especially at such a moment as this."

" Oh, well," said the officer laughing, " it is very natural that the fellow should have a spite against you, you seem to have given him a fine thrashing."

" But, sir, it was only in self-defence."

The Black Tulip

" Bah! " said the officer, with a shrug of the shoulders that was very philosophical, " bah! let him talk, what does it matter to you, now? "

A cold sweat broke out on Cornelius's forehead at this answer, which he regarded as ironical and rather brutal, especially from an officer who, he had been told, was attached to the person of the Prince.

The unfortunate man felt that he had no longer any resources, or any friends, and he resigned himself to his fate.

" Be it so," he murmured, bowing his head; " they offered many more insults to Christ, and though I am innocent, I must not compare myself with him. He would have allowed his jailer to strike him, and would not have struck in return."

Then turning towards the officer, who appeared to be politely waiting till he had finished his reflections, he said:

" Now, sir, where am I to go? "

The officer pointed out to him a carriage drawn by four horses, which reminded him strongly of the carriage which, under similar circumstances, he had once seen on the Buitenhof.

" Get into this," he said.

" Ah! " murmured Cornelius, " it seems that I am not to have the honour of the Esplanade, after all."

He said these words loud enough to be heard by the historian, who seemed to have attached himself to his person.

Doubtless he thought it his duty to give Cornelius

Van Baerle Settles with Gryphus

further information, for he approached the carriage-door, and while the officer, with his foot on the step, was giving some directions, he said, in a low voice:

"Condemned men have sometimes been taken to their own town and there, in order to make a better example of them, they have undergone their punishment in front of their own doors. It all depends on circumstances."

Cornelius thanked him by a sign.

Then to himself he said:

"Well, here, at any rate, is a fellow who never omits to give consolation when he has an opportunity. —My friend, I am indeed greatly obliged to you. Good-bye."

The carriage started.

"Ah! you scoundrel, you brigand!" shouted Gryphus, shaking his fist at the victim who was escaping him. "And to think that he goes off without giving me back my daughter!"

"If they take me to Dordrecht," said Cornelius, "I shall see, as I pass my house, whether my poor flower-beds have been ruined."

XXX

IN WHICH ONE BEGINS TO SUSPECT WHAT KIND OF
PUNISHMENT WAS RESERVED FOR CORNELIUS VAN
BAERLE

THE coach rolled on all day. It passed by Dordrecht, leaving it on the left hand, traversed Rotterdam, reached Delft. By five o'clock in the evening
it had gone at least twenty leagues.

Cornelius addressed some questions to the officer
who was, at once, his guard and his companion;
but circumspect as he was in his questions, he
was disappointed to find that they remained unan-
swered.

Cornelius regretted that he had not by his side the
guard who had so affably talked to him, without waiting to be asked.

He, no doubt, would have proffered, with regard
to the strange character of this third adventure,
details as pleasing, and explanations as precise, as
those which he had supplied with regard to the first
two.

They passed the night in the coach. The next
day, at dawn, Cornelius found himself beyond Leyden,

316

Cornelius Van Baerle's Punishment

having the North Sea on his left and the sea of Haarlem on his right.

Three hours later they entered Haarlem.

Cornelius did not know what was going on at Haarlem, and we will leave him in his ignorance until events enlighten him.

But with the reader, who has a right to know how things are going, even before our hero, it must be otherwise.

We have seen how Rosa and the tulip, like two orphan sisters, were left by Prince William of Orange in the care of President van Systens.

Rosa had heard nothing more of the Stadtholder till the evening of the day on which she had seen him at the president's.

Towards evening, an officer arrived at Van Systens's house; he came on behalf of his Highness to request Rosa to go to the Town Hall.

There, in the great council chamber into which she was taken, she found the Prince writing.

He was alone, and at his feet lay a large Frisian greyhound, which was looking fixedly at him, as though the faithful animal would have liked to try and do what no man was able to do, namely, read the thoughts of his master.

William continued to write for a moment longer; then, raising his eyes and seeing Rosa standing near the door:

"Come in," he said, and went on with his writing.

Rosa took a few steps towards the table.

" My Lord," she said, stopping short.

" That's right," said the Prince. " Sit down."

Rosa obeyed, for the Prince kept his eye on her; but scarcely had he turned them again to his papers, when she shyly retired.

The Prince finished his letter.

During this time the greyhound went over to Rosa, looked up at her, and licked her hand.

" Ah! " said William to the dog, " evidently this is a fellow-countrywoman; you recognise her."

Then, turning towards Rosa and fixing on her his gaze, which was at once searching and veiled, he said:

" Now then, my child."

The Prince was scarcely twenty-three; Rosa was about eighteen: he would have been nearer the mark if he had said " my sister."

" My child," said he, with that strangely imposing accent which chilled all who approached him, " we are alone, let us talk to each other."

Rosa trembled violently, and yet there was nothing but goodwill in the Prince's face.

" My Lord," she stammered.

" You have a father at Loevestein? "

" Yes, my Lord."

" Do you love him? "

" I do not love him, at least not as a daughter should, my Lord."

" It is wrong not to love one's father, my

Cornelius Van Baerle's Punishment

child, but it is right not to speak falsely to one's Prince."

Rosa lowered her eyes.

" And why do you not love your father?"

" My father is a bad man."

" And how does he show it?"

" My father ill-treats the prisoners."

" All of them?"

" All of them."

" But do you not reproach him with ill-treating some one in particular?"

" My father is particularly cruel to M. van Baerle, who . . ."

" Who is your lover."

Rosa stepped back.

" Whom I love, my Lord," she answered proudly.

" Since when?" asked the Prince.

" Since the first day I saw him."

" And you first saw him?"

" On the day after the Grand Pensionary and his brother Cornelius were put to death in such a horrible manner."

The lips of the Prince tightened, his face became pale, and his eye-lids dropped, so as for an instant to hide his eyes. After a moment's silence, he resumed:

" But what is the good of loving a man destined to live and die in prison?"

" There is this good in it, my Lord, that if he lives and dies in prison, I shall be able to help him to live and die."

The Black Tulip

"Then you would accept this position of wife of a prisoner?"

"I should be the proudest and happiest of human beings, if I were the wife of M. van Baerle; but . . ."

"But what?"

"I dare not say, my Lord."

"There is an accent of hope in your voice; what do you hope for?"

She raised her beautiful bright eyes to William's: there was in them a look so piercing that it found its way to the clemency which slept, with a sleep almost resembling that of death, in the depths of that gloomy heart.

"Ah! I understand."

Rosa smiled and clasped her hands.

"You hope in me," said the Prince.

"Yes, my Lord."

"Hum!"

The Prince sealed the letter which he had just written, and called one of his officers.

"M. van Deken," he said, "take this message to Loevestein. You will read the orders which I here give to the governor, and, as far as they concern you, you will execute them."

The officer saluted, and presently there was heard, echoing under the sonorous vault of the gateway, the gallop of a horse.

"My child," continued the Prince, "on Sunday there will be kept the Feast of the Tulip, and Sunday

Cornelius Van Baerle's Punishment

is the day after to-morrow. Dress yourself well, with
the help of these five hundred florins: for I wish that
day to be a great day for you."

"How would your Highness like me to be
dressed?"

"Wear the costume of a Frisian bride," said William; "it will suit you very well."

XXXI

HAARLEM

HAARLEM, which we entered three days ago with Rosa, and which we have just entered again with Cornelius, is a very pretty town, which prides itself with good reason on having more trees in it than any other town in Holland.

While other towns prided themselves on being remarkable for arsenals and dockyards, for shops and bazars, Haarlem made it her boast to surpass every town in the States in fine leafy elms, in tall poplars, and above all, in shady walks, above which the oak, the lime, and the chestnut spread a vaulted roof.

Seeing that Leyden, her neighbour, and Amsterdam, her queen, were on the way to becoming, the one a city of science and the other a city of commerce, Haarlem chose to be a city of agriculture, or rather, of horticulture.

And indeed, being well protected from the winds, and at the same time well supplied with air, and well warmed by the sun, she furnished gardeners with opportunities which other towns, with their sea-breezes or their too great exposure to the sky, were unable to afford.

Haarlem

And so at Haarlem were settled all those quiet, peaceable souls who loved the earth and its fruits, just as there were gathered together, at Rotterdam and at Amsterdam, all those restless and pushing spirits who loved commerce and voyages, and at The Hague, all the politicians and men of the world.

Leyden, as we have said, had been appropriated by the scholars.

Haarlem, then, cultivated a taste for pleasant things, for music, painting, orchards, walks, groves, and flower-beds.

Haarlem became crazed about flowers, and, among other flowers, about tulips. Haarlem offered prizes in honour of tulips; and thus we come, very naturally as one sees, to speak of the prize which the city offered on the 15th of May, 1673, in honour of the great black tulip, without spot or defect, which was to bring a hundred thousand florins to its discoverer.

Haarlem, having proclaimed its speciality, having made known its taste for flowers, at a time when the world was full of wars and seditions, having had the signal joy of seeing its special excellencies recognised, and the signal honour of seeing the ideal tulip actually flower, Haarlem, the pretty town, full of trees and of sunshine, of light and of shade, desired to celebrate the awarding of the prize by a festival the memory of which would long survive in the minds of men.

She had the more right to do so because Holland is the country of festivals; never did an idle nature show more ardour in shouting, singing, and dancing, than did that of the good republicans of the Seven Provinces on occasions of amusement.

We see this in the pictures of the two Teniers.

It is quite certain that lazy people are of all men the most eager to tire themselves out, not when they set themselves to work, but when they set themselves to enjoy anything.

Haarlem, then, had a threefold reason for exultation, inasmuch as she had to celebrate a threefold solemnity: the black tulip had been discovered; William of Orange, true Hollander that he was, intended to assist at the ceremony. And finally, it was a point of honour with the Dutch to show France that even after so disastrous a war as that of 1672, the flooring of the Batavian Republic was solid enough to dance on, to the accompaniment of the cannon of the fleets.

The Horticultural Society of Haarlem had shown itself worthy of its reputation by giving a hundred thousand florins for the bulb of a tulip. The city would not be behindhand, and had voted an equal sum, which had been intrusted to the leading men of the town to be expended on the festival.

Therefore it was that, on the Sunday fixed for the ceremony, there was such an eagerness in the crowd, such enthusiasm among the townsfolk, that even the quizzing French, who laugh everywhere and at everything, could not have helped admiring the character of these worthy Dutchmen, who were as ready to spend their money in building a ship to fight the enemy, that is, to sustain the national honour, as they were to spend it in rewarding the discovery of a new flower, destined to bloom for a single day, and during that day to amuse women, and scholars, and critics.

At the head of the influential citizens and of the Horticultural Committee shone M. van Systens in his very finest clothes. The worthy man had made every effort to resemble his favourite flower in the sombre and severe elegance of his attire, and, let us add at once, he had, to his honour, succeeded admirably.

Jet-black velvet, and pansy-coloured silk, with linen of dazzling whiteness, such was the ceremonial garb of the president, who walked at the head of his committee, holding in his hand an immense bouquet, similar to that which, a hundred and twenty-one years afterward, Robespierre carried at the Feast of the Supreme Being.

Only, the worthy president, instead of a heart filled, like that of the French tribune, with hatred and ambitious resentment, had within his breast a flower not less innocent than the most innocent of those which he carried in his hand.

Behind the committee, as variegated as a meadow and as perfumed as spring, one saw the learned men of the town, the magistrates, the military, the nobles, and the rustics.

The common people, even among the republicans of the Seven Provinces, had no place in the order of the procession; they only formed, as it were, a hedge along the sides of the streets. That, after all, is the best place to see from, and to be in. It is the place of the crowd, which waits, with true political philosophy, until the triumphal procession has passed by, before deciding what to say about it . . . and sometimes what to do with it.

But this time, it was not a question, either of the triumph of Cæsar, or of the triumph of Pompey. This time, it was neither the defeat of Mithridates that was celebrated, nor the conquest of Gaul. The procession was as calm and as inoffensive as the passing of a flock of sheep on the earth or of a flight of birds in the air.

Haarlem had no conquerors but its gardeners. Adoring flowers, Haarlem deified the florist.

One could see, in the midst of the peaceful and perfumed train, the black tulip, borne on a litter covered with white velvet fringed with gold. Four men carried the poles of the litter, and were followed by relays of other men, as was done at Rome in the case of those who carried the Mater Cybele, when, brought from Etruria, she entered the Eternal City amid the flourish of trumpets and the adoration of a whole people.

This exhibition of the tulip was a homage paid by a whole people, without culture and without taste, to the taste and culture of their superiors and leaders, whose blood they knew how to spill on the filthy pavement of the Buitenhof, while reserving the right to inscribe, at a later period, the names of their victims on the fairest stones of the Dutch Pantheon.

It was known that the Prince-Stadtholder would himself hand to the successful candidate the prize of a hundred thousand florins, a fact which interested people in general, and also that he would perhaps make a speech, a fact which interested his friends and his enemies in particular.

In fact, in the absolutely non-political speeches of statesmen, friends and enemies are always ready to see signs of hidden thoughts, and consequently always believe that they can tell what those thoughts are. As though the hat of a politician was not a bushel intended to cut off all light.

At last this great and long-looked-for day, of the 15th of May, 1673, had arrived, and all Haarlem, reenforced by its environs, ranged itself along the fine avenues of trees, resolved this time to applaud neither victors in war, nor victors in science, but simply the conquerors of Nature, who had forced this inexhaustible mother to produce what had hitherto been thought an impossibility, namely, the black tulip.

But no resolution is so seldom kept by the populace as that of applauding only one particular thing. When a town is in the mood to applaud, just as when it is in the mood to hiss, it never knows where to stop.

It applauded, then, first of all Van Systens and his bouquet, it applauded the corporations, it applauded itself; and finally, with good reason this time, we must admit, it applauded the excellent music which the authorities of the town provided in abundance at every halt.

Having seen the heroine of the festival, the black tulip, all eyes next sought for the hero, that is to say, the grower of the tulip.

This hero, making his appearance after the discourse which we have seen M. van Systens elaborating so conscientiously, would certainly produce a greater effect even than the Stadtholder himself.

For us the interest of the day is not centred in the weighty discourse of our friend Van Systens, eloquent though it was, nor in the young aristocrats in their holiday attire, crunching their heavy cakes, nor in the poor little plebeians, half dressed, and nibbling at smoked eels that looked like sticks of vanilla. Our interest is not even centred in the fair Dutch women with their rosy complexions, nor in the fat and stumpy mynheers who had never left their homes, nor in the thin and yellow travellers lately returned from Ceylon or Java, nor in the thirsty populace who refreshed themselves by swallowing cucumber pickled in brine. No; for us the interest, the powerful and dramatic interest, is in a radiant and animated figure walking in the midst of the Horticultural Committee; our interest is centred in a personage, sleek, well combed, wearing flowers in his belt, and clothed all in scarlet, a colour which showed up his black hair and his yellow complexion.

Haarlem

This radiant and excited conqueror, this hero of the day, destined to the signal honour of making the discourse of Van Systens and the presence of the Stadtholder mere secondary matters, is Isaac Boxtel, who sees in front of him, to the right, on a velvet cushion, the black tulip, his pretended child, and to the left, in a huge purse, the hundred thousand florins in good shining and glittering gold coins, towards which he is continually casting side glances, so as not to lose sight of them for a moment.

From time to time Boxtel hastens his steps so as to rub elbows with Van Systens. Boxtel takes from every one a little of his importance, to add it to his own, just as he had taken the tulip from Rosa, to make his own fortune and reputation by it.

In another quarter of an hour the Prince will arrive, the procession will halt at the final resting-place, the tulip will be placed on its throne, and the Prince, who in the worship of the public gives place to this rival, will take a magnificent illuminated parchment on which is written the name of the discoverer, and he will proclaim in a loud and clear voice that a marvel has been produced; that Holland, through the instrumentality of him, Isaac Boxtel, has forced Nature to produce a black flower, and that the flower will be called henceforth *tulipa nigra Boxtellea*.

From time to time nevertheless, Boxtel turned his eyes away from the tulip and the purse, and looked stealthily at the crowd, for in the crowd he dreaded above all things to see the pale face of the beautiful Frisian.

This would be a spectre that would spoil his festival, as thoroughly as the ghost of Banquo spoiled the feast of Macbeth.

And, let us add at once, this wretched man, who had climbed over a wall that was not his wall, who had clambered up to a window to enter his neighbour's house, who, by means of a false key, had sneaked into Rosa's room, this wretched man who, in fact, had stolen another man's reputation and a woman's dowry, did not regard himself as a thief.

He had so watched over the tulip, he had followed it so eagerly from Cornelius's drying-room to the scaffold on the Buitenhof, and from the scaffold on the Buitenhof to the fortress of Loevestein, he had so often looked at it springing up and growing on Rosa's window-sill, he had so frequently warmed the air around it with his breath that, to his mind, no one was more the author of it than he; any one who takes it from him now will have stolen it from him.

But he did not see Rosa.

Therefore Boxtel's delight was unalloyed.

The procession stopped in the middle of a circular space formed by magnificent trees, which were decorated with garlands and inscriptions: its stoppage was signalized by a burst of clamorous music, and the young girls of Haarlem came forward to escort the tulip as far as the elevated throne which it was to occupy on the platform, by the side of the gilt chair of his Highness the Stadtholder.

And the proud tulip, elevated on its pedestal, soon dominated the whole gathering of people, who clapped their hands and made the echoes of Haarlem ring with deafening applause.

XXXII

A LAST PRAYER

At this solemn moment, while the applause was still ringing in the air, a carriage was passing along the road which borders the wood; it advanced but slowly, owing to the numbers of children whom the pressure of the crowd had driven beyond the avenue of trees.

This carriage, wayworn, covered with dust and creaking on its axles, contained the unfortunate Van Baerle, who, through the open carriage window, began to observe the spectacle which we have tried, imperfectly no doubt, to bring before the eyes of the reader.

This crowd, this noise, this concatenation of all human and all natural splendours, dazzled the prisoner, as a sudden flash of light in his cell would have done.

In spite of the unwillingness to answer which his companion had shown, when he had questioned him regarding his own fate, he ventured to question him a last time regarding all this bustle, which he at first very naturally thought had nothing whatever to do with himself.

A Last Prayer

" Pray, lieutenant, what is this? " he asked of the officer who was escorting him.

" As you can see for yourself, sir," replied the latter, " it is a festival."

" Ah! a festival! " said Cornelius, with the gloomy and indifferent air of a man to whom pleasure of any kind has long been a stranger.

Then, after a moment's silence, when the carriage had gone a few yards farther, he asked:

" Is it the festival of the patron saint of Haarlem? for I see a great many flowers."

" As a matter of fact, it is a festival in which flowers play the chief part, sir."

" Oh, what sweet perfumes! what beautiful colours! " cried Cornelius.

" Stop! that this gentleman may look," said the officer to the soldier who was acting as postillion, with one of those impulses of kindliness which are found only among military men.

" I thank you, sir, for your kindness," replied Van Baerle, in a melancholy tone, " but the joy of others is only painful to me: spare me that, I beg of you."

" As you please. Go on, then. I told him to stop, because you asked me, and moreover because you pass for being a lover of flowers, especially those of which the feast is being kept to-day."

" And what flowers are they, sir, whose festival is being kept to-day? "

" Tulips."

The Black Tulip

"Tulips!" cried Van Baerle, "it is the festival of tulips, to-day?"

"Yes, sir, but since the spectacle is unpleasant to you, let us go on."

And the officer prepared to give the order for resuming their journey.

But Cornelius stopped him. A painful doubt had just come into his mind.

"Sir," said he, in a trembling voice, "is it to-day that they give the prize?"

"The prize for the black tulip? Yes."

The cheeks of Cornelius became purple, a shiver ran through his body, the perspiration stood out on his forehead. Then, reflecting that, in the absence of himself and his tulip, the festival would be a failure, for want of a man and a flower to be crowned, he said:

"Alas! all these good people will be as unfortunate as I, for they will not see this great ceremony to which they have been invited, or at least they will see it incomplete."

"What do you mean, sir?"

"I mean that the black tulip will never be found, except by one person whom I know," said Cornelius, flinging himself back in the carriage.

"Then, sir, this person, whom you know, has found it: for that which all Haarlem is looking at at this moment is the flower which you say cannot be found."

"The black tulip!" cried Van Baerle, thrusting his body half out of the window. "Where? where?"

A Last Prayer

"Down there, on the throne; do you see it?"

"Yes, I see it."

"Come along, sir, now we must go on."

"Oh, please, for pity's sake, sir," said Van Baerle, "do not drag me away! Let me look at it again. What! the thing I see down there, the black tulip, quite black . . . is it possible? Oh, sir, have you seen it? It must have some spots, it must be imperfect, perhaps it has only been dyed black. Oh, if I were there, sir, I should be able to tell at once. Let me get out, let me see it close to, I beg of you!"

"Are you mad, sir? How can I?"

"I beseech you!"

"But you forget you are a prisoner?"

"It is true I am a prisoner, but I am an honourable man, and on my honour, sir, I will not take to flight, I will not try to escape. Let me only look at the flower."

"But my orders, sir?"

And the officer again made as though he would order the soldier to drive on.

Cornelius again stopped him.

"Oh, be patient, be generous, my whole life depends on your pity. Alas! sir, my life will probably not be very long now. Ah! you do not know, sir, what I suffer: you do not know the struggle that is going on in my mind and in my heart. For," continued Cornelius, "if that should be my tulip, if it should be the one which was stolen from Rosa. . . . Oh, sir, think what it is to have found the black tulip,

335

to have seen it for a moment, to have recognised that it was perfect, that it was a masterpiece of Art and Nature combined, and then to lose it, to lose it forever! Oh, I must get out, sir, I must go and look at it! You may kill me afterwards, if you like, but I will see it, I will see it!"

"Be quiet, wretched man, be quiet, and come back into the carriage at once, for here is the escort of his Highness the Stadtholder coming towards us, and if the Prince were to notice anything disorderly, or hear any noise here, it would be all up with you, and with me too."

Van Baerle, more alarmed for his companion than for himself, flung himself back in the carriage, but he could not stay there half a minute, and the first twenty horsemen had scarcely passed when he was again at the window, gesticulating and beseeching the Stadtholder, just as the latter was passing.

William, impassive and calm as usual, was on his way to the appointed spot to preside over the ceremony. He held in his hand a roll of parchment, which had become, for this festival day, his field-marshal's baton.

Seeing this man gesticulating and entreating, perhaps also recognising the officer who was with him, the Stadtholder gave the order to stop.

On the instant, his horses, quivering on their sinewy hocks, halted six yards from the spot where Van Baerle was caged in his carriage.

"Who is that?" asked the Prince of the officer,

A Last Prayer

who had jumped out of the carriage on hearing the order of the Stadtholder, and was now respectfully approaching him.

"My Lord," said he, "it is the political prisoner whom I have been to fetch from Loevestein according to your orders; I am bringing him to you at Haarlem, as your Highness directed."

"What does he want?"

"He insists on being allowed to stop here for a moment."

"To see the black tulip, my Lord," cried Van Baerle, clasping his hands, "and afterwards, when I have seen it, when I have learnt what I have a right to know, I will die, if it must be so, but in dying I shall bless your merciful Highness for intervening, and allowing me to see my work brought to a proper conclusion and rewarded by the recognition which it deserves."

It was indeed a strange spectacle, that of the two men, each at the window of his carriage, surrounded by guards; the one all-powerful, the other helpless; the one about to mount a throne, the other believing himself on the point of mounting the scaffold.

While listening to his urgent prayer, William had looked coldly at Cornelius. Then, addressing the officer, he said:

"This man is the mutinous prisoner who tried to kill his jailer at Loevestein, is he not?"

Cornelius sighed and hung his head. His sweet-tempered, handsome face became red, and then pale.

337

The Black Tulip

These words of the omnipotent and omniscient Prince who, by means of some secret messenger unknown to other men, was already cognizant of his crime, led him to expect not only a more certain punishment, but also a refusal of his request.

He did not attempt to resist, he did not attempt to defend himself: he presented to the Prince a spectacle of unaffected despair which was quite intelligible, and must have been very touching, to so great a heart and so great a mind as that of the Stadtholder.

"Allow the prisoner to get down," said William; "he may go and see the tulip, which is well worth seeing at least once."

"Oh!" said Cornelius, nearly fainting with joy, and staggering on the step of the carriage, "oh, my Lord!"

He was unable to say more, and had it not been for the sustaining arm of the officer, it would have been on his knees and with his forehead in the dust that poor Cornelius would have thanked his Highness.

Having granted the request, the Prince resumed his drive through the wood, amidst the enthusiastic acclamations of the people.

He soon reached the platform, and the cannon awoke the echoes on the horizon.

CONCLUSION

VAN BAERLE, led by four guards, who opened out
a passage through the crowd, gradually approached
the tulip, which he gazed at more and more eagerly
the nearer he got to it.

He saw it at last, the unique flower which,
through the action of unknown combinations of heat,
of cold, of shade, and of light, was to appear for a
single day, only to disappear forever. He saw it
within six yards of him, and observed with delight
its perfections and its graces; he saw it surrounded
by the young girls who formed the guard of honour
of this queen of elegance and beauty. And yet, the
more he assured himself with his own eyes of the
perfection of the flower, the more wretched and distracted he felt.

He looked all round him in order to ask a question, a single question. But everywhere he saw only
strange faces, everywhere attention was directed ex-
clusively to the throne on which the Stadtholder had
just taken his seat.

William, who thus attracted the attention of all,

rose, cast a calm glance over the excited crowd, and allowed his piercing eye to rest in turn on the three extremities of a triangle, formed in front of him by three very different interests and three very different dramas.

At one angle was Boxtel, quivering with impatience, and devouring with eager eyes the Prince, the florins, the black tulip, and the assembled crowd; at another Cornelius, breathless, mute, with no thought or feeling for anything, except the black tulip—his child.

Finally, at the third, standing on the raised step of a daïs, amid the young girls of Haarlem, was a beautiful Frisian maiden, clothed in fine red woollen cloth, embroidered with silver, and covered with a lace veil which fell in waves from her head-dress of cloth-of-gold—Rosa, in fact, who, half-fainting and with her eyes full of tears, was leaning on the arm of one of William's officers.

The Prince, seeing all his audience in their places, slowly unrolled his parchment, and, in a calm clear voice, which, though not strong, was heard distinctly by every one, thanks to the respectful silence which suddenly fell on the fifty thousand spectators and kept them breathless,

" You know," said he, " with what object you have been called together here. A prize of a hundred thousand florins has been promised to the person who should produce the black tulip. The black tulip! and this wonder of Holland is here, before your eyes:

Conclusion

the black tulip has been produced, and produced in accordance with all the conditions laid down in the programme of the Horticultural Society of Haarlem.

" The history of its origin and the name of its grower will be inscribed in the roll of honour of the town.

" Let the person who is the owner of the black tulip come forward."

And as he pronounced these words, the Prince, in order to judge of the effect which they produced, cast a searching glance over the three extremities of the triangle.

He saw Boxtel start forward from his place.

He saw Cornelius make an involuntary movement.

Finally, he saw the officer who had charge of Rosa, lead her, or rather push her, in front of the throne.

A double cry burst forth, at the same moment, on the right and on the left of the Prince.

Boxtel, thunderstruck, Cornelius, lost in amazement, had both cried out, " Rosa!" " Rosa!"

" This tulip is yours, young woman, is it not? " said the Prince.

" Yes, my Lord," stammered Rosa, whose beauty and charm were greeted by a general murmur of admiration.

" Oh! " murmured Cornelius, " she was lying, then, when she said that this flower had been stolen from her. Oh! that is why she left Loevestein! I am forgotten, betrayed by her! by her whom I thought my best friend."

"Oh!" groaned Boxtel, "I am lost!"

"This tulip," continued the Prince, "will therefore bear the name of its producer, and will be inscribed in the catalogue of flowers under the name of *tulipa nigra Rosa Baerlensis*, by reason of the name Van Baerle, which will very shortly become, through her marriage, the name of this young woman."

And, at the same time, William took Rosa's hand, and placed it in the hand of a man who had rushed forward, pale, astounded, and overcome with joy, to the foot of the throne, thanking in turn the Prince, his betrothed, and God, who from on high was watching with a fatherly smile this spectacle of two hearts made happy.

At the same time there fell at the feet of President van Systens another man, struck down by a very different emotion.

Boxtel, overwhelmed by the ruin of his hopes, had fainted.

They lifted him up; they felt his pulse and his heart; he was dead.

This incident did not interrupt the festival, for neither the president nor the Prince appeared to pay much attention to it.

Cornelius started back, appalled. In the thief, in the pretended Jacob, he recognised the true Isaac Boxtel, his neighbour, whom, in the innocence of his

Conclusion

heart, he had never for a moment suspected of such wickedness.

This sudden stroke of apoplexy was a blessing for Boxtel, in so far, at any rate, as it saved him from having any longer to contemplate things so painful to his pride and his avarice.

Then, to the sound of trumpets, the procession resumed its march without any change in the ceremonial, except that Boxtel was dead and that Cornelius and Rosa walked in triumph, side by side and hand in hand.

When they had re-entered the Town Hall, the Prince, pointing out with his finger to Cornelius the purse with the hundred thousand florins, said:

"One does not very well know by whom this money has been gained, by you or by Rosa: for if you found the black tulip, she reared it and made it flower: therefore she ought not to offer it as her dowry, for that would be unjust. Besides it is the gift of the city of Haarlem to the tulip."

Cornelius waited to see what the Prince was leading up to. The latter continued:

"I myself will give Rosa a hundred thousand florins, which she will have well earned, and which she can offer to you: they are the prize won by her love, her courage, and her honesty.

"As to you, sir, thanks again to Rosa, who has brought forward the proof of your innocence "—and saying this, the Prince handed to Cornelius the famous leaf of the Bible on which the letter of Cornelius de Witt had been written and which had served as a cover for the third bulb—"as to you, it is now clear that you have been imprisoned for a crime which you did not commit. You are therefore free, and since the goods of an innocent man cannot be confiscated, your property is restored to you.

"M. van Baerle, you are the godson of Cornelius de Witt and the friend of John. Remain worthy of the name which the one gave you at the baptismal font, and of the friendship with which the other honoured you. Preserve the tradition of the merits of both, for the De Witts, wrongly judged and wrongly punished, in a moment of error on the part of the people, were two great patriots of whom Holland to-day is proud."

The Prince, after these words which, contrary to his usual custom, he uttered in a voice full of feeling, gave his two hands to the bride and bridegroom to kiss, as they knelt on each side of him.

Then, with a sigh, he added:

"Alas! you are indeed happy, you who, thinking perhaps of the true glory of Holland and, above all, of her true happiness, seek to conquer for her only new colours in tulips."

And looking towards France, as though he saw new clouds gathering in that direction, he got into his carriage and drove away.

.   .   .   .

Cornelius, too, set off the same day for Dordrecht; with him went Rosa, who had sent on old Zug as an

Conclusion

ambassador to her father, to inform him of all that
had happened.

Those who, thanks to the account we have given,
know the character of old Gryphus, will understand
that it was only with great difficulty that he was recon-
ciled to his son-in-law. He still felt, in his heart, the
blows he had received from the stick: he had counted
them by the bruises they caused: they numbered, he
said, forty-one. But in the end he yielded, in order,
as he put it, not to be less generous than his Highness
the Stadtholder.

Made a guardian of tulips, after having been a
jailer of men, he was the harshest jailer of flowers
that had ever been seen in Flanders. It was a sight
to see him, keeping an eye on dangerous butterflies,
killing field-mice, and putting to flight the too hungry bees.

As he had learnt the true story of Boxtel, and was
furious at having been the dupe of the pretended
Jacob, he demolished the observatory formerly raised
by that envious man behind the sycamore-tree; for
Boxtel's ground, being sold by auction, was turned
into flower-beds by Cornelius, who thus rounded off
his property in such a manner as to bid defiance to all
the telescopes in Dordrecht.

Rosa, growing more and more beautiful, became
also more and more proficient in learning, and at the
end of two years of marriage she knew so well how to
read and to write, that she was able to undertake
alone the education of two fine children, to which she

gave birth in the years 1673 and 1674. They were both born, like tulips, in the month of May, and gave her much less trouble than the famous flower to which she owed it that she had them at all.

It need hardly be stated that, one being a boy and the other a girl, the first received the name of Cornelius, and the second that of Rosa.

Van Baerle remained faithful to Rosa and to his tulips: his whole life was devoted to the happiness of his wife and to the cultivation of flowers, and thanks to his devotion to the latter, he produced a large number of varieties which are inscribed in the Dutch catalogue.

The two chief ornaments of his drawing-room were the two leaves of the Bible of Cornelius de Witt, in large gold frames: on one, it will be remembered, his godfather had written to him, begging him to burn the correspondence of the Marquis of Louvois; on the other, he himself had bequeathed to Rosa the bulb of the black tulip, on condition that, with her dowry of a hundred thousand florins, she should marry a handsome young man of from twenty-six to twenty-eight years of age, who should love her and whom she should love.

This condition was strictly fulfilled, although Cornelius had not died, and in fact just because he had not.

Finally, to ward off jealousy in the future, from which Providence might not think fit to save him as it had saved him from Mynheer Isaac Boxtel, he

Conclusion

wrote above his door these words, which Grotius, on the day of his escape, had carved on the wall of his cell:

"One has sometimes suffered enough to have the right never afterwards to say, ' I am too happy.' "

NOTE ON THE PORTRAITS OF ALEXANDRE DUMAS THE ELDER

NOTE ON THE PORTRAITS OF
ALEXANDRE DUMAS THE ELDER

ALEXANDRE DUMAS
About 1833.
Published by the *Voleur*.

IT is not the intention of the author of this note to make any attempt to define the rightful position of Alexandre Dumas the Elder, in the great literary movement of 1830, nor the value to be set upon his work. His sole object is to supplement Dr. Garnett's study of the author by a chapter dealing with his portraits, and to call up the various aspects under which Alexandre Dumas was known to several generations of his readers. What we offer is rather a sort of hastily arranged dissolving-view, wherein the chief pictorial transformations of one type, and an occasional recollection of the exaggerations with which the caricaturist's fancy has adorned it, may be reviewed. The most succinct of descriptions will be found below each portrait.

351

The Portraits of

ALEXANDRE DUMAS.
Lithograph by Déveria, 1832.

The elder Dumas is first presented to us by Déveria's admirable lithograph, published in 1832. In this picture the young man's elongated face, worn by the effervescence of his youthful passions, speaks to us clearly of the sensual temperament, the physical audacity, and the intellectual energy, which were the peculiarities of this wondrous "half-breed." Antony in the flesh, hot-spirited, vehement, the very essence of the lover.

Another lithograph, probably several months later in date, and published in *Le Voleur*, gives us Dumas in evening dress, the face fuller, the eye calm, and the kindly thick lips drawn together, and slightly smiling, with

ALEXANDRE DUMAS
About 1836.
Biographie des hommes du jour,
of Saru and Saint-Edme.

352

Alexandre Dumas the Elder

an expression at once satirical and good-natured. He looks the celebrity who has already tasted his success. He feels his own strength, and remembering his past victories, feels no doubt as to his future triumphs: a young Alexander, in repose.

On page 356 we see him, in a different frame of mind, draped in a great cloak, tossed over his left shoulder haughtily; his mouth, pouting a little under the soft mustache, bespeaks defiance and disdain, as well as a hunger for woman's kisses. This time, he is in the heat of some struggle. With what is he wrestling? With some woman's heart, or with

ALEXANDRE DUMAS.
Aged 29 years.
Lithograph by Maurin, 1833.

Fame herself? Unless, indeed—and nothing seems more likely—it be with both! This is the copper-plate engraving which forms our frontispiece to *The Black Tulip*. It is one of the most life-like of the portraits of the author of *Les Trois Mousquetaires*, at the flood-tide of his success, when he was enriching the stage with *Henri III et sa Cour*.

The portrait after Eugène Giraud, which must

have been executed at about the same time, is also exceedingly life-like and luminous, but it is rather Oriental-looking and fantastic.

In 1840 we have a fine drawing by Maurin, which gives us a rather more mature Alexandre Dumas. The forehead is well modelled, and bears the fine

ALEXANDRE DUMAS.
Aged 35 years.
After Giraud, lithograph of 1838 published in the *Echo des Feuilletons.*

longitudinal furrow of the man who uses his brain. The eyes look upward, the expression of the mouth is grave: this is Dumas, the man of sentiment and poetry.

The *Biographie des hommes du jour* reveals a man who is still young, though not a young man. There is a bitterness in the smile, a melancholy in the eye. The curly hair seems thinner, and looks as if it had been crimped with irons. In this picture, Alexandre Dumas has been fined down, sand-papered, rubbed up with chamois leather: a "got-up" figure for the smart society folk.

It is impossible to explain why, from 1840 to 1860, practically no portraits of the elder Dumas are to be found. This was a time when his impetuosity was at its height, when he wandered all over

Alexandre Dumas the Elder

Europe like a happy commercial traveller, displaying everywhere his extraordinary culinary gifts. Did he leave any portraits of himself in Switzerland, Italy, or Spain? Had he time to sit to be painted or sketched between two journeys? Would he risk having his face reproduced in view of the

ALEXANDRE DUMAS
In 1840.
After a lithograph by Maurin.

then imperfect processes of Daguerre and Niepce? It is difficult to say, but between 1840 and 1860 there is a gap in which caricatures predominate to the detriment of authentic portraits.

Infinitely more truthful, and older-looking too, is the

ALEXANDRE DUMAS.
Aged 26 years.
Medallion by David d'Angers, 1829.

cheery "bonvivant" engraved by Geoffroy in *L'Alliance des Arts* for 1858, a most attractive portrait, show-

ALEXANDRE DUMAS
About 1842.
After a lithograph by Eugène Giraud.

ing us Dumas the lover of life and its enjoyments, the antithesis to which is to be seen in the photograph taken in 1869, wherein we perceive " Père Dumas," as full of swagger as when he was twenty, endeavouring to look severe, and my readers will forgive the slang expression *il la fait à la pose.*

From 1868 onwards, the portraits of the elder Dumas literally swarm. Hundreds of them are to be found in the illustrated periodicals and magazines, caricature sketches by Cham, by Benjamin, by Carjat, by Adrén Gill, abound : a good-sized album would hardly suffice to hold a complete series of the pictures which this big, curly-headed, jovial, laughter-loving man inspired his contemporaries to pro-

ALEXANDRE DUMAS.
After a lithograph, 1834.

Alexandre Dumas the Elder

duce. He set every pen and pencil at work, whether in France or out of it. Everywhere he travelled with enjoyment, and everywhere his good humour won him friends.

After 1865, photography fixed the elder Dumas's features oftener than ever. In

ALEXANDRE DUMAS.
By Grévin, 1866.

his desire to oblige everyone, he posed unhesitatingly before every camera presented to him, and photographic portraits of " Père Alexandre," as he was called, were largely sold by stationers and photograph venders.

Some of these were exceedingly compromising, as when, though over sixty years of age, he allowed himself to be taken with a circus-rider, Mme. Adah Menken, famous at that time for her beauty of form, in quasi-paternal and undignified attitude, the fair lady seated on his knee clad in tights, just as she was then appearing at the circus, bound on a horse's back, in the part of Mazeppa, in a pose of ideal and romantic beauty.

ALEXANDRE DUMAS.
Caricature by Étienne Carjat, published by the *Diogène* in 1860.

357

ALEXANDRE DUMAS.
By Geoffroy, 1858.

The later portraits of the elder Dumas abound. No old man was ever more gay, more overflowing with life, more fully awake than was the author of *The Three Musketeers* at the age of sixty. The sculptors who undertook his statue after his death did not dream of having recourse to the young mulatto hero so forcibly depicted by Déveria; all—Gustave Doré, Chapu and other sculptors—reproduced the old Dumas with frizzly hair, his broad face radiant with the joy of living. So we find his bust by Chapu at the Théâtre français, his statue by the same sculptor in the Odéon, and thus he also appears above his pedestal upon that place Malherbes which was soon to see the statue of the splendid General Du-

ALEXANDRE DUMAS.
From a photograph, 1869.

mas, that of Dumas the Younger, and to be called "La Place des trois Dumas."

In every section of society, Dumas' wit, his brilliant sayings, his love of show, his theatrical quarrels, his debts, his fondness for good eating, his culinary talent, his peregrination, and his serial novels, made him the fashion. No man roused more curiosity, and during the later period of his life his portraits and caricatures numbered many hundreds. As regards photography, he broke the record. None

ALEXANDRE DUMAS.
About 1870.

of his contemporaries were photographed, sketched, engraved, deformed by caricature in the comic papers, to such an extent as he.

We can make no attempt in this place to analyze even in the most summary way, this enormous series of portraits. The chief types of the man, those which mark the principal stages in his appearance, are reproduced in the course of this short notice. They express the suitor for the hand of Glory, the Courtier of Fame, the only phases of a man's appearance which possess any real interest, after he himself has departed. Once the hero espouses fame, and lives in lawful wedlock with her, he ceases to be interesting because all his battles have been won. The real value of illustrious writers, as of great warriors, lies in their seasons of struggle and of action. Once they have attained their ends, they live on the legend of what they once were, in the

The Portraits of Alexandre Dumas

effort to reach their goal. They wax fat, they become self-satisfied, they grow old. No longer do their faces shine with the glory of the man who goes forth to fight and conquer fortune.

OCTAVE UZANNE.

ALEXANDRE DUMAS.
Statue by Gustave Doré.